W9-DFS-255

SAVING WRIGHT

The Freeman House and
the Preservation of
Meaning, Materials, and Modernity

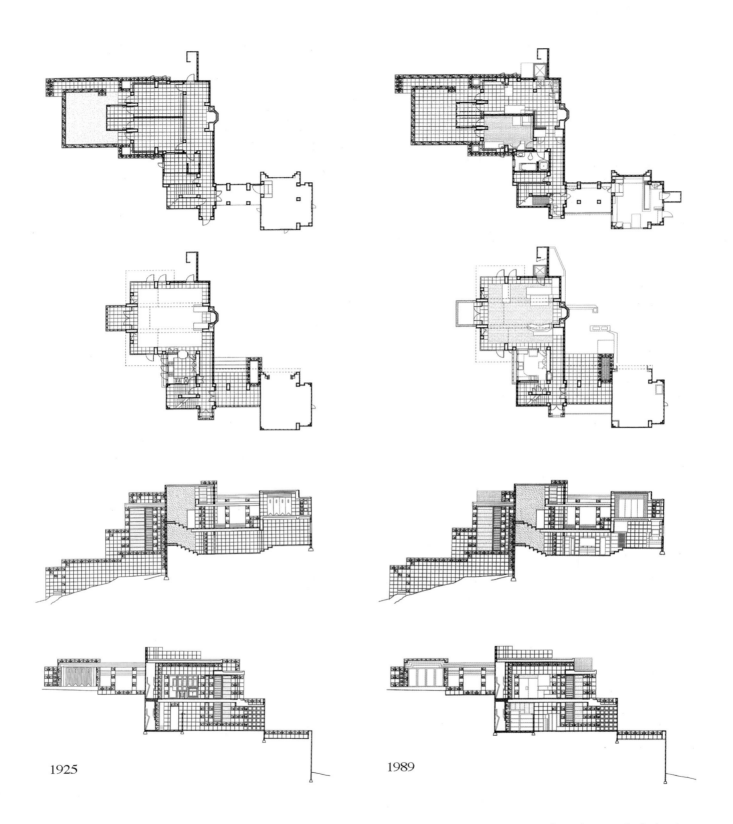

1925

1989

Over time the Freeman House changed significantly as different architects responded to its owners' wishes. These as-built drawings come from a set documenting the house as constructed, and when USC took possession. Alterations are noted in red. Top to Bottom: first-floor plan; main-level plan, section through stair tower looking west, section through living room looking east.

SAVING WRIGHT

The Freeman House and
the Preservation of
Meaning, Materials, and Modernity

JEFFREY M. CHUSID

W. W. Norton & Company

New York • London

For information about permission to reproduce selections from this book, write to
Permissions, W. W. Norton & Company, Inc., 500 Fifth Avenue, New York, NY 10110

For information about special discounts for bulk purchases, please contact
W. W. Norton Special Sales at specialsales@wwnorton.com or 800-233-4830

Manufacturing by Walsworth Print Group
Book design by Jonathan Lippincott
Production manager: Leeann Graham

Library of Congress Cataloging-in-Publication Data

Chusid, Jeffrey M.
Saving Wright : the Freeman House and the preservation of meaning, materials,
and modernity / Jeffrey M. Chusid. — 1st ed.
p. cm.
Includes bibliographical references and index.
ISBN 978-0-393-73302-0 (hardcover)
1. Freeman House (Hollywood, Los Angeles, Calif.) 2. Wright, Frank Lloyd, 1867–1959.
3. Architecture, Domestic—Conservation and restoration—California—Los Angeles.
4. Historic buildings—Conservation and restoration—California—Los Angeles.
5. Los Angeles (Calif.)—Buildings, structures, etc. I. Wright, Frank Lloyd, 1867–1959.
II. Title. III. Title: Freeman House and the preservation of meaning, materials, and modernity.
NA7238.L6C49 2011
728'.370979494028— dc22
2011010950

ISBN: 978-0-393-73302-0

W. W. Norton & Company, Inc., 500 Fifth Avenue, New York, N.Y. 10110
www.wwnorton.com
W. W. Norton & Company Ltd., Castle House, 75/76 Wells Street, London W1T 3QT

0 2 4 6 8 9 7 5 3 1

CONTENTS

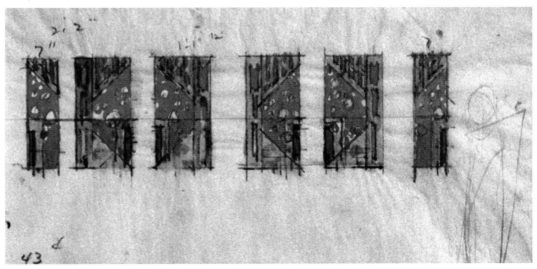

The story of the Freeman House has been assembled from diverse sources, including those seen here, which chart the course of color on the building. Top: south façade photographed by the architect John Reed, ca. 1940, showing the green fascia close to its original appearance; center: a strip of cloth tape removed from the fascia over the garage in 1989 revealed the bronze powder originally applied to the lowest band of the fascia, but largely covered over by 1940; bottom: during the course of design in 1923 or 1924, this watercolor incorporated the block pattern into a series of panels. While it is believed to come from Lloyd Wright's hand, its purpose or intended place in the house remains a mystery.

PREFACE

In 1984, Harriet Freeman gave her house, designed by Frank Lloyd Wright in late 1923 and early 1924, to the School of Architecture at the University of Southern California. She continued to live in the house until her death two years later. This book is an outgrowth of the research on the house undertaken subsequently, and a discussion of the structural rehabilitation project in 2000–2001, which was both a result of that research and a direct response to the Northridge earthquake of 1994. It is a case study in historic preservation, and a tribute to the powerful woman who played a critical role in the building's creation and its decades as a crucible of modernist art and politics. As it happened, she transformed my life as well.

In the summer of 1985, I was a young faculty member teaching an architecture "summer camp" for high school students at USC when Robert Harris, the dean of the School of Architecture, told me that he had just received a call from Harriet Freeman. She was looking for someone to rent the apartment in her house. When he asked me if I knew of anyone who might be interested, I replied, "Yes, me." He gave me her number, and I made arrangements to go to the house.

As I walked down the dark hallway with its glimpse of light at the end, and then turned left into the spectacular living room with its wall of glass facing the city, I was struck as much by the view of Harriet, clad in bright orange and sitting at the dining table at the far end of the room, as I was by the extraordinary architecture. With her hair dyed a blazing hue of red and a bright streak of lipstick across her mouth, Harriet Freeman presented a fierce, almost alarming image. We talked briefly, probably about the rent, who I was, and when I could start living there, and then I went downstairs. The apartment turned out to be a work of infill by the architect Rudolph Schindler, assembled from a former laundry room, hallway, and loggia. It was not particularly prepossessing. Its concrete-block walls, painted a glossy white, were dirty. Crude built-in furniture had drawers that bound. A tiny kitchenette included a refrigerator housed in a rickety wooden box that was actually outside the house with access through a glass door and two steps. The little terrace outside the front door was two feet deep in leaves and other debris. The ceiling in the supposed bedroom was 6'8" high. The apartment was half underground, and felt it. But the large windows along the east wall featured an expansive view through treetops of the neighboring hillsides.

The apartment was nowhere near as glamorous as I had hoped a Frank Lloyd Wright–designed dwelling would be. It felt almost like a mechanical room inside some giant piece of urban infrastructure. And yet . . . it was unusual, it was inexpensive, and it was in the Hollywood Hills (by one steep block). Despite its somewhat run-down condition and ad hoc character, it was also fascinating. My greatest hesitation arose from a presentiment that my life would change profoundly if I moved in. In the end, though, I couldn't turn it down.

My first "preservation" project at the Freeman House—the repair and repainting of the apartment—was spontaneous and shaped only by my sensibilities as an architect. I selected a muted palette of colors that would show off to best effect the interventions made by Schindler in the 1930s and '40s while restoring some of the earthy character that I thought the once-bare concrete-block walls had conveyed. Doors and windows were next: making them operable, cleaning the glass, and installing wooden blinds. (I discovered later that blinds were there originally.) A piece of black-painted plywood in one of the closets turned out to be an original Schindler dining table, meant to be screwed into a window sill. I put it in place. Two chairs and two little side tables came out of closets in the main house and were restored to the apartment for which they were designed. I found and repaired a half-dozen lighting fixtures, one or two in each of the built-in furnishings in the space.

After a few months, I told Dean Harris that I wanted an ongoing role at the house once it passed into the school's hands, and as the planned transformation into a visiting faculty residence began. Perhaps I could be a friend of the house and serve as the client's representative in the rehabilitation process. The dean was amenable. There were no plans at that time for a major restoration—just as well, because it was only two years since I had received my Masters of Architecture from the University of California at Berkeley, and I was neither a preservation architect nor a Wright scholar.

I met Harriet infrequently. If she wanted to talk to me, her companion, Noel Osheroff, would knock on the little door in the bathroom that connected my apartment to the main house, or telephone me, and I would go outside, up the stairs, and through the front door of the house to see Harriet. (Osheroff, a noted ceramic artist and daughter of the Freemans' friends Bill and Stephanie Oliver, took care of Harriet after she was confined to a wheelchair by degenerative discs in her neck and a stroke.) Sometimes I would stop and talk to Harriet when she was sitting in her wheelchair outside the front door, getting some sun. Our final conversation took place in early 1986, shortly after the stroke that would finally take her life. She was lying in a bed in the living room of the house, unable to talk yet still completely lucid. I fed her ice chips and communicated with her by spelling words letter by letter, going through the alphabet until she nodded.

I regret not getting to know Harriet better, but I owe to her my involvement with historic preservation. I remained at the Freeman House as the site's tenant, director, and preservation architect for another eleven years. During that time, I learned about preservation and cultural resource management on the job, aided by many professionals who gave generously of their time, expertise, and support to help the cause of the house. As a result, I determined to return the gift that Harriet and the experience had given me by making the stewardship and preservation of the house a learning experience for students in the School of Architecture, for members of the design community in Southern California, and for preservationists everywhere. This book is part of that commitment.

The decision to make the house a teaching laboratory, and to use it to support the development of a preservation program at USC, had two other important consequences. First, it allowed the school, and outside scholars, to undertake research and explore conservation techniques and ideas that a more narrowly focused project might not have. Second, it encouraged reflection and discussion about what we were doing and why. As will be seen, it also made some of our own limitations into virtues.

In the twenty-five years since I first moved into the Freeman House, my career as a preservation architect and educator has flourished, and I have practiced and taught around the country and in a number of places abroad. Meanwhile, the theory and practice of preservation has developed to an extraordinary extent. The passage of time has given me a certain degree of reflection and perspective and provided some useful distance from the events and decisions. But it is striking just how challenging Wright's work remains for preservationists: not merely the seemingly impossible technical difficulties of the textile-block construction system, but also the theoretical challenges to accepted preservation practice. One could assemble a fascinating and heuristic series of case studies in preservation using Unity Temple, Florida Southern College, the Johnson Wax Buildings, the Darwin Martin House, Auldbrass Plantation, the Meyer May House, Robie House, the Guggenheim, and Taliesin, to name just a few of the recent projects at Wright sites.

The chapters in this book alternate between the historical narrative and a discussion of the preservation issues just raised. "Setting the Scene" and the even-numbered chapters ("Design," "Construction," "Inhabitation and Change," and "Implementation") tell the story of the Freeman House from original vision through the structural rehabilitation project of 2001. The odd-numbered chapters ("Interpreting the Design," "Material Realities," "Stewardship," and "Wright and Historic Preservation") examine theoretical issues, interpretation, preservation practice, and conservation implications. I invite readers to proceed through the book in sequence, or to read sets of alternating chapters, whichever might be most interesting and useful.

ACKNOWLEDGMENTS

This book would not have been possible without the help and support of many people and institutions. First, my gratitude to the School of Architecture at the University of Southern California and Dean Robert Harris for entrusting me with the house, and to subsequent deans Victor Regnier, Robert Timme, and Qingyun Ma for their ongoing encouragement and support, as well as to Ken Breisch, who "inherited the mantle" of the house and the preservation program, and has continued to be a generous colleague and articulate advocate. I thank Harriet and Sam Freeman's many acquaintances, friends, and family members who spoke or wrote to me—Gary and Hap Lovell, Hazel Roy, Wyn Evans, Murray Niedich, Esther Dekker, Noel Osheroff, Dorothi Bock Pierre, Dione Neutra, Sharon DeKeyser, Bella Lewitzky, Margot Wellington Zausner, and Newell Reynolds among them—and made life at the house come alive. Robert Clark, Wally Newiadamsky, and James Reneau all shared their experiences as architects and contractors for Harriet and Sam. Robert Sweeney and Kathryn Smith generously shared what they learned from spending years studying Frank Lloyd Wright's work in Los Angeles. Their books are still the basic texts for understanding the period, and provided much of the context for the events described in this study. Other Wright experts, among them

Anthony Alofsin, Donald Kalec, Virginia Kazor, Neil Levine, Carla Lind, Jack Quinan, John Reed, and William Storer, welcomed me into their fold and helped me understand the larger world of Wright and Wright sites. Esther McCoy, David Gebhardt, and Judith Sheine helped me to understand the role played by Rudolph Schindler; Thomas Hines was my guide for Irving Gill and Richard Neutra. Julius Shulman not only took extraordinary photographs of the Freeman House over the years, and generously shared them, but also came to the house and lectured to support its preservation. Bruce Pfeiffer, Oskar Muñoz, and the staff at the Frank Lloyd Wright Archives allowed me to study the drawings for three wonderful days I will never forget, and also shared photographs and other material they had about the Freeman House. Finally, among the Wright circle one stands out: Eric Lloyd Wright. It is hard to conceive of a kinder, more generous, more devoted architect and colleague. He has always been forthcoming with anything he had, or knew, or could do to help the house. All three Los Angeles textile-block houses owe him an enormous debt of gratitude.

Many others in Los Angeles helped me learn preservation, worked professionally on the Freeman house, assisted students doing research, and gave willingly of their time and energy in the cause, among them: Christie McAvoy, David Charlebois, Melvyn Green, Peyton Hall, and two who are, alas, no longer with us, Linda Lefevre and Martin Eli Weil. Martin was a mentor, an important contributor to the Historic Structure Report, and a dear friend. Additional conservation guidance came from Frances Gayle, Stephen Gottlieb, and American preservation's equivalent of a living national treasure, Norman Weiss, whose knowledge would be intimidating if he weren't such a nice guy. In the realm of scholars who support, advise, encourage, and take mentorship and collegiality seriously, no one has done more for me, and this book, than Richard Cleary.

Four people, in particular, spent many years supporting the effort to save the Freeman House as board members for the Friends of the Freeman House, organizing events and exhibitions, serving as docents and hosts, and raising significant amounts of money: Ann Gray, Daniel Adams, Bettie Wagner, and John Gray. They made possible the research that went into this book. Dottie O'Carroll was the person at USC who worked with the board most closely, and implemented many of the programs envisioned by them. The phrases "indefatigable" and "generous to a fault" seem completely inadequate in describing her years of effort.

I thank the dozens of students who worked on the project, drawing and measuring, photographing, picking things apart, staffing programs and events, and mounting exhibits. Among them were Adam Smith, Gregory Downs, Luis Carranza, Denise Dea, Jeff Samudio, Paul Hoffman, and Lambert Giessinger. This book includes many of their contributions.

Several organizations provided substantial financial support for my research at the house. Without them, little could have been accomplished. The Getty Grants Program under John Sanday underwrote much of the Historic Structure Report. Steelcase matched their grant. The Graham Foundation for Advanced Studies in the Fine Arts, the Domino Center for Architecture and Design, the National Endowment for the Arts, and the Andy Warhol Foundation gave generous grants that supported specific programs, research, and preservation projects. Thank you, and though it has taken a while for this book to see the light of day, I hope it still counts as an acceptable grant product!

And, finally, to my parents: role models and fans, no matter what.

1

SETTING THE SCENE

Thursday Eve 1956

Happy New Year Mr. Wright

    For 32 years or more, I'm sure every student you've ever had who visits Los Angeles, visits our wonderful home. Every interested architect from New York, Holland, Ireland, Germany, Denmark etc. who comes to LA sooner or later comes to see too. . . . Many more wonderful New Years to you. In case you don't know it, I love every minute I spend in our home and after so many years too. Thank you.

    Harriet Press Freeman.

January 21st 1957

Dear Mrs. Freeman: I am glad to know that you are still happily "at home."

    Sincerely, Frank Lloyd Wright[1]

INTRODUCTION

This book is a case study on the preservation of an important work of modern architecture. The story of the Freeman House, and of the attempt to save it, entails almost all of the provocative issues that make historic preservation so fascinating, technologically and theoretically complex, and politically charged. Built in twelve months between March 1924 and March 1925, the Freeman House has been the site of a struggle between architecture and entropy ever since. After the death in 1986 of Harriet Freeman, who with her husband, Sam, commissioned the house, it became the property of the University of Southern California School of Architecture. Since then, the school, along with numerous architects, preservation consultants, engineers, students, and volunteers, has been bound up in the cause of keeping the house standing. For much of that time, there has been an enthusiastic public debate about its condition, its importance, and what should be done. Multiple interested parties have voiced their opinions, from the building's neighbors to preservation professionals to Wright scholars and aficionados, not to mention a plethora of city, state, and federal agencies. Inevitably, controversy has accompanied every decision and physical intervention, not to mention things not done or left undecided.

It turns out that there is no simple answer to the question of how to save this house—nor is there any single answer. The Freeman House is a valuable case study because it serves as a test of established preservation procedures and protocols, of building forensics and conservation techniques, and of the meaning of a historic site to overlapping and not necessarily compatible communities.

The Freeman House was an experiment born out of Frank Lloyd Wright's polemical vision of a new kind of architecture for the middle class, for modern America and, in particular, for the Los Angeles foothills. Its design and construction were difficult; those circumstances, as well as many poor decisions, planted within a beautiful work of architecture the seeds of its own destruction. Or, to use the poetic term common in conservation, it was a site rich in "inherent vice," flaws that become the root causes of building failures in later years.

The house was also, not coincidentally, commissioned and inhabited by a couple who were thoroughly modern in their lifestyle, artistic enthusiasms, and politics; people who were themselves the products of experiences and ideas born in the crucible of revolution that marked the end of the nineteenth century. Upon moving in, these clients almost immediately began to transform their new home into a salon of modern dance and art, as well as a guesthouse and a refuge for friends down on their luck or victims of the McCarthy-era blacklist. To accommodate their needs, changes took place over a period of fifty-plus years under a series of architects, some of whom were as important to the development of Southern California architecture as the team that designed the house, Frank Lloyd Wright and his son Lloyd.

1-1. The Freeman House in 2007, after the seismic rehabilitation project.

These included Rudolph Schindler, Gregory Ain, Robert Clark, John Lautner, James Reneau, and Eric Lloyd Wright, all of whom—with the exception of Ain, who had worked for both Schindler and Neutra, and James Reneau, who was brought in later by Harriet's nephews— had worked or studied with Wright.

Sixty years after the house was built, as Harriet Freeman was about to die—apparently the Wright client who occupied her home longer than any other—she gave it to USC "so that it would be used for educational enrichment in the architectural field."[2] For several years, the house was open to the public for tours, hosted a variety of special events and educational programs, and was the subject of research by professional conservators, engineers, architects, students, and faculty. During that time, the house underwent additional changes, mostly minor, with the author as architect. In 1994, the Northridge earthquake hit the Los Angeles region, taking fifty-seven lives and injuring some nine thousand people, as well as significantly damaging the Freeman House and many other structures. Six years later, the Freeman House underwent a substantial structural rehabilitation—designed by Robert Timme, Frank Dimster, Eric Wright, and Jeff Guh—that both saved and forever altered it. Smaller incremental projects have continued since then. Much more is needed.

But this is getting ahead of the story. Let us go back some nine decades to Los Angeles before the Freeman House, as a middle-aged architect in search of a new home and a new direction for his career arrived, hopeful and determined to transform himself and the landscape of Southern California.

WRIGHT

Frank Lloyd Wright was born in Richland Center, Wisconsin, on June 8, 1869.[3] His father, William Cary Wright, was Amherst- and Yale-educated, a man of many talents, but prone to drifting and melancholia. Frank's mother, Anna Lloyd Jones, a teacher, was William Wright's second wife and considerably younger than he. They led an itinerant life. When Frank was sixteen, his father, then a Baptist minister in Weymouth, Massachusetts, walked out, never to be seen again. Anna, on the other hand, played an almost mythic role in Wright's life, reportedly choosing his career for him while he was still in the womb. When Wright was seven, she gave him a drawing board subdivided into four-inch squares; according to one biographer, "This established in his consciousness the grid system that he later used to establish order and rhythm in his architecture."[4] Two years later, Anna brought the youngster Froebel blocks, a system of educational toys (called "gifts" by their creator), about which Wright himself wrote extensively, crediting them for teaching him fundamental principles of nature and design.[5] They too were based on simple geometries in both two and three dimensions.

At sixteen, Wright apprenticed to a local engineer while taking classes at the University of Wisconsin. Unhappy with the experience, he left home two years later, financing his departure for Chicago by selling various personal belongings. He found work first with the architect Joseph Silsbee, and then with the firm of Adler and Sullivan. Louis Sullivan's influence on him was profound. Wright always referred to Sullivan as his *lieber meister*, or "beloved master." From 1893 on, Wright headed his own practice, which was based in Chicago and Wisconsin until the 1930s, when he also operated out of Arizona during the winter.

Wright designed many of his best-known works as a pioneer of the Prairie School, which flowered during the first decade of the twentieth century, including the Larkin Soap Company (1903), Unity Temple (1904), Darwin Martin House (1904), and Frederick Robie House (1906).[6] In 1909, Wright left his first wife, Catherine Tobin, and their six children, for Mamah Cheney, the wife of a client. The two traveled to Europe accompanied by Wright's oldest son, Lloyd. There, Wright oversaw the publication of the *Wasmuth Portfolio*, which introduced his work in Europe to great acclaim; his ideas were absorbed by architects across the Continent, among them future apprentices such as Rudolph Schindler and Richard Neutra. Although he continued to design in the Prairie idiom sporadically, Wright's work after his return to the U.S. in 1910 was transformed by his interaction with various proponents of European modernist movements in art and architecture. Primitivist formal gestures and cubist compositions that would later appear in Wright's Los Angeles designs are first explored in projects such as the Midway Gardens in Chicago (1913), the A. D. German Warehouse in Richland Center, Wisconsin (1915), and the Bogk House in Milwaukee (1916).

In August 1914, while Wright was in Chicago, a servant at Taliesin, Wright's home in Spring Green, Wisconsin, set fire to the house and attacked its residents with an ax. Mamah Cheney and her two children were among the seven victims. This nationally notorious event began a decade marked by great turmoil in Wright's personal life, extraordinary developments in his architectural ideas and projects, and an expansion of his practice to Tokyo and Los Angeles. From 1914 to 1922, Wright's involvement with the Imperial Hotel, a school, and several residences in Japan, and with oil heiress and arts patron Aline Barnsdall in California, served as a welcome distraction from the pain and condemnation he faced in the Midwest as a result of the slayings.[7]

1-2. Hollyhock House, west facade. The Ennis House is faintly visible in the distance, just to the left of the rightmost tree trunk.

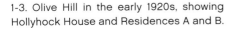

1-3. Olive Hill in the early 1920s, showing Hollyhock House and Residences A and B.

Still, Wright undertook one of his most ambitious projects in his native region during the late teens. In conjunction with Wisconsin developer Arthur Richards, Wright embarked on a multiyear effort to develop a new wood-frame construction system for single and multiple housing units, the American System-Built Homes. This was intended to develop a new way of building that would rival in quality and affordability not just traditional construction but also the popular mail-order homes available from Sears Roebuck and others. Only a few of the System-Built units were constructed, however, the effort curtailed at least in part by World War I.[8] Nonetheless, they serve as an important precedent for the textile-block houses.

Wright apparently first visited Southern California in 1905, on his initial trip to Japan. When he returned to the region a dozen years later, Aline Barnsdall had bought Olive Hill in Hollywood and commissioned Wright to design Hollyhock House, Residence A, and Residence B (Oleanders, since demolished), as well as unrealized theaters and other structures intended to complete Barnsdall's vision of an ambitious arts complex. Wright's early meetings with Barnsdall roughly coincided with his receiving the commission for the Imperial Hotel, however, and so he spent much of the period between 1917 and 1921, when Olive Hill was under construction, in Japan, working on the hotel, as well as the school and several residences.

When Frank Lloyd Wright arrived in Los Angeles after his last trip to Japan, it was with the intention of settling there permanently. He was fifty-five, ready after seven years of traveling between the United States and Japan to live and practice in a burgeoning region that promised work and renewal. Together with his son Lloyd, Wright established an office in the Homer Laughlin Building in downtown Los Angeles; they soon relocated the practice to West Hollywood. Wright himself briefly lived on Olive Hill, in Oleanders.

Wright's first designs upon his arrival in Los Angeles were for the Doheny Ranch, a planned development for what is now Trousdale Estates in Beverly Hills, and a second home nearby for Aline Barnsdall. These houses and their associated infrastructure (roads, bridges, and retaining walls) were to be built of a single modern material, concrete block, which incorporated the ancient material of the site, decomposed granite, in a construction technology that would be easy and inexpensive to employ—what he later named the textile-block system.

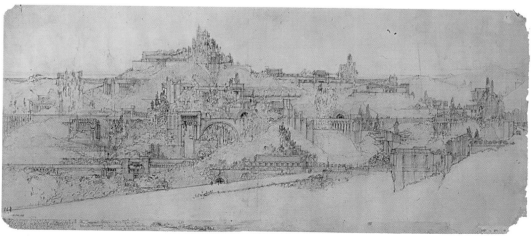

1-4. The Doheny Ranch project, Frank Lloyd Wright, 1923.

None of these initial projects was realized, however, and it is not evident that any client actually existed for the first or that Barnsdall ever intended to live in the second,[9] but, as David DeLong has pointed out, the four houses that were built shortly afterward—Millard, Storer, Freeman, and Ennis—should be seen as constructed manifestations of this initial vision, as should the partially constructed Little Dipper School from the same time.[10]

Wright's lofty ambitions for these projects came in part from his need to reestablish himself as a "brand" in American architecture, especially in his new home town; more important, they came from his desire to transform the nature of his own work and ideas, to remain current and visionary. But these ambitions, expressed in a radical departure from traditional building practice, would also contribute to the difficulties the buildings have experienced in the decades since their construction.[11] At the same time, for all their idiosyncrasies of design and construction, the four houses are directly connected to a lifelong set of interests Wright had in low-cost housing, the development of a simplified system of building, and the use of concrete as a building material. The houses are, in spite of—or because of—Wright's ambitions, among his most beautiful and powerful works.

The first, designed in 1921, was La Miniatura, built in a streambed in Pasadena. It was a residence for a repeat client, Alice Millard. The house is striking for several features besides its compelling presence in the landscape. It is a cubist composition, an organic outgrowth of the square blocks used to make it; and its section introduced a series of staggered floors that produced diagonal moves long familiar from Wright's plans but hitherto not seen in the vertical dimension to this extent. The material and setting give the building a rough, organic feel; at the same time, its form and spatial organization connect it to contemporary projects by Adolf Loos and other European Modernists. La Miniatura was constructed using a system of two interlocking 16"-square blocks that formed a double-wythe wall (that is, a wall formed of two parallel layers of masonry units with a narrow insulating space in between), reinforced only by a strip of steel mesh laid in the horizontal joints. This particular system was used only once.

At essentially the same time, Wright designed the Little Dipper, a new home for a kindergarten at Olive Hill, where Barnsdall's daughter, Sugar Top, was a student. The principal client seems to have been Harriet Freeman's sister Leah Lovell, who was teaching there with Pauline Schindler, Rudolph Schindler's wife.[12] This project became Harriet's introduction to Wright. It was also the first site at which Wright used the construction system (described below) that he later employed for the Storer, Freeman, and Ennis houses. However, shortly after work started on the Little Dipper, the already fragile relations between Barnsdall and Wright ruptured, and the project was abandoned.

In 1923, Wright began work on a house for Dr. John Storer. This project apparently arose quickly because, rather than designing a new building from scratch, Wright took out of the drawer an unbuilt design recently proposed for another client, C. P. Lowes, in Eagle Rock (another hillside neighborhood in Los Angeles). The Storer House became a larger, concrete-block version of the wood-frame and stucco original.

Though the Storer House was not originally designed with the textile-block system in mind, it adapted comfortably; of all the block houses, it survives in the best condition, and has had the fewest problems. Still, construction was difficult, running over budget and testing the many as yet un-designed and poorly conceived details of the new system. Lloyd Wright

1-5. Storer House, Frank Lloyd Wright, 1923.

1-6. Ennis House, Frank Lloyd Wright, 1924.

became the supervising architect. Before the Storer House was completed, work began on both the Freeman House and the Ennis House.

The Storer, Freeman, and Ennis houses form a line from west to east in the Hollywood Hills, sited approximately two miles apart. The Freeman House, designed in late 1923 and early 1924, was the first completed structure designed from the beginning in the textile-block system; the Ennis House, which was designed just a few months later, was the largest. The wealthy Ennises received a design in the Mayanesque California Romanza style used at Hollyhock House, while the decidedly middle-class Freemans received a modernist gem.

Wright continued to build in concrete block through the 1950s, although it remained an often problematic material. Still, in the ensuing decades, Wright's block system became the basis for the Arizona Biltmore Hotel, numerous other homes, many unbuilt projects, and his largest single collection of work in one location, Florida Southern College.

HOLLYWOOD

To understand why Wright saw opportunity in Los Angeles and why he took the approach he did, it helps to look at what was happening at the time he arrived and established his new practice. It is also important to understand the context in which his Los Angeles experiments were conducted, and in which the Freeman House was built and existed. The house is not just a work of architecture by Frank Lloyd Wright but also an example of the development of Hollywood, physically and culturally, during the 1920s: a creation of the avant-garde at a time and place when creating something new and progressive was a widely held community aspiration.

Between 1900 and 1930, the population of Los Angeles County increased thirteen times, from 170,298 to 2,208,492.[13] The region was "population mad, annexation mad, and speculation mad."[14] People came because of climate and health, fleeing the Spanish flu, tuberculosis, and winter; because land was cheap, as were one-way train tickets; and because of jobs.

And they came because California was open to a wide range of lifestyles, including many not accepted back home; because there was the freedom to do what you wanted, live how you wanted, believe in what you wanted. These intellectual and social renegades were the kind of people who were likely to appreciate and hire Wright. Furthermore, the rapid influx had created the first city in which the dominant residential building type was the single-family house. It was a landscape of isolated homes and pockets of commerce sprawled across fertile plains that were crisscrossed by wide roads a mile apart, all set against a backdrop of dramatic hills, a "strange 'metropolitan area,' . . . characterized neither as urban nor as rural, but . . . everywhere a combination of both,"[15] an apt description not only of Los Angeles in the teens and twenties, but of Broadacre City, the idealized model for American life that Wright created a decade after he left the region.

Hollywood was also growing rapidly, expanding from 7,500 to 36,000 inhabitants just in the decade between 1910 and 1920. There, and in the surrounding neighborhoods—a zone little more than a mile wide and five miles long running east–west along the southern flanks of the Santa Monica mountains—Frank Lloyd Wright, Lloyd Wright, Rudolph Schindler, Richard Neutra, and Irving Gill designed and built more than thirty structures in the teens and twenties.[16] For the architects as well as their clients, this zone represented the quintessential California site, a cultural landscape of extraordinary potency and potentiality in which natural features were equal players with the hand of man.

Until the mid-nineteenth century, the area of the future community of Hollywood, some ten miles northwest of the small town of Los Angeles, was largely in the hands of the Cahuenga Indians. The first European settler, Don Tomás Urquidez, arrived in the area in 1853 (his adobe home survived at Cahuenga and Vine until 1924, when it was demolished for the construction of a parking lot while the Freeman House was under construction a half mile away).[17] Developer Henry Wilcox founded the city of Hollywood in 1887. It was primarily an agricultural community until the beginning of the twentieth century, when the first large homes started appearing, along with a sprinkling of resort hotels used by day-trippers and weekenders who came out on the streetcar from Los Angeles. In 1903, Hollywood requested annexation by the city of Los Angeles, in order to hook into its outfall sewer.

The movie industry arrived in Hollywood around 1910. By the end of the decade, its presence was felt not only economically and culturally, but physically as well. The massive sets for D. W. Griffith's *Intolerance* stood at the base of Olive Hill when Barnsdall and Wright arrived to design their arts complex, and the sets for *The Thief of Baghdad* dominated the skyline just below the Freeman House as it was being built in 1924. The great movie palaces were rising on Hollywood Boulevard, including the Egyptian and the Chinese. The eclecticism and fantasy of movie sets, studios, and theaters spilled over into the realm of home and interior design. Kevin Starr, a California historian, wrote about the connection: "The more sets Hollywood created . . . the more expressively scenic became the popular architecture of the Southland."[18] Louis Adamic, the contemporary chronicler

1-7. Morgan House, Irving Gill, Hollywood, 1917.

of Southern California, described the resulting housing stock: "Almost unimaginable combinations of old Spanish, Bulgarian, Swiss Alpine, Italian, Slovak, French and other peasant houses and silly battlemented castles with a tower on each corner and flying banners on each tower."[19]

One development being constructed in 1921, right next to the Hollywood Bowl and within a few blocks of the future site of the Freeman House above Highland and Franklin Avenues, featured a Bolognese-style elevator tower set in the steep slopes to provide access to the surrounding homes—which included Lloyd Wright's Otto Bollman House. Just across Highland Avenue, Whitley Heights, which was developed starting in 1918 and was the home to many stars of the early movie era, covered its hillsides with a Mediterranean Revival village—along with a medieval castle. Many people wanted to own a piece of Los Angeles and to change it at the same time—to present it and then represent it. This was as true of architects with high-art aspirations and reputations as it was for land speculators and movie magnates—not to mention the overwhelming numbers of immigrant residents themselves.

Part of what fueled the sprawling growth of Southern California in the 1920s was the transformation of the automobile from an expensive rarity into a universal appliance of domestic life. Angelenos bought cars; vehicle registration in the region soon came to surpass that in any other urban center in the country, and the city began to acquire a worldwide reputation for being, among other things, the most motor-conscious on earth.[20] Cars made it possible for Wright (and others) to imagine developments in the foothills, areas not served by public transportation and too steep for pedestrian or horse. Just as critically, along with the automobile came the truck, which noted writer J. B. Jackson viewed as at least equally responsible for transforming American life and landscape.[21] The truck was essential to the new hillside building boom, because it made possible the easy movement of building materials, equipment, and even cubic yards of dirt to and from construction sites, permitting the relatively large amounts of cutting and filling required by the new houses and streets.

Automobile growth went hand in hand with the growth of the area's roads. In 1923, Mulholland Drive, the twisting, scenic road running along the top of the foothills from Hollywood west toward the Pacific, was opened to great fanfare. The next year, a highway opened through the Cahuenga Pass, connecting the Los Angeles Basin to the San Fernando Valley, and "erasing the last traces of the native Indians from the lands they had occupied in the area for generations."[22] The pass starts just below the site of the Freeman House.

When Wright arrived in California in 1921, his hopes were based on more than census data or an affinity for the landscape, however. Hollywood was essentially bracketed by two ambitious developments, each located on its own hill, unimpeded by surrounding ridges. Each was a block from Hollywood Boulevard, the major commercial spine of Hollywood. Each included both a residence for its owners and other buildings and amenities intended for the public (both had zoos, for example). And each possessed a distinctive and exotic architectural style, a major factor in its popularity and fame. The property at the western end of Hollywood was the Yama Shiro, crowned by a reproduction of a palace near Kyoto. It was built in 1913 for two brothers, Adolph and Eugene Bernheimer, who were in the import-export business. The house, surrounded by seven acres of Japanese gardens containing 30,000 varieties of trees and shrubs, waterfalls, goldfish ponds, and a 600-year-old temple shipped over from Japan, quickly became the largest tourist attraction in the

1-8. A view of Highland and Franklin, the intersection just below the Freeman House, in 1905, twenty years before the house was built.

1-9. The Hollywood Heights neighborhood, ca. 1950, showing major landmarks. Highland Avenue runs top to bottom in this image, joining the Hollywood Freeway in the Cahuenga Pass. North is down. The intersection shown in fig. 1-8 is just above the Freeman House in this photograph.

region. The property at the eastern end was Olive Hill, crowned by Hollyhock House, which evoked the Nunnery at Uxmal on the Yucatán Peninsula. It was set in its own formal gardens, and flanked by two other residences and a giant olive grove—with plans for a theater, school, cinema, and other arts-related facilities underway. Aline Barnsdall was the center of an important artistic circle, many of whose members were associated with the powerful new movie industry, and Wright apparently had every intention of joining and exploiting those relationships, as his son already had.

THE CLIENTS

Sam and Harriet Freeman resembled many of Frank Lloyd Wright's clients: young, left-wing, Jewish, artistically inclined, and supportive of the cultural and political avant-garde.[23] Both Sam and Harriet were from families that had immigrated to the United States during the 1880s to escape oppression in their native lands. Sam was born Samuel Friedman in New York City on August 2, 1889. He had two sisters, Ettie and Bertha, who were respectively six and four years older than he. Neither of them would marry. Their parents, Adolf and Sally, came to the United States in 1881, having married just before the voyage. When Sam was a boy, the family lived in a third-floor walk-up on the eastern fringes of the Upper East Side. One of Sally's brothers, Isidore Weisenberger, lived a few blocks away.

The Friedmans and Weisenbergers came from the province of Trencsén in Slovakia, then a part of the Hungarian portion of the Austro-Hungarian Empire.[24] The province just to the south of Trencsén was Nitra, the ancestral home of Richard Neutra, while the families that produced Harriet's sister Leah's husband, Phillip Lovell,[25] emigrated from the Austrian province of Galicia, which bordered Trencsén on the north.[26]

Adolf Friedman, like so many of his fellow immigrants, found work as a tailor. His daughter Ettie worked as a milliner. Sam yearned for something different. Upon graduating from high school in 1906, he moved to Los Angeles to work for his mother's younger brother, Julius Weisenberger, who was comfortably established as a jeweler. Two years later, Sam had changed his last name to Freeman. He never went to college.

When he first arrived in California, seventeen-year-old Sam Friedman moved into Julius's apartment just south of downtown Los Angeles. The other members of the household were Julius's wife, Addie; her parents, Leopold and Alice Cohn; two of her younger siblings, Winnie and Sam; and a Japanese servant named Dauzo Saito. Weisenberger co-owned a store with several of his in-laws in the downtown jewelry district near 7th and Hill streets. By the late 1920s, Sam was apparently a full partner in the business. However, as the Depression took hold, something happened to the family firm and Sam became a salesman for the EA George Company, another downtown jeweler, and sold real estate on the side.

1-10. The Friedmans, ca. 1918. Sitting, left to right: Adolf, Sally, Sam; standing: Ettie and Bertha. Sam was the only one in the family to change his name to Freeman.

Within ten years of Sam's departure from New York, his parents and sisters had joined him in Los Angeles. Adolf and Sally Friedman moved into a house at 8368 Romaine at Orlando Street in what is now West Hollywood.[27] Despite his modest profession, Adolf seemed to be relatively comfortable economically, able not only to move his wife and two daughters to a new home across the country but also apparently to contribute some or all of the money required to build Samuel and Harriet's house. When Adolf died in 1934, his bequest to Samuel and his sisters included shares of Union Oil stock.[28] By the advent of World War II, Sam was able to retire from sales and devote his life to left-wing politics and the care of the house.

Harriet was the youngest of six children of Mose and Sarah Press.[29] Her older siblings, three boys and two girls, were Abe, Bernard, David, Leah, and Marie. The two oldest children were born in the town of Grodno, Russia (now Belarus). In 1883, Mose emigrated to the United States and shortly afterward brought Sarah, Abe, and Bernard over to join him; they then settled in the Midwest, where other members of their extended family had been established since the 1870s. David was born in Iowa in 1884; Leah and Marie, in Missouri in 1885 and 1886, respectively. The large gap between oldest and youngest siblings made it feel "like two different families."[30] Shortly after Harriet's birth in Omaha, Nebraska, on January 16, 1890, the family moved east to Chariton, Iowa, a town some fifty miles south of Des Moines.[31]

Some family members were involved in agriculture, but most were merchants. The area in which Harriet and her siblings grew up was booming at the end of the nineteenth century, and Chariton was an important commercial center, arranged around a classic courthouse square and situated on major rail lines. Its importance was further bolstered by the nearby presence of a number of large coal mines. When Harriet was still in high school, the family moved once again, this time to New York City. Both Harriet and Leah were interested in teaching. Leah enrolled at New York University, where she received a degree in education and was a New York City public school teacher by the time she was in her early twenties. When Harriet was in high school, she and her friends would go to the gymnasium at Leah's school and sit on the wooden floor to

1-11. Portrait of Mose Press, Harriet's father, by Edward Weston.

watch Leah teach. "It was like going to the theater," she later said. "My sister wasn't just a teacher. She was a very rare educator. She was known all over New York. She had her kids so well trained, the kids would go to the different classrooms and teach, and the teachers would watch."[32]

One summer Harriet worked as a counselor for disabled children, helping the students grow tomatoes, swim, and engage in other life skills and recreational activities. Upon graduation from high school, Harriet took courses at Hunter College that allowed her to receive a teaching certificate from the State of New York in 1911, and she obtained a degree in physical education from Savage's Normal School in 1915. She taught in a New York public school for several years.

In 1914, while still at Savage's, Harriet spent nine months in Bermuda as a member of the cast of *Neptune's Daughter*, a silent film starring Annette Kellerman. She played one of the mermaids battling the evil minions of the Witch of the Sea.[33] The film was a great success, and helped launch Kellerman's career as the "million-dollar mermaid." A champion swimmer and the popularizer of synchronized swimming, as well as the "inventor" of the one-piece bathing suit for women, Kellerman pioneered the connection between entertainment, health, beauty, and mass merchandising with her books and short films about exercise and diet. Harriet, who was also an excellent swimmer (she participated in the annual swim around Balboa Island well into middle age), clearly found an early role model in the young Kellerman; she even developed her own exercise routines in later years. "Before women's lib was invented," Harriet later said, "I was doing my own thing, never dressing like anyone else, not even carrying a regular pocketbook."[34]

Harriet pursued a part-time career in entertainment for the rest of the decade, interspersing dance engagements around New York with teaching. She seems to have been inspired in part by her brother David, the sibling to whom she was closest. David had left home as a teenager, earning a living as an itinerant piano player. Married by twenty, he and his wife, Myrtle, made their way to Goldfield, Nevada, where they shared rented rooms with a musician named Charles Hall. Goldfield was a gold-strike boomtown, founded in 1902 and the biggest city in the state by 1910, when the couple arrived. But the gold mines soon petered out, and the town shriveled up. David died there from causes unknown, and Harriet took the loss of her soul mate hard.

In her late twenties, Harriet and a friend from the Savage School, Margary (or Margarie) Lane formed a dance team and toured with different musical comedy revues.[35] Their notices were positive: "Harriet Press and Margarie Lane, billed as a couple of Broadway Trippers, are also deserving of special mention."[36] The two then joined the road show production of *Glorianna*, starring former Austrian opera star turned Broadway actress Fritzi Scheff. The company played in over a dozen cities, including Chicago, Savannah, Lynchburg (". . . while the specialty dancing of Margaret [*sic*] Lane and Harriet Press blazoned out in a performance that laid 'Listen, Lester' in the shade with odds to spare"), Vicksburg ("The dancing of Misses Lane and Press was especially a feature and won

1-12. Harriet as a mermaid, while filming *Neptune's Daughter*, starring Annette Kellerman, in 1914.

much applause"), Toledo, Omaha, and Pittsburgh. Cleveland—where both Eubie Blake and the Vatican choir were performing at the same time in other theaters—had a more qualified response to the show. "Some of the dancing is light and zippy, particularly that of the Misses Margary Lane and Harriet Press . . . [but] a fog of depression settled over a considerable part of the audience Monday."

In 1919, just before the tour took off, Harriet's mother and sisters had followed the oldest sibling, Abraham, to Los Angeles, where his tuberculosis was cured in the California sunshine using "natural" methods, and he was operating a health spa in Hollywood and farming. Sarah, Leah, and Marie moved in with Abe in a house on Myra Avenue, not far from Olive Hill. Through Abe, Leah met the future "naturopath" doctor and *Los Angeles Times* columnist Philip Lovell, perhaps ten years her junior and at the time working as a research chemist.[37] By 1920, they had married, although they continued living with Leah's mother and siblings.[38] After her tour, Harriet joined her family. It seems possible that she was hoping to continue her entertainment career in Hollywood. But entering her thirties, Harriet was competing with thousands of young women from around the country, and despite her dance skills she was not enough of a beauty to do so successfully. *Glorianna* was her last turn as a performer.

Where and how Harriet and Sam met is not known, but they married on April 18, 1921, and moved into an apartment at 4150 Santa Monica Boulevard, just a few blocks from the rest of the Press clan. Two years later, following a visit by Harriet to her sister's school on Olive Hill, they commissioned Frank Lloyd Wright to design their house. "After seeing Wright's buildings there, I couldn't imagine choosing another architect."[39]

Because of the passions of its owners, the Freeman House would play a significant role in the history of the avant-garde in Los Angeles. For many years, a wide range of artists, architects, actors, scientists, and political figures visited Harriet's "salon." She became an important supporter of modern dancers, especially the Lester Horton Dance Theater and Bella Lewitzky. She hosted a dinner for Martha Graham in the living room.[40] Harriet herself led dance and exercise classes at the house and in several colleges in the area. Sam became immersed in political activities. And like many of their friends, he was labeled a Communist by the FBI.[41] Later, one acquaintance complained, "The Freemans were always trying to recruit young girls to their cause."[42] Perhaps as a result of the controversy and danger attached to liberal activities at the time, much of the story of Sam's daily life remains a bit elusive. But we do know that at various times he supported left-wing theater groups in Hollywood and was a part-owner of a leftist bookstore, and that he included among his friends such politically engaged figures as the socialist Unitarian minister Stephen Fritchman and Augustus Hawkins, the first African American congressman from California. Early discussions about how to force integration of the federal government's proposed public housing project for Chavez Ravine

1-13. Harriet and Margary Lane during their tour with Fritzi Scheff in *Glorianna* in 1919.

1-14. Sam and Harriet Freeman, ca. 1930.

were held in the living room of the Freeman House, attended by a mix of clergy and political activists. And several of the wives of the Hollywood Ten were regulars in Harriet's exercise classes at the house.

Almost continuously after 1928, the Freemans were hosts to an assortment of guests and tenants. Some, such as the actor Albert van Dekker and his wife and child, and the actress Helen Walker, were invited to stay because their fortunes were low—or political activities had led to their being blacklisted in the movie industry. Others, such as bandleader Xavier Cugat, collector Galka Scheyer, and actor Claude Rains, were friends involved with the arts. Still others, such as Clark Gable's agent or the Swiss mathematician Fritz Zwicky, were just interesting, rent-paying tenants. At one point in 1939, four different "households," totaling seven people, resided in the little house. Later, as this first generation of friends moved on or passed away, the childless Freemans welcomed young people who aspired to either artistic or political careers.

Though Sam and Harriet's funds and desires caused the house to happen, it is unclear how much influence they had on Wright's design. Sam said that Wright was more interested in who they were than in what they wanted, which was fine with the young couple. On the other hand, the house undoubtedly achieved Harriet's primary objective: to serve as her entrée into the world of the avant-garde and to continue for decades to attract artists and other interesting people with whom she could engage. Still, the house required ongoing modifications over the years to accommodate the evolving needs of the couple and their guests. In addition, the building itself was a demanding artifact, owing to the experimental nature of the textile-block system and the many difficulties that accompanied its design and construction. The result is a history of change that transformed Frank Lloyd Wright's modernist conception into a much messier but ultimately even more interesting place.

OTHER HANDS AT THE FREEMAN HOUSE

From the very beginning, the Freeman House was a product of multiple hands. Frank Lloyd Wright, Jr., commonly known as Lloyd Wright, played two roles at the Freeman House: he was a partner in the design firm that created the house and its contractor. Because of his lesser fame, Lloyd Wright's role in and importance to the house and to Los Angeles is easy to overlook. The oldest of Wright's children, Lloyd was born in 1890 to Wright and his first wife, Catherine Tobin. He had a beautiful hand, producing many of the illustrations for the *Wasmuth Portfolio,* as well as other work in his father's office.[43] Lloyd attended the University of Wisconsin but, like his father, dropped out before graduation. Upon his return from the European trip with his father and Mamah Cheney, Lloyd joined the distinguished landscape architecture firm of Olmsted and Olmsted in Boston, moving to California shortly afterward to work with John Olmsted and Irving Gill on the San Diego Panamanian Exposition. (Gill had worked with Frank Lloyd Wright in the office of Adler and Sullivan.) When Bertram Goodhue ended up taking the exposition commission away from Gill, Lloyd went to work directly for Gill from 1912 to 1915, becoming involved with several of Gill's most important projects, which, significantly, were constructed of concrete. Then Lloyd went into practice as a landscape architect with Paul Thiene, designed the landscape at Olive Hill for Aline Barnsdall, worked briefly as director of the Design and Drafting Department at Paramount Pictures, married an actress from Barnsdall's circle (Martha Taggart), and moved to New York. In 1919, he returned to Los Angeles to supervise construction of Hollyhock House for his father. That responsibility lasted only a year, however, before the elder Wright replaced him.

Two years later, Lloyd designed his first built residence, the Prairie-style W. J. Weber House, apparently completing a commission originally intended for his father. During the early 1920s, he worked on his own, with his father, and with others. He continued to be heavily involved with Aline Barnsdall's circle, working on theatrical designs with Norman Bel Geddes, acoustical shells for the Hollywood Bowl, and the bookstore of the renowned cultural maven Jacob Zeitlin. He joined Gill, Rudolph Schindler, and his father in exploring new ways of building in concrete, first in 1922 for two romantic expressionistic residences for a pair of contractor brothers, Otto and Henry Bollman, and then in 1924 for the Oasis Hotel in Palm Springs, which used shallow concrete pours to give the tower its distinctive banded appearance. The Henry Bollman House is notable for being ornamented with areas of concrete block wired together and attached to the wood-frame and stucco building. In later years, Lloyd would point to this as the progenitor of the textile-block system. Lloyd also worked on the Millard House in 1923. After supervising the construction of the Storer, Freeman, and Ennis houses, Lloyd embarked on his own practice, and designed a series of strong, evocative houses in the late 1920s that employed textile blocks, although only to accent openings and other special elements. These included the Derby, Sowden, and Samuels-Navarro houses, as well as his own home and studio. In 1928, he also designed what could be described as the model for automobile-oriented commercial-strip architecture, the Yucca-Vine Market. Lloyd continued working in Southern California until his death in 1978, designing for important figures in the arts, such as Jasha Heifetz and Claudette Colbert. Perhaps his most well-known work is the Wayfarers Chapel in Palos Verdes, begun in 1946.

The Freemans took a harsh view of Lloyd, making him the scapegoat for all that went wrong with their house, and any features or furnishings they did not like. This would seem to reinforce Lloyd's importance to the project, but probably was also a way for Harriet to deflect any responsibility for having selected Frank Lloyd Wright as her architect. In any case, when the Freemans wanted some more work done on their house in 1926, they did not turn to Lloyd, who was theoretically both available and knowledgeable, but to another former Wright apprentice and a family friend, Rudolph Michael Schindler.

Of all the architects who worked on the Freeman House after Frank Lloyd Wright and Lloyd Wright, Schindler was by far the most important. The relationship came about because of Schindler's deep involvement with Harriet Freeman's sister and brother-in-law Leah and Philip Lovell, for whom he designed three houses (in Wrightwood, Fallbrook, and Newport Beach), a school, and an office. Schindler's first project for the Freemans actually predated the house; it was a shower remodel in April 1924 in the newlyweds' apartment on Santa Monica Boulevard.[44] He became the Freemans' architect again a year after their new house was finished, and remained so until his death in 1953.

Schindler was an Austrian architect who had come to the United Sates in 1914 to join Chicago architecture firm Ottenheimer, Stern and Reichert, with

1-15. Oasis Hotel, Lloyd Wright, Palm Springs, 1923.

the hope that they would provide an entrée to Frank Lloyd Wright.[45] Although the two met and talked, it was several years before Wright was in a position to hire the ardent applicant. Schindler finally got the job in early 1918, and Wright immediately placed him "in charge of my affairs during my absence."[46] Schindler worked on the Imperial Hotel and the Barnsdall projects, and essentially replaced Wright's son John, who had been in charge of the Chicago office but accompanied his father to Japan.[47]

In 1919, Schindler met and married Pauline Gibling, who had been a teacher at the progressive Hull House in Chicago and had broad interests and a family background in music, politics, and architecture. When problems arose in the construction of the Barnsdall buildings at Olive Hill in 1920, Wright asked Schindler to come out to Los Angeles to supervise the project personally—replacing Lloyd. Pauline Schindler met Leah Press at Olive Hill, where Leah had started the kindergarten that Sugar Top, Aline's daughter, attended. After the collapse of the Little Dipper project, the two women started an elementary school in Hollywood. Schindler became the Lovells' architect. In 1921, Schindler and Clyde Chace, the engineer for Irving Gill's Horatio Court apartments in Santa Monica, began work on a house in West Hollywood for their two families. Considered by many to be among the most original and important works of modern architecture, the Schindler-Chace Double House on Kings Road was inspired in part by the rock and canvas lean-tos of Yosemite, and was built half of redwood and canvas, half of concrete. Equally important, it was organized in a way that gave each of the four adults his or her own room, and each family its own outdoor space. A shared kitchen and small guest apartment were also included; sleeping took place in open-air structures on the roof. This house became the venue for decades of salons, performances, and lectures, and was often paired with the Freeman House in an evening's festivities.[48]

In 1927, after four years of collaboration, Philip Lovell and Schindler fell out, whereupon Lovell, then a successful entrepreneur and media figure, turned to Richard Neutra to design

1-16. Schindler-Chace Double House, West Hollywood, 1921.

his Hollywood Hills home, the Health House. Neutra had been a fellow student and friend of Schindler in Austria, and remained an intellectual companion through correspondence over the years. In 1923, Schindler was able to help Neutra escape the devastation of postwar Europe and come to the United States. Like Schindler, it took Neutra some time to get work at Wright's office, which he did for a few months beginning in late 1924. (During that brief period, Neutra even did some drawings of the textile-block construction system.) The next year, Neutra and his wife, Dione, moved to Los Angeles, where they took up residence with the Schindlers in the Kings Road house, the Chaces having left. However, the relationship between the two friends deteriorated following Neutra's "betrayal," as the Freemans would later characterize Neutra's supplanting of Schindler as the Lovells' architect and his taking all of the credit for a jointly designed submission to the League of Nations competition the same year. In their choice of language, the Freemans were obviously reflecting a sentiment conveyed to them by Schindler. The Freemans' annoyance was exacerbated by the fact that Schindler had previously asked them, as a favor to him, to employ Neutra to design a landscape plan for the house (see fig. 6-33), as he had done for the Lovells, also at Schindler's request.

Harriet and Schindler were lovers; the affair most likely started not long after they first met and continued for years.[49] It was an open secret; many of their friends knew, and it seems hard to believe the respective spouses did not. Nevertheless, both Harriet and Sam remained fervent admirers and supporters of Schindler their entire lives, and he designed projects for twenty of the Freemans' friends and family members.[50] Three of these were immediately adjacent to the Freeman House, transforming both the physical and social context in which the building existed for most of its history, and in which we seek to understand the house today.

It is difficult to overemphasize the importance of Schindler to the story of the Freeman House. During the late teens and twenties, he wove in and out of Wright's work and practice in ways that eventually

1-17. Harriet Freeman and Rudolph Schindler at his Wolf House, Catalina, ca. 1928.

angered the elder architect, from whom Schindler became estranged until 1953, when Schindler lay dying and Wright made a gesture of reconciliation. Schindler was in charge of Wright's Chicago and Los Angeles offices while Wright was in Japan, and he worked on Olive Hill, both as designer and construction supervisor, and on the Millard House, which clearly shows Schindler's influence.[51] He was the designer in Wright's office for the early version of the C. P. Lowes House, which later became the Storer House, as well as the architect for the house the Loweses finally did build the next year. He continued to work for Aline Barnsdall even after she would have nothing more to do with the Wrights. He was involved with the Freeman House within months of the Wrights leaving the project, and also remodeled the interior of the Storer House shortly after its completion. And he was the architect who, perhaps more than any other, brought Wright's California work into the next iteration of modernist architecture through his own remarkable body of work, almost all of which was built in the Los Angeles region. One only needs to look at Schindler's How House or Puebla Ribera Court, for example, both from 1925, to see how Schindler developed his own response to the technological and formal ideas of the Freeman House.

Following Schindler's death, the Freemans hired other architects to make repairs and relatively minor modifications to their home. The list is a minor history of Los Angeles architecture and includes Gregory Ain, a student of both Schindler and Neutra as well as a political buddy of Sam Freeman's; Taliesin graduate Robert Clark; John Lautner, another former Wright apprentice and notable designer; James Reneau, a local architect; and Eric Lloyd Wright, Frank Lloyd Wright's grandson, who also trained at Taliesin and to this day both works on his own projects and helps restore the buildings of his father and grandfather.

THE TEXTILE-BLOCK SYSTEM

Concrete was a favorite material of modern architects, and Wright was no exception. He helped to pioneer poured-in-place concrete construction with Unity Temple in 1904, and used both poured concrete and concrete block in numerous other designs from that date on. Thus, the textile-block system Wright used in Los Angeles in the 1920s was one answer to a set of practical and ideological issues with which he had been concerned for years. Like virtually all modern architects—and most of the American construction industry since the nineteenth century—Wright was searching for a building technology that reduced costs and construction time by allowing the use of cheap, unskilled labor (even, perhaps, the home-owner himself) and machine-made materials. Toward that end, he sought a system that could simplify construction both conceptually and in practice, and a material that would be struc-ture, skin, and ornament all at the same time: a "mono-material" that was organic rather than contrived. Wright's goal was to integrate his process of designing a space (which relied on regular geometries) with a technology based on an equally rigorous geometry for building that space: a grid both formal and structural.

It is important to recognize that concrete-block construction had become common at the end of the nineteenth century, though much of it prior to Wright had involved concrete masonry made to resemble stone. This history included buildings designed by noted architects as well as vernacular construction using machinery widely sold by Sears Roebuck and oth-ers. In fact, Wright's system failed to obtain a patent because it so closely resembled another system, called Nel-Stone, which had been invented by William Nelson. Wright scholar Rob-ert Sweeney has written about this, making the case that the similarities were probably not coincidental.[52]

Wright described the textile-block system in 1927: "The system consists of concrete block slabs about 2 or 3 inches thick of unit sizes which can be handled, laid on end with interlock-ing grooves, reinforced horizontally and vertically by means of steel rods tying the inner to the outer shell of the walls. Concrete is poured into the holes through which the rods extend, forming a complete, weatherproof, structural bond of spidery steel reinforcement between the various units making up the general system of design. The pattern or design of the face and the size of the blocks may be varied to suit any particular plan condition or exterior treat-ment. Floors and roofs of these buildings are reinforced concrete tiles and joists knitted to the exterior and interior walls, forming a continuous construction. Walls may be made of varying reveals with the air space between the vertical slabs of the interior and outside wall face, mak-ing for warmth in the winter and coolness in the summer."[53]

Wright apparently first used the term *textile-block* in this same article.[54] In the specifications for the Freeman House from early 1924, he variously refers to the "reinforced concrete construction," "cement blocks," "cement tiles," and "pre-cast slabs or blocks."[55] He refers to the wythes of the block walls as "outer and inner shells." As it happens, just as the origins of the system are a bit murky,[56] so is the origin of the term we use today. "Tex-tile" was a brand name used by the National Tile Company (NATCO) to describe a construction system that employed terra-cotta tiles with steel reinforcing in a manner not too dissimilar from Wright's. A construction manual from 1919 described the NATCO system: "The Textile block is a hollow-tile block in which the exposed faces are finished like a rough face brick. . . . The exterior effect of this wall is distinctive, as the faces of the Textile blocks showing in the face of the wall are about three times the size of a standard brick. . . . The wall has the appearance of having been built of very large bricks, which gives it a peculiar attractiveness."[57] Many aspects of the NATCO system are shared by Wright's: the use of the exposed face in a distinctive finish as the final surface, the use of a larger-than-standard masonry unit, and the structural interweaving of block and steel. NATCO's system preceded Wright's by at least five years, and continued in use through the 1920s.

In the textile-block system used at the Storer, Freeman, and Ennis houses (and the abandoned Little Dipper school), the basic component was a 16" x 16" concrete tile, held in a matrix of ¼"-diameter steel bars (the warp and weft of the textile). The tiles were frequently coffered

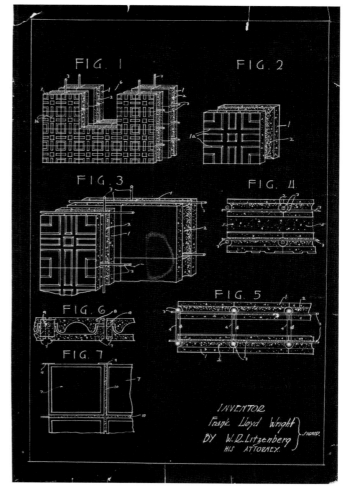

1-18. Patent drawing for the textile-block system.

on the back, so that they ranged in thickness between 3½" at the edges and 1½" in the middle. A semicircular channel ran the length of each edge.

After several blocks were stacked edge to edge horizontally, steel bars were placed in the vertical channels between them, and another bar was laid in the continuous channel running along the top. Another horizontal row of blocks was set on top, and a soupy grout was poured into the channels, anchoring both vertical and horizontal sets of bars. The result is a set of blocks made from a dry-tamped cementitious material, anchored by a set of grout tubes made from a poured cementitious material with steel embedded.

In a typical wall, two wythes of blocks were to be set back to back, an inch apart, with the hollow areas serving as insulating air space (and lessening the blocks' weight). Additional steel rods periodically tied the wythes together. This assembly would be 8" thick, half the width of a block module. Single-wythe walls were also used in the Freeman House, especially in areas, such as closets or the garage, where a finished look was not critical but the extra 4" of space would be welcome.

Blocks were made by preparing a concrete mix so dry that "it left no moisture when squeezed in the palm of the hand," according to the specifications. (This is why the mix is called a dry tamp.) On occasion, a hand-operated mixer was used to make the concrete; otherwise, it was mixed with a hoe in a six-foot-long wooden box.[58] The mix was then placed into a cast-aluminum mold that consisted of a plain or patterned face plate, a coffered back plate covered with a lightweight tin liner, and a hinged flask or surround that held the two plates together. Ribs along the inner sides of the flask impressed the channels into the edges of the block. The filled mold was set on a table, topped with a piece of wood, and the entire setup hit with a six-pound sledgehammer. The top plate was then taken off, the flask unhinged, and the block removed from the mold by means of the tin liner. Using the dry mix and tin liner meant that the block did not require any significant time to assume its final shape: it could be (carefully) removed from the mold and set out to dry almost immediately. After a few hours, when it had achieved an early set, the block was separated from the liner and set on edge in rows on the site, to be kept moist while curing for three or more weeks. Seventy-five or more blocks could be made this way each day.

While new blocks cured, the crew constructed wooden frameworks wherever work was going on to support the wobbly block walls until the interconnecting grout tubes had time to set. (They also built regular formwork for cast-in-place footings, columns, and beams.) Once the framework was in place and an area was ready to receive new blocks, the crew had to find the appropriate variants from among thousands lying around the site and install them.

While by far the most common type of block made for the Freeman House was a plain 16"-square tile (4,496 out of a total of roughly 10,000), there are actually 74 types of block in the building. What was supposed to be a simple, "mono-material" system required such complexity because of the need for different block dimensions (full, half, or quarter modules) and patterns (left-facing, right-facing, or plain), as well as special perforated blocks for screens and mitered blocks for corners. Forming the variants necessitated the addition of certain pieces to the basic molds, or even separate specialized molds.

1-19. Mason Peter Purens demonstrating block making using the original Freeman House mold.

1-20. Components for a Freeman House block mold, including plain and patterned face plates, coffered back, flask, and tin liner.

All the block houses actually relied to a significant extent on other construction systems and materials. For example, only in one 24-square-foot area in the "tool shed" (a small structure attached to the exterior of the Freeman House) did the textile-block system form a ceiling plane. Most horizontal surfaces above grade were built using the joists and sheathing of traditional wood-frame construction. The major structural elements at the block houses were typically poured-in-place concrete columns and beams. Even block bearing walls were supported in part by poured-concrete members running both vertically and horizontally. And in more visible locations inside the Freeman House, the backs of single-wythe walls were faced with plaster (the stairwell), gypsum wallboard (some closets), or wood paneling (the downstairs lounge). Ceilings were finished in wood panels or plaster.

The textile-block system and its construction are discussed in more detail in subsequent chapters, especially Chapter 5, because the system is central to many of the conservation issues at the Freeman House.

A DESCRIPTION OF THE HOUSE

The Freeman House, as noted earlier, is the smallest of the block houses (approximately 2,500 square feet), constructed on the smallest site (about 7,000 square feet). The constraints of size and budget may have helped make it, of all four houses, the clearest, most efficient expression of Wright's ideas for the type and for affordable middle-class housing. The house is situated on a dramatic hillside lot, close to "downtown" Hollywood. The uphill (northern) elevation of the house fronts a small, winding residential street; it is mostly solid wall and modestly scaled to fit the narrow street and its neighbors. The downhill (southern) elevation is larger, more open, and more impressive, as if in response to its visibility from the surrounding city. Although only a few yards from one of the busiest intersections in Los Angeles, and only three blocks from Grauman's Chinese Theater and other Hollywood landmarks, the Freeman House is nestled among eucalyptus and pine trees and connected by winding paths and stairs to several other historic homes nearby. It is a pastoral setting complete with skunks, possums, raccoons, deer, coyotes, hawks, mountain lions, owls, and other wild animals. These contrasting realms make the house paradigmatic for generations of Los Angeles hillside homes to follow, with their ambiguous relationships between independent country life and the dynamic city(scape) from which they draw their very existence. It is also an example of the kind of urban/suburban conflation that Wright envisioned in his Broadacre City designs of the 1930s.

The massing of the two-story Freeman House consists of two cubes: a living/dining room set over two bedrooms and a sitting room, and a detached garage over (originally) a laundry/storeroom. The cubes are set at right angles to each other at a bend in the street, and connected at both levels by circulation and services via walkways and a three-story stair tower. The geometries are simple, and clearly deliberate. The main portion of the house is 26'8" on a side, and throughout the house proportions of rooms or elements on the facades are 1:1 or 1:$\sqrt{2}$.

The living room of the Freeman House is one of the greatest of Wright's small spaces: it contains elements of a basilica (the raised central roof lined by clerestories) and of a modern skyscraper (curtain walls of glass). At its core lies the oppositional relationship

1-21. North façade of the Freeman House and garage during construction, late 1924. The north wall of the main house is essentially solid along the street, punctuated only by perforated blocks and the folded planes of the chimney.

of the "tree house" vistas of the city and the "cave"-like hearth. This symbolic linking of the world as seen from a high perch to the family gathered around the sacred fire was an important and consistent formal dialogue in Wright's residential architecture, effectively uniting two distinct approaches to place making. The living room also powerfully demonstrates Wright's desire to connect design inextricably to materiality and construction through its cubist geometry, the play of solid and void along the walls, the celebration of light and patterning caused by the perforated blocks. The double-height strips of glass, interrupted by the projecting volumes of the balconies on both south and east, and capped by the dramatic horizontal roof plane slicing through the south facade, makes the house an abstract modernist composition of space and movement, of light and dark, of introversion and explosion. It is as radical as its iconic contemporaries in Europe, such as Le Corbusier's Ozenfant Studio or Loos's Villa Lido or Rietveld's Schroeder House, and demonstrates Wright's intention to be not just Modernism's forebear but an able practitioner of the new movement's forms and ideas, albeit with a primitivist earthiness replacing the factory aesthetic of the Europeans.

THE HOUSE IN 1986

When Harriet Freeman decided to give the Freeman House to USC in 1984, the School of Architecture conducted a quick evaluation of the building and developed a scope of work so that Dean Robert Harris could request additional funds from her to accompany the gift for the purpose of fixing any problems. That study was clearly preliminary and sketchy, in large part because Harriet was very skittish, having previously given the house away to the Trust for the Preservation of Cultural Heritage (basically, Augustus Brown, the owner of the Ennis House) and then yanked it back. Still, the issues were easily identified. There were cracks in floors, walls, and ceilings, myriad leaks, plants growing all over the exterior of the

1-22. Freeman House from the southeast, ca. 1928.

building, and damage from both dry-wood and subterranean termites. Cockroaches, potato bugs, spiders, and mice rounded out the nonhuman residents of the house. (The bats had, fortunately, already been encouraged to depart a few years before.) Veneers were peeling off furniture, electrical outlets were sparking or dead, walls bore black stains, efflorescence, or damp patches. Windows sagged, especially at the living room corners, or barely closed. The only heat came from unvented gas heaters. Kitchen appliances barely worked; the same was true of the bathroom fixtures. The garage had lost its doors, and many of those in the rest of the house were flimsy at best. The yard was overgrown with weeds; trash and plant debris littered the apartment terrace.

The Freeman House's location in the border zone between downtown Hollywood and the Hills meant that the urban decay of the 1970s and 1980s regularly washed up against it. It had been broken into several times; at one point Harriet, already in a wheelchair, had been tied up. Drug addicts regularly used the hillside to shoot up or deal, prostitutes used the dead-end street for encounters, and shortly after USC took over the house, a murder occurred nearby.

Concern about these issues among residents in the neighborhood influenced their attitudes toward the house; they feared it might attract a transient crowd of students and architecture buffs and tax the narrow streets with more cars parking, yet they welcomed the idea of the surrogate presence of a major institution. All three fronts had to be addressed: the condition of the house, the condition of the community, and the role of the house within its multiple contexts. While we are concerned here with the first of these almost exclusively, considerable time and energy went into the other two as well. Today, the neighborhood is safer, the community supportive and protective, and the house still stands.

A PRESERVATION PROJECT

This book tells the story of a preservation project. Frank Lloyd Wright's work provides great case studies because any preservation effort involving his work is a challenge. The technical aspects are often daunting. The audience watching is large and vociferous. There is both a theoretical—even polemical—component to the architect's designs and a high level of artistry in the composition, materials, and craftsmanship of the building. And preserving the work can be very expensive.

While many of these issues are discussed in the course of our story, two dilemmas underlie much of the debate concerning what should be done at the Freeman House. The first is centered on integrity; the second concerns authorship.

In America, historic preservation is based on the principle that the *authenticity* of a site is related to its integrity, which the National Park Service notes is "evidenced by the survival of physical characteristics that existed during the property's prehistoric or historic period. . . . [This means that] not only must a property resemble its historic appearance, but it must also retain physical materials, design features, and aspects of construction dating from the period when it attained significance today."[59]

For most people, the Freeman House is valuable because of the beauty and originality of the design by Frank Lloyd Wright, and the distinctive character of his experiment in a new low-cost construction system that responded both to the landscape of Southern California and to the need to house the American middle class affordably. However, the home's original construction was deeply flawed, in both design and execution. Restoring the Freeman House in a way that maximizes its integrity, and hence its "authenticity," implies attempting to preserve something that did not work from the beginning, the building's particular experimental construction system, which is admittedly one of the most important historical aspects of the building.

The second dilemma, authorship, also arises from the fact the building's principal significance for most people lies in its design by Frank Lloyd Wright. It is easy to demonstrate the importance of the house to the development of Wright's own career and work. Yet, within only a few years of construction, the house began to change at the hands of its original clients, and what they did to the house in support of their salons, their gallery of guests and tenants, their political meetings, classes, and other events, transformed the house Wright designed for them, sometimes rudely. The architect for most of the changes was Rudolph Schindler, who over a period of twenty-five years created out of the Wright house a typical Schindler house: a single-family residence that could, with a few simple partitions and entries to the outside at different levels, suddenly become a duplex, or even a triplex. The Freeman House ended up the single largest collection of Schindler's design work, one that spanned virtually his entire career. Other important architects were involved later.

In sum, Harriet and her sister Leah Lovell were clients for three great houses of modern architecture: the Freeman House, the Lovell Beach house by Rudolph Schindler, and the Health House by Richard Neutra. Yet the Freemans' continual program of alterations both diminished Wright's vision and gave a physical form to the history of Hollywood in the twentieth century. The house has evolved continuously over its nearly ninety years. An accurate history of this "historic" site would keep those changes; a restoration that took popular sentiment into account, and sought to bring back the glory of Wright's genius, would not.

The dilemmas of authorship and authenticity echo throughout this book. They are still unresolved today, although much of the preservation work done to date on the house has taken them into account in some fashion—at the same time as that very work has also altered both the context for the debate and its subject.

2-1. The site of the Freeman House, ca. 1922, looking northeast toward the Hollywood Hills. The arrow marks the grove of eucalyptus in which the house will be set. The Yama Shiro is visible on the left. Highland Avenue runs from lower right to upper left, into the Cahuenga Pass. Whitley Heights is across Highland.

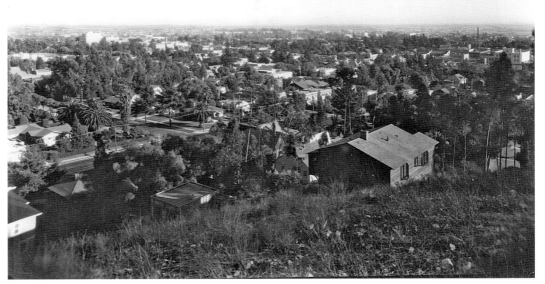

2-2. The site of the Freeman House, ca. 1922, looking southeast. The wood cabin in the foreground is still there today. This view is taken approximately from the location of the bend in as yet unbuilt Glencoe Way. The intersection of Highland and Franklin seen in fig. 1-8 is visible at the base of the hill.

2

DESIGN

The story of the Freeman House begins at a point full of hope and excitement. A young pair of newlyweds is embarking on the adventure of building a house to be designed by a world-famous architect, a house that will express their culturally and politically avant-garde sentiments and aspirations and provide them with a home in the heart of the thriving arts community of the Hollywood Hills. As for the architect, after a decade of turmoil in both his professional and personal life, he is counting on this and other nearby projects, as well as his new textile-block construction system, to launch a revitalized career in the boomtown of Los Angeles.

Sam Freeman was evidently content to leave the choice of architect to his wife, who picked Frank Lloyd Wright because of his work at Olive Hill—even though her sister's employment there should have revealed to Harriet at least some of the personal, economic, and technical difficulties that were bedeviling Wright and Aline Barnsdall's relationship. Still, Harriet was persuaded by Wright's great personal charm and by the case he made for his new construction system, promising the young couple a work of innovative architecture for "no more than the price of an ordinary bungalow."[1] The decision likely was cemented by a bit of competition with Harriet's sister and brother-in-law, who had hired the apprentice (Schindler), not the master, as their architect.

Wright was actively involved in choosing where to build his homes for Millard, Storer, and, later, Oboler (the last built in Malibu in 1941); it is tempting to speculate that he was similarly involved with the Freeman House. As noted, both he and Lloyd lived, worked, and had clients in the area. However, in an interview in 1974, Sam Freeman implied that he had purchased the property himself, before hiring Wright.[2] Whichever the case, Lot 3 of Tract 6687 was purchased from L. W. Walker and his wife on September 28, 1923.[3]

The site was a relatively small parcel on a newly constructed street, Glencoe Way, which was not even paved until construction on the house was almost complete. Finding the site must have entailed a degree of hiking around the hillsides and familiarity with the development patterns of the area. Evidently, three lots were surveyed before the final selection was made. The one chosen was located at a 90-degree bend in the street, providing the potential for two front elevations, as well as views to both south and east.

Though the site was spectacular, it was also a difficult one on which to build. At its high-

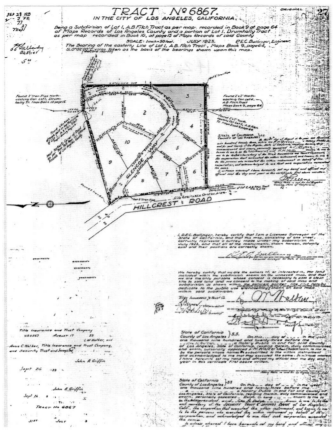

2-3. Title document for the sale of the lot, 1923.

est point, the property lies 8 feet below the short, winding street that serves the property and is supported by a stone retaining wall for its entire length of some 150 yards. The street also climbs 8 feet from west to east across the northern edge of the property, while curving in a large arc of constantly changing radius. The site slopes steeply away from the street in three directions—to the south, west, and east—36 feet over its length and up to 10 feet across its width. Its east and west boundaries are both close to true north–south, but they are not parallel. The southern boundary forms a right angle with the eastern edge, the only right angle on the property. This complicated site seriously bedeviled the project surveyors, and the designers as well.

Wright produced three iterations of the design for the Freeman House: a schematic design on three sheets in the late fall of 1923, followed by two sets of working drawings, in January and February 1924, the first consisting of seven sheets, the second of nine (with two variations of sheet 8). Produced over the course of the development of the schematic design and working drawings were seven drawings of the site itself, both plans and sections, which were attempts to figure out the site's geometries from the survey data.[4] Two pages of specifications—written descriptions of materials, products, and procedures—accompa-

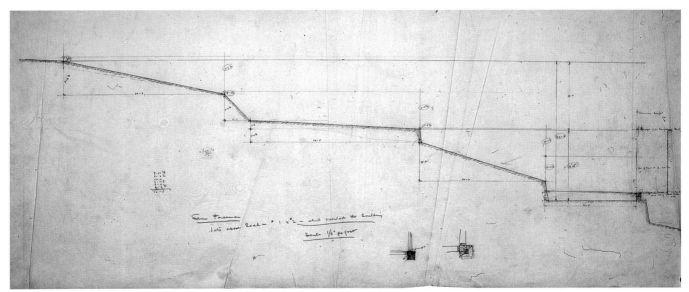

2-4. Site section from survey. This section is cut through a portion of the property (far right), the retaining wall for the street and Glencoe Way, and the two lots above the street, perhaps while the Freemans were considering which lot to purchase. Many section cuts were made through the site over the course of the design.

nied each set of working drawings as well. Four formal presentation drawings, consisting of two plans and two perspective views, seem to have paralleled the production of the working drawings, created along with the first set and modified as the design changed during the second. (These have continued to be altered or redrawn over the years for various publications produced at Taliesin.) Additional sketches and several sheets of details for the kitchen, living room furniture, and doors and windows were produced during construction.

THE SCHEMATIC DESIGN OF THE FREEMAN HOUSE

The north elevation on one of the three pages of schematic design drawings appears to be the earliest sketch for the Freeman House. If so, then the building began life looking much like the Hollyhock and Ennis houses—a Mayan/Amerindian-style temple with battered walls and stepped openings trimmed with ornamental blocks—in what Wright called the California Romanza style. But the Freeman House was a miniature, at best a third the size of the other two. The elevation and the two schematic plans are related formally through the use of stepped squares and rectangles, the way those forms mass together, and the use of low wings to the side. The repetition of formal moves in different parts of a building, at different scales, is one of the fundamental principles of Wright's organic architecture.

Even the most casual observer would find the two drawings on the elevations sheet incongruous, however. Although both façades share a vocabulary of stepped forms, the stylistic differences between the north and south elevations are so strong that if they had not been drawn on the same sheet of paper they would seem to be from different projects. Walls that appear in both drawings are shown inclined in one and straight in the other. The north façade evokes a romantic exoticism, whereas the south façade is an abstract modernist composition of cubes, cantilevers, and tall planes of glass. The latter even seems (and may well have been) drawn by a different, and cruder, hand than the one that drew the north elevation (and lettered the sheet).[5] While the north elevation is drawn as a single, long, horizontal band with a stepped skyline and with the front door set into a stepped opening as at Hollyhock House, the south elevation is organized as a series of four partially overlapping vertical towers, each seven blocks wide. Patterning on the perimeter and central band of blocks on each tower provides the ornamentation. Four wider background elements connect and set off the towers. The façade of the main block of the house is further articulated into three horizontal bands seven blocks tall: the ground floor, main floor, and roof and chimney. In combination with the seven-block-wide towers, these establish six squares across the south façade, and imply three more above the roofline. The resulting nine-square composition remained central to the design throughout its development. The south elevation also includes shadows and vegetation, while the north elevation does not.

A number of basic concepts of the completed Freeman house are visible in the schematic drawings:

1. The division of the program into two buildings, a two-story main house and a two-story accessory building, set at right angles to each other at the bend in Glencoe Way, connected by a covered walkway at each level
2. The division of the main building's structural system into a solid bearing wall

along the street to the north, and a pier-and-beam assembly with cantilevers and glass walls to the south

3. The use of the square-block module as the progenitor of the design and structural grids, starting with the division of the site into four large squares; and the use of the octagon as a secondary geometric element

4. The placement of the public rooms on the upper level and private rooms on the lower

5. Overhangs to shade the windows and control light on the upper floor, and smaller windows without overhangs on the lower level

6. The basic "tadpole" *parti*, or organizational scheme, in which a large head (the public room), is connected to a tail consisting of a series of smaller private rooms linked by a single-loaded corridor

The top floor of the main house contains the living room, reached by a narrow hallway, and the kitchen, reached through a small pantry set across from the front door. A small,

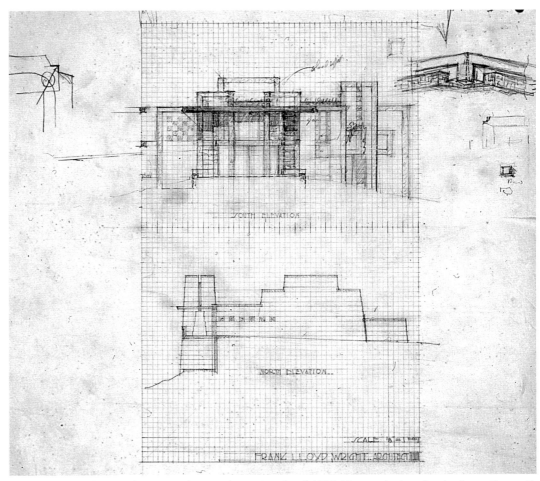

2-5. Schematic design: elevations sheet, with cornice detail, 1923. The south elevation is above; the north elevation, below, appears to be the earliest design for the house.

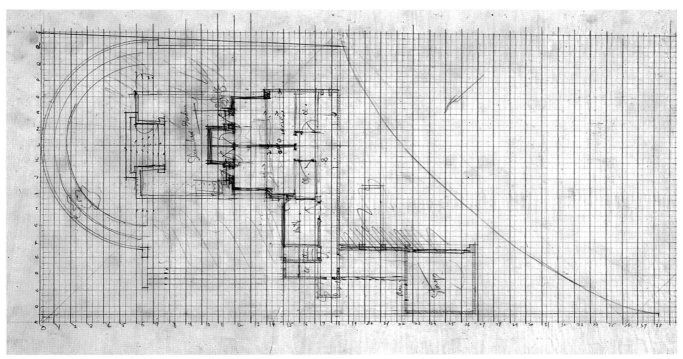

2-6. Schematic design: first- (or lower-) floor plan, 1923.

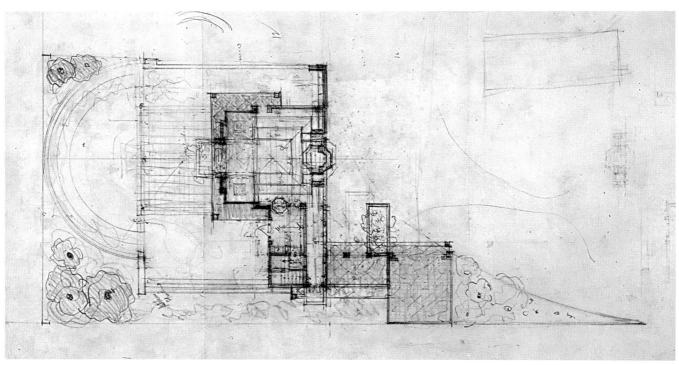

2-7. Schematic design: main- (upper- or street-) floor plan, 1923.

cantilevered balcony immediately adjacent to the front door terminates the east end of the main-floor hallway, and another balcony opens from the middle of the south wall of the living room. Facing the balcony, on the north wall of the living room, is an octagonal inglenook. A smaller octagonal element, a movable dining table, is set in the wall between living room and kitchen (fig 2-7).

The living room is basically square in plan. The reflected-ceiling plan, drawn on the upper-floor plan, divides the ceiling into two sections, one twice the size of the other. The larger portion, which covers the northern two-thirds of the room, is made of a series of concentric wood steps rising toward a square in the middle of the room. An essentially flat, plastered ceiling covers the southern third of the room and continues onto the soffits of the overhangs outside. Two large, recessed panels are set into the plastered ceiling.

Downstairs are two bedrooms (below the living room) and a bathroom (below the kitchen). A set of closets placed between the bedrooms and the hallway creates a small entry for the two bedrooms. The bedrooms open in back to a square outdoor terrace. French doors at either end of the hallways on both levels demonstrate two of Wright's ideas for the house: that every axis should terminate outdoors, and that the California house should be half-inside, half-outside (fig 2-6).

A detail sketched on the elevations sheet shows that the plaster ceiling was to wrap up and over the edge of the roof overhangs, with a high-relief pattern on the fascias, or vertical roof edges. This was similar in concept to the block fascias that lined the edges of the roofs at the Storer House, although the plaster version would probably have been lighter and easier to build. These elements were to be polychromed, again recalling the fabric awnings and painted soffits designed for the Storer House, which added touches of color to warm up the mono-lithic gray blocks.[6] The specific design of these articulated fascias resembled the polychrome, geometricized reinterpretations of classic Greek architectural elements found on the balcony posts of Residence B at Olive Hill. A similar colorfully patterned detail at the edge of the roof can be found in the designs for the Little Dipper. The two recessed ceiling coffers, with their repetitive inset squares, as well as the stepped elements in the rest of the room, also echoed some of the façade elements from Residence B, as well as the similar elements of "stripped classicism" in the work of Adolf Loos, such as the ceiling of the American Bar in Vienna. This stepped-square motif was connected to the design for the block pattern that was developing at the time: a series of squares within squares linked to other squares by diagonals. The entire living room ceiling formed a nine-square grid, composed of 8' x 8' sections.

The cement plaster on the soffits and ceiling furthered the concept of the mono-material house. By using patterned plaster to hide the wooden framing employed to construct the horizontal surfaces in the house, and by patterning it in ways that mimicked the patterns on the block, Wright was clearly striving for a sense of material continuity. A central goal of the system was to address a wide range of construction conditions. Or, as he put it succinctly: "Floors, ceilings, walls all the same."[7] However, as previously mentioned, at that time Wright succeeded in using blocks structurally only in a few horizontal locations above the ground plane: in the garage and hallways at the Ennis House, in a part of the dining room at the Storer House, and in the roof of the "tools" structure at the Freeman House. The latter may be the only location where the block system itself does the spanning, as opposed to being supported by wood joists.

There was also a pragmatic consideration: covering the exterior soffits and roof edges with plaster would help make the house fireproof according to contemporary codes, not only protecting it from the hillside fires so common in Southern California but also reducing the insurance costs for the Freemans. Wright was well aware of this benefit, and used the alleged fireproof nature of the construction to help sell Alice Millard on concrete block.[8] Indeed, the Sanborn insurance maps of the time do note the Freeman House as fireproof.[9]

The north wall of the main house runs straight across the site in the schematic design, and the area designated for "tools" (a semi-enclosed outdoor area for utility connections and storage at the west end of the house) is shown as a simple extension of the north facade to the west on the plan. (It is shown as stepped back on the north elevation.) The garage was designed to accommodate two cars, and an entry pool extended out to create a strong welcoming presence beyond the line of the garage. At some point during this part of the design process, however, it was realized that the actual location of the street was different from what had been assumed, because an alternative floor plan can be seen drawn on the upper-floor plan, shifted about four feet to the southwest. This ghost plan appears to have come second, because it is closer to the house as built and better accommodates the street edge. However, it is not clear whether the floor plan was moved in its totality or only in pieces. Erasures and other marks show several other instances where the drawing of both the exterior and interior of the house was reworked.

An important element of the design of the house was the pattern that was to be cast into some of the blocks; it was meant to provide a visual metonym of both the house and its decoration. The first version of the block pattern was a simple, geometric design. On the façades, ornamental blocks most commonly formed the edges of large areas of plain blocks, usually along the top; occasionally there is a checkerboard of plain and patterned blocks. Patterned blocks were also placed in vertical stripes in the middle of the planes on the south façade. Visually, the blocks were a device to articulate the masses of the architecture, like shadows on drawings. The roughened, and therefore darker, band at the edge of a wall would help it to stand out from adjacent surfaces in the bright Southern California sunshine.

The schematic design plan extends the house into the landscape with a series of low walls and steps that form rectangular terraces echoing the cubic volume of the house, although they actually cover more area. A large semicircular form recalling the east pool at Hollyhock House completes the composition. This semicircle was the lowest of the outdoor terraces, and a terminus for the great north–south axis of circulation and vistas that began within the house but continued visually along Highland Avenue. Romantic clumps of trees or shrubs are set into the drawing to frame the round terrace and complete the triangle of the site to the north.

Had the terraces been built as shown in the schematic design, the result would likely have been similar to that of the Ennis House, where a series of living pavilions are arranged atop a concrete platform rivaling the interior of the house in size, and with retaining walls in places taller than the vertical planes of the house.[10] However, the design of the terraces at the Freeman House was based on a flawed survey; it did not match the actual conditions, and substantive changes would have been required to fit the terraces to the real site.

There were other difficulties with the terraces in the schematic design. Besides their considerable expense, the large expanses of unshaded concrete would have formed spaces too hot and too bright for occupancy for much of the year. And constructing the terraces would have placed the textile-block system in its least successful and most vulnerable structural position, as a retaining wall, although the schematic plan shows them double-wythe, from the footings to the top of the parapets.

The two-car garage sits above a laundry or storeroom, which is connected to the lower-level bedrooms by a covered loggia. The garage is connected to the main house by a single, flat roof that also covers the entry courtyard set between the two buildings.

Two things in the schematic design drawings for the Freeman House hint at the coming storm. One is the way the plan overlapped the street at the upper level. The second is that it depicted the lower-floor plan all on one level, despite the significant slope across the site. At least as ominous as these discrepancies, however, was Frank Lloyd Wright's two-month absence from Los Angeles in October and November 1923, shortly after the Freemans chose him as their architect. While it was putatively for the purpose of marrying Miriam Noel at Taliesin, his family home in Wisconsin, it marked the start of a heightened period of personal and professional turmoil and the beginning of the end of the Los Angeles experiment.

Catherine Tobin had finally granted Wright a divorce in 1921, more than a decade after he had left her and his children to go to Europe with Mamah Cheney. The divorce enabled Wright to marry Noel, his mistress for the past six years, even though he was aware she was mentally ill and a drug addict.[11] In fact, their time together as a married couple lasted only months. But besides his stated hope that the marriage would somehow solve Noel's problems, Wright may also have been seeking to fill a void caused by the death of his mother in February 1923. Anna Wright was not only the central authority figure of Wright's youth but had remained close enough to her son to come to Japan to take care of him when he was ill with dysentery.

A month after the wedding, in December 1923, Wright returned to Los Angeles only to face the consequences of another of his failed long-time relationships, the one with Aline Barnsdall. Despairing over the unrealized state of her grand vision for Olive Hill, and deeply disappointed in her architect, in whom she had invested so much confidence, Barnsdall gave Wright a list of items she wanted completed by the beginning of February. Then she pulled the plug on the Little Dipper project, even though construction had already begun, and proceeded with plans to give much of Olive Hill to the City of Los Angeles. At the end of January 1924, Wright was served with papers in the first of a series of lawsuits that commenced a three-year round of litigation between him, Barnsdall, and the contractor at Olive Hill.[12]

Meanwhile, there were three new projects to get off the ground: Storer, for which construction had already started, Freeman, and Ennis. In addition, Wright and his son were desperately trying to expand their practice with a series of other proposals, none of which bore fruit, including, in 1923, an inn and summer cottages for Lake Tahoe and the Nakoma Country Club for Madison, Wisconsin; and in 1924, the Gordon Strong Planetarium for Sugarloaf Mountain, Maryland, and two projects for wealthy businessman A. M. Johnson: a high-rise headquarters tower for his National Life Insurance company in Chicago, and a residential compound for Grapevine Canyon, near Death Valley.

THE FIRST SET OF WORKING DRAWINGS

Despite everything, in early 1924, Wright (or more accurately, Frank, Lloyd, and the others working in both the Los Angeles and Midwest offices) produced a set of seven working drawings for the Freeman House—the second major iteration of the design. This version included most of the concepts from the schematic design, as well as new elements and a number of significant changes. The drawings incorporated a more realistic understanding of the site's topography, the geometric and technological requirements of the textile-block system, and budget implications. They were presented to the Freemans on January 29, 1924.

The couple indicated their approval of the design by signing the drawings, as did the proposed contractors for the job, H. J. D. Wolff and Emil Hackenschmidt. At the same time, Wright and the Freemans signed an agreement between client and architect.[13] The couple gave Wright $682.50, "being first payment of 7½% of Contract for Residence", and were given a signed receipt in return. (The architect's fee was 10 percent of the construction cost. The Freemans were supposed to pay the remaining 2½ percent upon completion of construction.) Finally, all parties signed a contract with Wolff and Hackenschmidt to build the house for $9,500, "and to complete same by August First." It is interesting that the first legal agreement, and exchange of money between the Freemans and their architect, did not take place until after a set of working drawings had been delivered. Perhaps the Freemans had learned something from the situation at Olive Hill after all.

But numerous problems plagued the design of the house, and many changes lay ahead. Some sheets of the January working drawings are so covered with notes and revisions that it is difficult to separate the various versions being depicted. Emendations include sketches off to the side and on the backs of the sheets, written comments, and revisions drawn over the original images—identifiable because they are drawn more crudely or hastily, are lighter (because they were drawn with a different medium or by a different hand), or are called out with written notes. In brief, what the Freemans might have envisioned as a ceremony marking the commencement of construction actually ended up becoming an interim review of a project still in progress.

The seven sheets in the January working drawings are 1: First Floor Plan [the bedroom, or lower, level], 2: Main Floor Plan [the street, or upper, level], 3: Roof Plan, 4: South Elevation and East [actually, West] Elevation, 5: North Elevation and West [actually, East] Elevation, 6: Cross Section and Section Thru the Staircase, and 7: Longitudinal Section and Partial Section Thru West Wall of LR and Bed Room. In the following discussion of the building imagined in the drawings, descriptions of the revisions that were added to the set are in italics. (This is necessarily only a partial description of the contents of the drawings and of the myriad iterations of the design found within this one set.)

Outside the house, the large semicircular terrace at the southern edge of the property, seen culminating the site composition in the schematic design, remains, although large terraces on the east and west sides of the main house have been dropped, and the semicircular terrace exits to the natural site instead. A heroic central stair connects this lowest terrace to the slumber terrace, which barely exists except as

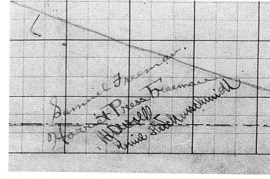

2-8. Signature of the Freemans and the original contractors.

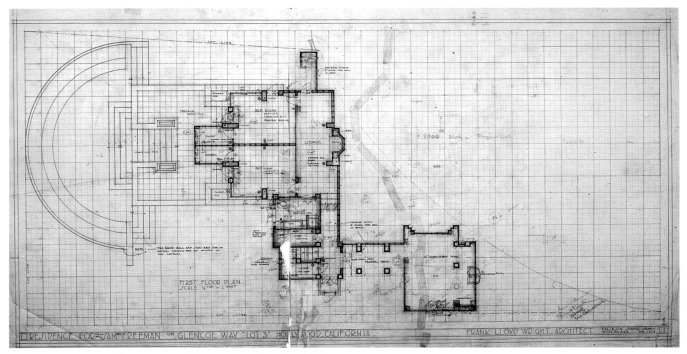

2-9. January working drawings set, Sheet 1: First Floor Plan, 1924.

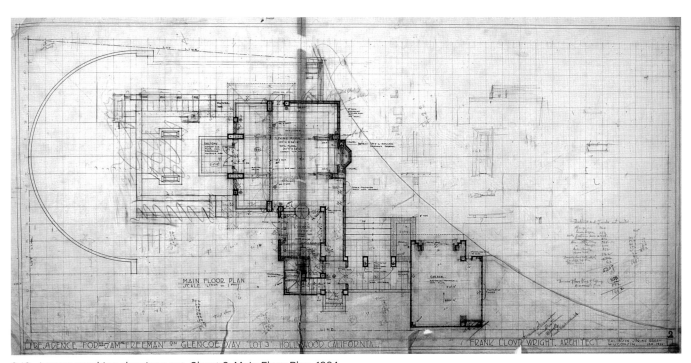

2-10. January working drawings set, Sheet 2: Main Floor Plan, 1924.

a landing for the stair. The slumber terrace sits six steps below the level of the bedrooms. *The slumber terrace is repositioned by redrawing it two blocks higher on sheets 4, 5, and 6, which causes the south wall of the terrace to be taller than originally planned but eliminates the need for two steps inside the bedroom doors. This also reduces the height of the bedroom doors from 8' to 6'8", although they remain 8' on the elevations. The planters to either side of the slumber terrace are also raised 4'. Meanwhile, four extra steps are added to the large central stair connecting the slumber terrace to the semicircular terrace to help it reach the new slumber terrace elevation on sheets 4 and 6, while the main- (upper-) floor plan shows a completely new stair off to the side of the slumber terrace, the central stair crossed out, and a note added: "This round wall and steps each side of central terrace are not included in the contract."*

Instead of running straight, the north wall of the house now jogs twice to the south, at both the upper and lower levels, acknowledging the actual location of the street. The first jog happens at the chimney, the second at the wall of the "tool" area. At the same time, the plan of the main volume of the house is subtly altered at the main columns on the east and west sides, so that the slightly thrusting shape of the schematic design, which carried the momentum of the overall composition of building and terrace toward the great semicircle to the south, is replaced by a perfect square. Inside the house, the basic configuration laid out in the schematic design continues into the working drawings, but downstairs, a lounge has been added for the paired bedrooms, replacing the large closets in the hallway in the schematic design, and the closets attached to the south side of the bedrooms have been considerably enlarged. The lounge includes a new fireplace that aligns with the one directly above it in the living room. The wall between the lounge and the bedrooms is drawn as a double-wythe wall, 8" thick. *It is made into a single-wythe wall by erasing the wythe facing the lounge. The north–south section drawing, sheet 6, continues to show the wall between lounge and bedrooms as a full-height double-wythe block wall; all the other drawings show it as single-wythe, with the top four feet glazed.*

The entry to the bathroom moves from the hallway to the lounge area, which is closer to the bedrooms and allows the bathroom to be on the same floor level. The walls of the bathroom and an adjacent large hall closet are shown as double-wythe. *Most of these are made into single-wythe walls.*

Three steps are introduced in the middle of the lower hallway leading to the bedrooms; *one is crossed out.* The doors opening from the bedrooms to the slumber terrace sit on the second of five steps leading down four feet to the level outside. (The idea of placing the door partway down the stairs is repeated at the living room balcony upstairs.) As noted above, *this condition is altered when the slumber terrace is raised.*

The bedrooms and lounge have a ceiling height of 10'8". The bathroom has a plaster ceiling suspended at 9'4". *The entire lower floor is raised one block (16") on sheets 6 and 7. The ceiling in the bathroom is raised as well, and attached directly to the underside of the upper-floor joists. This leaves the ceiling height at 9'4" throughout the lower level, with the doors a full 8' tall. Because the bathroom window was located according to its role in the composition of the south façade, it was not moved when the floor level changed. Thus, the sill drops from 48" to 32" above the floor.*

The east end of the lower hall ends at the façade of the stair tower with a set of double french doors facing out. *The end of the hallway is moved 3' farther east, aligning it with the end of the balcony above, which is enlarged as well, removing the cantilevered balcony seen in the schematic design set.* This seemingly minor change highlights the challenge of finding appro-

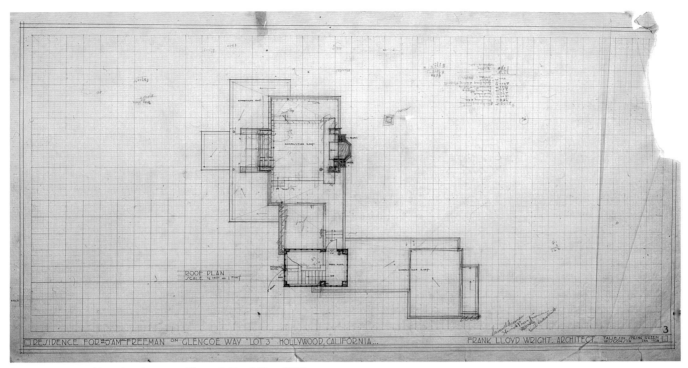

2-11. January working drawings set, Sheet 3: Roof Plan, 1924.

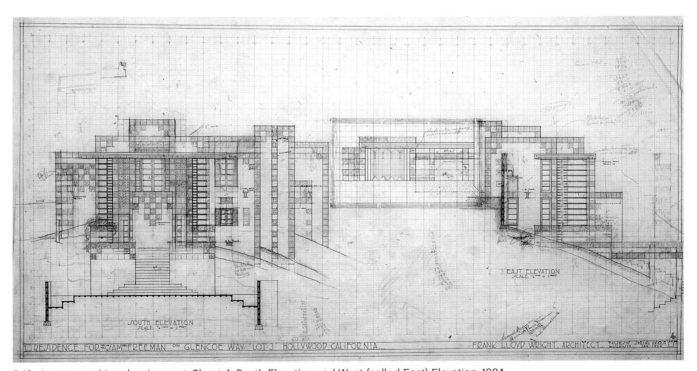

2-12. January working drawings set, Sheet 4: South Elevation and West (called East) Elevation, 1924.

priate ways to accommodate desired design features within the structural constraints and compositional implications of the textile-block system. It was not well suited to a cantilevered element, despite its supposed origins in exactly that condition at the Bollman House, and so as the balcony grew large enough to be functional, the lower floor was brought out to support it. (On the other hand, the living room balcony always rested on the bedroom closets, which partially blocked the view of the slumber terrace from the bedrooms but kept the outdoor space above them structurally sound.)

The storeroom has a column to support the floor of the garage overhead. The main staircase inside the house has 12" wood treads and triangular steps at the corners. *The stair tower is enclosed with double-wythe walls in some drawings in the set, and with single-wythe, except at the corners, in others. The simple wood and glass window units that sit behind the perforated block thus project into the inhabited space.* An 8"-wide strip window runs down the east façade of the stair tower from one block below the top all the way to the lower-floor level. One purpose of this window is to shift the 16" grid a half module. This move has to occur at a number of places around the house, where jogs or wall thicknesses cause portions of the building to misalign.

No details show how the block floor pavers are to be laid on the lower level. They are drawn in the sections, sheets 6 and 7, as if they sit directly on the dirt. Most walls terminate in a small, continuous concrete footing, set in the dirt. In a detail drawn on sheet 7, the 32"-wide windowsill for Sam's bedroom is shown somehow wrapping up and over walls of unexcavated earth.

The main-floor plan (sheet 2) has extensive notations and redrawings, including some that address conditions at the lower level. This is likely the drawing upon which Lloyd Wright relied most to track changes he needed to reach the next stage in the design process. The drawing is in two pieces, taped together, allowing a modified lower-level plan to be used for the south half of the upper-floor plan.

The living room ceiling maintains the use of plaster and wood shown in the schematics, with the room clearly divided into two zones by the strong east–west line where the materials meet. The southern third has the low plaster ceiling (at 8'), while the northern two-thirds is covered by a shallow, three-sided wooden ziggurat made of three steps, each 16" wide and 8" tall, with a 4"-wide inset reveal around the edge. *The two lower steps are crossed out in the partial wall section on sheet 7, and replaced in the cross section on sheet 6 with a simple, flat ceiling at 10'8".* Above the juncture of the wood and plaster ceilings, a 15" steel I beam spans the room from column to column, providing the major structural support for the roof. *This structural solution is dropped, and its replacement, a system of concrete beams, is penciled in lightly on the plan.* The plaster continues outside on the soffits under the roof overhangs with the comment "color decoration on fascia edge and 1'-0" wide on soffits" written on sheet 4 beside the garage roof as well as next to the main cantilevered roof.

The floor of the square room consists of strips of oak running north to south, bordered by a row of blocks. Paired sets of benches and bookcases, noted as "removable," project from either side of the hearth, sitting on both the block border and the oak flooring. In the building sections, the two materials are shown level. However, the large-scale wall section of the living room on sheet 7 makes it clear that the concrete and wood were to join at the plane of the block's perimeter channels, about ¾" lower than the main block face. No molding is depicted. The edges of the furniture align with the steps in the ceiling.

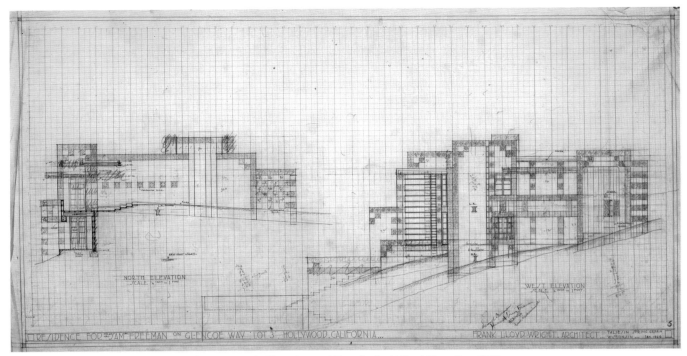

2-13. January working drawings set, Sheet 5: North Elevation and East (called West) Elevation, 1924.

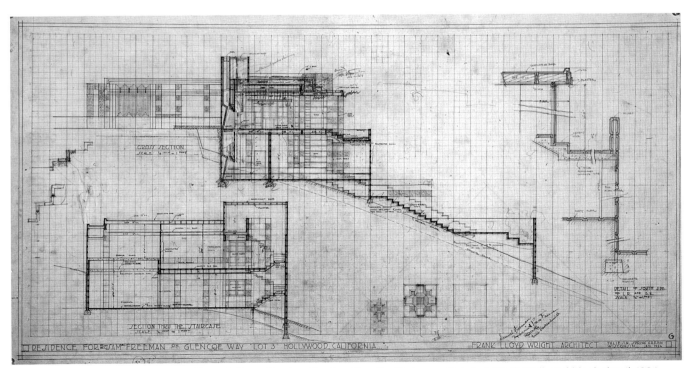

2-14. January working drawings Set, Sheet 6: Cross Section, Section Thru the Staircase, Detail of South Wall, and block detail, 1924.

50   SAVING WRIGHT

Above the hearth is a 2' x 4' skylight, similar to those above the hearths at Hollyhock House and Residence B. It is aligned with the furniture below, and seems to consist of two pieces of glass at the top and bottom of a shaft, which in turn is set in a large box on the roof of the house that is 16' long, 5'4" tall, and either 32" or 48" wide. How the skylight intersects the wood ceiling is not clear. In the schematic design, it seems simply to replace part of the wood step closest to the hearth. *A completely different configuration for the wooden ceiling is drawn in the cross section and plan.* As noted above, *the area of the roof above the central part of the wood ceiling is raised one block, and the flat ceiling spans between two block beams that form the east and west sides of that central area. The top row of each beam is made from perforated blocks, which become clerestory windows. The box on the roof is reduced 5'4" in length. The skylight disappears.*

The northwest quadrant of the living room has no openings. *A note calls for the use of perforated block in the west wall near the corner. Two different sizes of a window opening are penciled in just south of the proposed perforations.*

Three steps lead from the living room down to the balcony. The parapet at the edge of the balcony is at the same height as the floor level of the living room. *The raising of the lower floor forces a change in the living room balcony, since the original balcony slab height allowed only about 7'2" headroom in the bedroom closets. Therefore, one of the steps down to the balcony is crossed out, raising it 8". Because the balcony parapet cannot be higher than the floor of the living room without violating one of the most important aesthetic decisions in the house—the uninterrupted flow of space from house to surrounding land and cityscape—the parapet height drops from 32" to 24".* The balcony is paved with block and lacks drainage.

The french doors from the living room to the balcony have operable sidelights. The entire assembly sits at the front edge of the middle of the three steps, allowing the 16" sidelights to swing inward. *The raising of the balcony floor puts the door on the lower of two steps. In the large-scale wall section on sheet 6, the door is drawn on the inside edge of the lowest step, against the riser, making an inward-swinging window impossible.*

The plaster fascias on the edge of the cantilevered roof have a low-relief pattern, which repeats every 16". The pattern is offset 8" from the blocks on the south façade, but comes into alignment with the blocks on the east and west façades because each of those elevations inserts a half block into the grid. *A similar design is sketched on the edge of the garage roof in the elevations.*

The two-story corner windows begin with a 16"-wide vertical band of 8" glass strips to either side of the perforated-block screens on the south façade. Similar double-height columns of 8" windows are drawn on the west and east elevations just south of the piers on the east and west side of the living room. On all three elevations these 8" window strips extend down to the bedroom floors. *They are erased and redrawn, or drawn over, so as to stop at the level of the window ledges, 32" above the floor.*

The wall between the kitchen and the living room is a development of the schematic design for this area; a set of glass and wood panels, 6'8" tall, is faintly depicted in the cross section on sheet 6. The panels seem to be simply french doors and casement windows, similar to the exterior doors and windows elsewhere in the house. Essentially, the east wall of the living room consists of three columns, with either glass or panels of wood and glass making up the rest of the enclosure. *Only after the ceiling was altered could the kitchen wall be built as shown on the cross section: set beneath a 9'4"-long lintel of vertical glass lights, each 8" wide by*

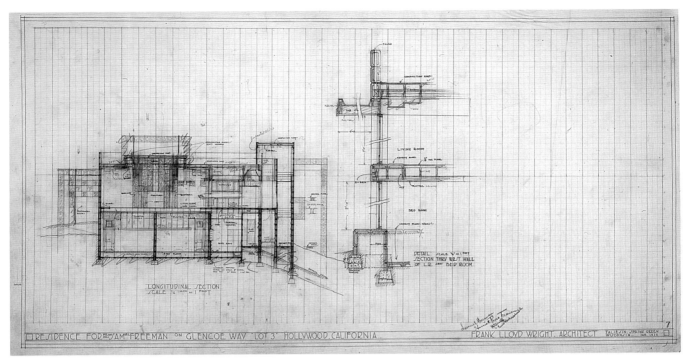

2-15. January working drawings set, Sheet 7: Longitudinal Section and Detail Section Thru West Wall of LR and Bed Room, 1924.

24" tall. This band of vertical glass panes echoes the frosted-glass screen set in the wall between the lounge and the bedrooms downstairs, visible in the Longitudinal Section on sheet 7. Those windows are twice as large, however, at 16" x 48". The most interesting feature of the wall remains the octagonal table, which projects into both spaces as a counter, or can be moved into the living room to serve as a dining table.

The exterior wall of the kitchen aligns with the wall of the bathroom below. There is a double-casement window, 4' tall and 32" wide, with fixed glass on either side. On the south elevation the sidelights are divided vertically every eight inches, similar to the doors and sidelights in the living room. *These divisions are erased, both in the kitchen sidelights and in those on either side of the door to the living room balcony.* The kitchen has a suspended ceiling, with a four-foot attic space between it and the roof. The attic accommodates a large hood for the stove. On the wall opposite the window are cabinets with glass doors that echo the design of the window. There is a sink set in a long counter under the window, as well as a stove and space for an icebox.

The balcony at the east end of the upper hallway, adjacent to the front door, cantilevers 32" from the face of the building; a cantilevered roof partially shelters the space. An 8'-tall pair of doors opens out. *The east balcony is redrawn to cantilever 48" and becomes the roof of an extension of the lower-floor hallway, with walls extending vertically down the hillside to the natural grade. The roof is erased. The doors are lowered to 6'8".*

The main stairs go from near the front door up to a "penthouse" and the roof, which consists of two sections: a large, flat area (almost 500 square feet) enclosed by double-wythe parapet walls 32" high, and a lower part—extending to the south, east, and west—above the overhangs and the plaster ceilings of the living room. There are 360-degree views, from the snow-capped San Bernardino Mountains and downtown Los Angeles to the east, to the HOLLYWOODLAND sign and hills to the north, to the miles of city ending at the Pacific Ocean to the west and south.[14] Along the north edge of the roof, the fireplace chimneys are partially enclosed in the long rectangular box described earlier.

The changes to the living room ceiling force major changes to the roof, most designed to accommodate the new clerestory windows that run north to south. *The upper area is divided into three sections: a high area over the center of the living room, with a lower area to each side (east and west). A couple of steps on each side allow walking up and over the center section. At the south end of the raised area, a set of steps leads down to the lowest roof—and thin air. This stair, echoing the one proposed for the slumber terrace directly on axis two floors below, provides a great—if terrifying—panorama of Hollywood. There are alternative versions of these steps on sections, elevation, and roof plan, and they are identified variously as cement and wood. The roof over the kitchen is dropped to the same level as the low roof of the overhangs, further diminishing the usable space on the roof, and eliminating the attic space. All parapets become single-wythe.* As noted above, *the box on the roof is reduced 5'4" in length.*

The house is entered from a terrace set between the garage and the main house. The eastern portion of this terrace also forms the roof of the loggia, which connects the lower-floor bedrooms to the storeroom. The terrace comprises two parts separated by a set of three (or four, depending on the drawing) shallow steps: an area outside the front door, 12' x 14'8", paved in blocks, and a larger triangle of land bounded by the house, the garage, and the curving street. (No surface is specified for the larger area on the plan, although in section it is shown as a concrete slab.) Between the steps and the garage sits a pool set in a container made from the blocks. The main floor of the house and the floor of the garage are at the same elevation.

The garage is connected to the main house by a roof, set 8' above the level of the entry terrace, which also forms the roof of the garage. It spans 14'8" from building to building, and 9'4" from its eastern edge at the terrace parapet to the front façade of the garage. The underside is to be plastered. The vehicle entry to the garage is partially offset, due to the curvature of the street, and there is no longer capacity for two cars. Even though the interior is still over 16' wide, the opening, with its folding doors in place, is barely 7'. *The garage is raised 32". In the north–south section, the lower part of the garage is erased, and the upper part redrawn. On the west elevation, the garage is cut out of the page and reinserted two blocks higher. A second roof now spans from the south face of the garage to the main house, 32" above the first. It, too, is to be plastered underneath. The two roofs are 9'4" from east to west, and offset 5'4" from each other in plan. A row of blocks is drawn in above this new roof where it intersects the west façade of the garage.* (Meanwhile, a third, even higher, roof for the garage itself is drawn on the roof plan, sheet 3.) *At the front of the garage, on the roof plan, the upper of the two entry roofs is shown extending 32" past the façade, which puts it over the street. In the upper-floor plan, however, that roof only extends 16" from the façade because of the curvature of the street. No redesign of the drainage accompanies the transformation of the single entry roof into three separate pieces.*

The design of garages, and their relationship to a house, was the subject of much discussion in architectural circles, especially in car-conscious Los Angeles in 1924. Placing the garage apart from the house, with a covered pedestrian walkway connecting them, especially one that helped to create a grand entry to the main house, was a highly praised solution. The arrangement of house and garage in the upper-floor plan of the Freeman House and the location of the roofs over the entry connecting the two implied an ability to walk, under shelter, between the two structures. There is clearly space for a door from the garage to be set in the wall opposite the front door to the house, and even space for the steps needed once the garage floor was raised. Faint marks on the plan in both the schematic design and January working drawings seem to suggest both an intention for a door in the south wall of the garage, and steps leading down from the garage to the entry terrace; but the only clear attempt at a connection between the two is a note on the upper-floor plan to set a 4'-wide panel of perforated blocks in the garage wall at that location.

Lights are placed in the back of the piers at the entry to shine on the portion of the entry directly in front of the door. Like the various balcony doors and french windows, the front door is drawn as french doors in the north elevation. Interior doors are more solid, with concentric wood bands framing a small window (the bedrooms) or with wood bands but no window (the bathroom). The garage doors are like the bedroom doors, but with no bottom rails, so that the bottom of the door steps up in the middle, recalling the shape of the living room ceiling. This provides one of the few instances of ornament at the house, aside from the decorative blocks.

The design used for the patterned blocks is a symmetrical cruciform figure, similar to that found on the blocks of the other block houses. An enlarged detail on sheet 6 reveals a composition of nine squares, the arrangement obtained by dividing a square into thirds vertically and horizontally. This is the basic organization of both the south façade of the main cube of the house and the ceiling of the living room. The block pattern is further manipulated so that within each of the nine sections of the block, new squares appear, varying in size. The center square in each section is the largest, with four intermediate-sized squares at the cardinal points, and four smaller squares at the corners. Besides providing an interesting pattern, the varying size of the squares allows manipulation of the surface in three dimensions. The center square is highest; the intermediate squares lowest. The diagonals that mark the intersection of planes in the block design form octagons, as in the shape of the hearth and of the dining table set in the kitchen wall. The dominant center square also echoes the living room ceiling (in its initial conception), in which the center square is the highest portion of that composition.[15] All of these ideas come together on the south elevation (sheet 4), where a patterned block sits at the apex of a triangle of checkerboarded plain and patterned blocks on the wall supporting the living room balcony, and that block also sits at the center of a set of implied squares formed by elements of the façade.

The most distinctive aspect of the blocks at the Freeman House, however, is not their pattern or placement, but rather how they form a corner. At the Millard, Storer, and Ennis houses, L- or U-shaped blocks create corners. The Little Dipper also had special corner blocks, as did later block projects, such as Florida Southern College. At the Freeman House, however, corners are formed by mitering the edges of two separate blocks (or three in the case of the tops of some columns and piers). This is clearly shown in the full-size drawing of the block produced in order to create the molds, see fig. 4-2.

Continuous concrete spread footings under virtually all walls and piers are shown on the lower-floor plan and in the sections. *Some are scratched out, others redrawn in a new location vertically, reflecting the uncertainty over the actual and final ground and floor levels.* Most of the footings are located just below soil level. Their size and the desired concrete mix are noted as well. The wood framing of floors and roofs is dimensioned directly on the drawings.

In several locations they are resized upward through additional notations. The architects were clearly struggling to fit the required structural capacity for the horizontal surfaces within the tight tolerances imposed by the block module and the increasing complexity of the massing. In numerous instances, practical necessities were sacrificed to the grid, the most glaring example being the inadequate accommodation for roof flashing. Fascias, doors and windows, and overhangs were all being pushed to, and beyond, their performance limits in order to fit the relentless textile-block system.

The January plans begin to locate electrical fixtures, such as outlets and lights. These are relatively sparse, as might be expected in a house of the era. Electrical wiring is noted as running under the floor, implying that at the lower level it ran under the blocks resting in the dirt. Outlets are set in the floor; the light fixtures are probably not yet designed, as none are shown in the sections or elevations. Gas cocks are shown in four locations, "for emergency light and heat" according to the specifications.

Also on the plans are penciled counts of blocks and windows and doors. On the roof plan, sheet 3, there is a project cost estimate of $7,375 total that includes the rather optimistic calculation that the 9,000 blocks would cost 30 cents each installed, for a total of $2,700.

The specifications include additional information about the house (see Appendix). All terrace walls, floors, and steps are to be cement blocks. All the framing in the house is to be Oregon pine (now known as Douglas fir) or redwood. The wooden areas of the living room ceiling are also to be made of redwood boards. The plaster ceilings and exterior soffits are to be plaster, "two coats rough and sand finish colored in box to suit and applied without laps." Terrace floors are to be "formed same as roof and cement tile laid thereon." The "doors and sash" throughout the house are to be redwood, "coated with oil stain or other approved coating, inside and outside." All wood inside to then have a "coat of hot Johnson Prepared Wax brushed on and wiped smooth." The door and window hardware is to be "first class in every respect," with cast-iron hinges and bronze hangers, thresholds, and lever handles. All "moveable" windows are to have copper-mesh screens. The number and, in many cases, brand of electrical outlets, heaters, pieces of glazing, and plumbing fixtures are also itemized.

The specifications also contain a significant comment about the roof. "All roofs to be flashed clear through beneath the coping walls and counter-flashed where necessary to guarantee no leaks." After construction is finished, all horizontal block applications, such as at the bedroom windowsills, are to be "waterproofed with Bar-lith or other approved compound."

What were the reasons for the revisions that covered the January drawings? First and foremost were continuing problems with the survey. The actual ground level at the south end of the house was 3'–4' lower than the architects had assumed, and some 30" higher at the garage to the north. Parts of the house ended up as much as 4' taller than originally intended, requiring several hundred additional blocks during construction. Second, financial realities forced a number of edits, primary being the elimination of the large semicircular terrace. That allowed the slumber terrace to come into its own as a major outdoor space. And that in turn may have provided some rationale for the third major change, which was the elimination of the roof as a practical venue for outdoor living.

The roof changes originated in the decision to replace the skylight in the roof in front of the fireplace with two rows of clerestories. In order to accomplish that, the center of the roof had to be raised; the part over the kitchen, lowered. But it continued with the decision to make the parapets single- instead of double-wythe, probably for budget reasons. That decision had two unfortunate consequences: any usable space on the roof would be surrounded with the less attractive, coffered sides of the blocks, and it would make flashing and roofing more difficult. (A double-wythe parapet might have been better able to integrate through-the-wall flashing, counter flashing, and/or reglets—horizontal channels into which the flashing or counterflashing can be set—on the relatively flat front face of unpatterned blocks.) The functionality of the roof was further compromised by the fact that it was only 8" thick, including ceiling, structure and roofing, and any slopes for drainage. This resulted from the need for the roof to fit both within the block module and in the spaces determined by the clerestories.

The changes to the design of the living room ceiling that took place during the course of the January working drawings may be the most significant departure from the initial schematic design; it seems to have arisen from two concerns: light and structure. Initially, there was no source of natural light in the northern half of the room, except for the skylight, hence the notes about adding perforated blocks and another window to the west wall. Questions may also have been raised about the quality of light to be expected from the skylight, which was set at the bottom of a tall shaft and was also fairly low, because of the way the ceiling stepped down toward the hearth. At the same time, Wright, or someone else in his office, may have decided that the major structural element in the roof, the steel beam that spanned from east to west, did not work. Because of the building's location on the hillside, the structural system had to tie the southern part of the house, which sits on fill, back to the part that rests directly on bedrock, an especially important consideration because of the region's seismicity. The change may also have been made because Wright did not want a steel beam as a major element in what was supposed to be a mono-material system, or because he hoped that the clerestories and block beams would be less expensive than the pyramidal ceiling, elaborate skylight, and steel beam.

THE FEBRUARY WORKING DRAWINGS

Though the contract signed on January 29 by the Freemans and their contractors, Wolff and Hackenschmidt, called for work to begin "immediately," February instead was devoted to the production of a new set of working drawings that incorporated the hand-drawn revisions from the January set and other changes. The February drawings are somewhat cleaner, more precise, and more professional, even as the building moves further away from the schematic design. Two new sheets are added to this set: sheet 8, Kitchen Details, which has two versions, and sheet 9, which is unlabeled but contains door and window details.[16] Like the January set, the February drawings are labeled "Frank Lloyd Wright Architect, Taliesin, Spring Green, Wisconsin," underscoring the fact that by the end of February 1924, Wright had abandoned Los Angeles for good, ending his attempt at a new practice in the West—even while the Storer, Ennis, and Freeman Houses were under way. Lloyd Wright was left with most of the responsibility for developing the design of the Freeman House as the project moved forward (and for managing the design and construction of the other two houses as well). These drawings are again signed by Harriet and Sam, but no builder's signature joins theirs.

As was the case with the January set, the February working drawings contain revisions and notes, although they are fewer in number. These changes constitute clarifications and additional information, however, rather than major revisions. There are also penciled block counts on virtually every sheet. The copy of the February working drawings used by Lloyd Wright during the construction of the Freeman House contains additional annotations, many likely made on site. These include revisions to the dimensions of openings, layouts for reinforcing steel within poured-concrete members, more information on utilities, and additional construction details. As in the description of the January set, items added by hand to the drawings after they were printed are signalled in italics here. While many of these revisions were made during construction, they are described here for the sake of better understanding the evolution of the design of the house.

The great semicircular terrace below the slumber terrace is largely gone from the February drawings, although it still appears faintly on the lower-floor plan (sheet 1), and on the elevation (sheet 4) along with the note, "these are not included in the contract." The slumber terrace is now a simple rectangular space, and a single stair on the west side of the terrace descends to the bare hillside below. The number of steps from the slumber terrace to the bedrooms is reduced from five to three, allowing the bedroom doors to be placed at the level of the bedroom floor instead of on one of the steps. Inside the house, two steps lead from the lounge up to the lower-floor hallway, and another four from the loggia under the entry porch down to the laundry, or storeroom.

The storeroom is a generous space, over 250 square feet, furnished with only a double sink, a floor drain, some shelves and an ironing board. Access to it is by the loggia, which actually provides a third private outdoor area, sheltered under a roof, with a beautiful view through the eucalyptus of Whitley Heights in the distance. But together the loggia and storeroom seem curiously unresolved. While it would be easy to envision the latter as a dance studio (except that it lacks a wood floor), there is no indication that it was designed as anything other than the support for the garage overhead. Both north and east sides of the room have a set of windows consisting of three perforated blocks on either side of a 16" x 48" casement. The south side of the room has a row of three perforated blocks. *The double sink is drawn in two locations: against the south wall, and more faintly against the north. There are several long curved lines penciled on sheet 1 that seem to indicate contour lines.*

The wood staircase in the stair tower is replaced by concrete block steps with an 8" rise and a 16" run. The dimensions of the stair tower and lower-hall closet change as a result of changing the stairs' tread-to-riser ratio. In the plans, the walls of the stair tower are still drawn as a single wythe of block. *The sections show the addition of an inner wythe to the stair tower at the east and south walls.*

Furniture is drawn lightly on sheet 1 in the area of the lounge: a couch set between the west wall and the fireplace opposite the door to the west bedroom, with an armchair set against the partition wall facing the couch, and a square coffee table between them. Other lines suggest additional furnishings, perhaps a bench or another couch, opposite the hearth.

Added to the structural system is a network of "deadmen," concrete beams that extend from the retaining walls on the lower level into the dirt fill, where they resist the horizontal loads by

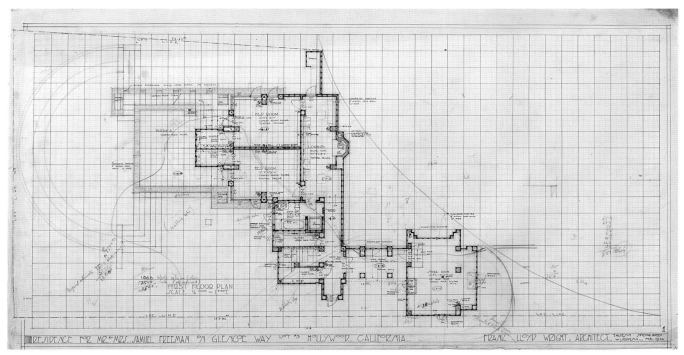

2-16. February working drawings set, Sheet 1: First Floor Plan, 1924.

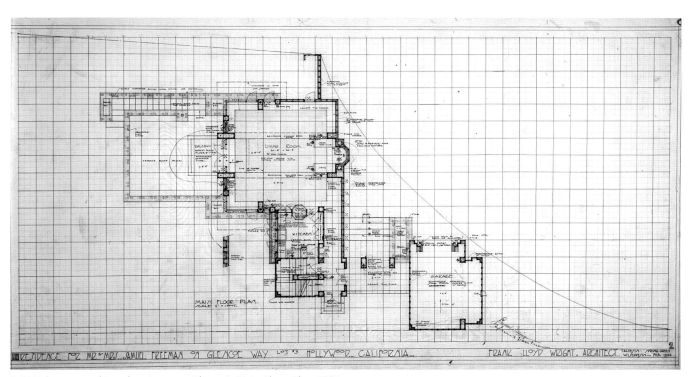

2-17. February working drawings set, Sheet 2: Main Floor Plan, 1924.

friction. These are drawn on sheet 1 to the north of the lower-floor hallway and to the west of the loggia and storeroom. The deadmen are 4' to 5'4" long, spaced between 32" and 5'4" apart, and connected at their free end by an 8"-wide continuous concrete member running parallel to the retaining wall. One set of deadmen appears in the Taliesin set on the North Elevation on sheet 5, while Lloyd's copy of that same sheet shows two sets of deadmen, one 32" higher than the other. Lloyd's set also includes a couple of diagonal beams connecting the retaining walls at the joint between the two portions of the house under the entry terrace.

The living room is configured according to the revisions on the January set, the hidden east–west steel beam replaced by two large, visually dominating, reinforced-concrete beams spanning between the columns at the north and south of the room. Though the room is still divided into a northern section with two levels of higher ceilings and a smaller, southern section with a lower ceiling, the introduction of the massive concrete beams completely changes the character of the room, focusing attention much more on the duality of the hearth to the north and the glass wall overlooking the city to the south. The two rows of perforated blocks that form a clerestory on each side of the central, raised portion of the living room are now connected by another clerestory of perforated blocks to the south.

The nine-square division of the room seen on the previous schemes still prevails, but more subtly. In the revisions on the January drawings, the central, raised area of the living room ceiling was wider than the raised area lined with clerestories in the February set. In the previous iteration with the stepped ceiling, three edges of the central square did not line up with the columns or any other structural elements. This, along with the strong line of the plaster ceiling running east to west, made for a more complex spatial composition than the unidirectional February design. Now, all the various elements—columns, beams, clerestories, ceiling panels, hearth, and balcony—are gathered together in a more ordered, more powerful experience. Reinforcing this change, the plaster areas of the overhangs and living room ceiling are gone, and the entire ceiling, all four different planes, become board-and-batten panels of redwood with trim pieces that echo the tripartite step-and-panel design on the french doors and windows.

Lloyd's job set copy of sheet 2 shows that in order to construct the lower ceiling at the south end of the room, three small 8"-wide concrete beams, hidden in the ceiling, connect the columns on each side to the new massive concrete beams, and those beams to each other. Two of these new beams are also drawn in the Longitudinal Section on his copy of sheet 7. The lowest ceiling in the living room covers the southern third of the room, including the area of the corner windows. Its northern edge is a straight line running east–west between two large columns. *In Lloyd's set, the middle of the three new concrete beams is moved 3' to the south, breaking the line of the low ceiling so that now the high center area extends farther to the south, toward the new clerestory window and the balcony.*

Another window is added to the west wall of the living room, roughly on axis with the entry hall. With the removal of the skylight, the window provides the bright glow that would attract people down the hallway from the front door. It also provides some natural light for the northern third of the room, which otherwise would get light only from the clerestories and the small glazed areas of the kitchen wall, to balance the wall of glass to the south. The south-facing clerestory results in the elimination of the "grandstand" stairs on the roof.

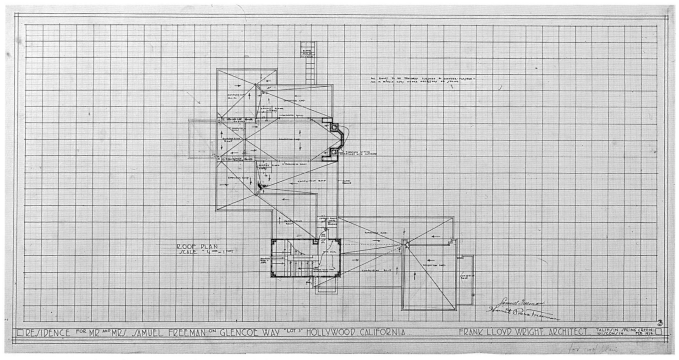

2-18. February working drawings set, Sheet 3: Roof Plan, 1924.

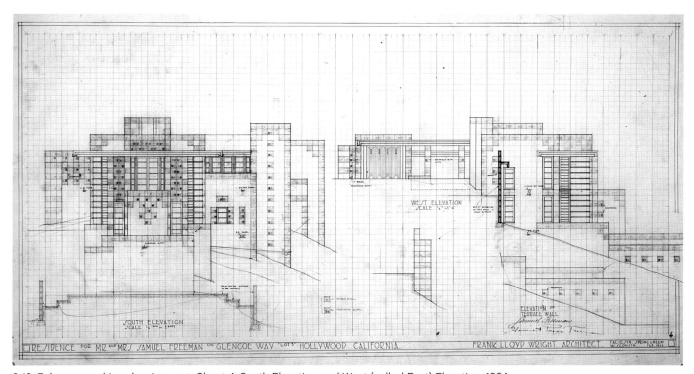

2-19. February working drawings set, Sheet 4: South Elevation and West (called East) Elevation, 1924.

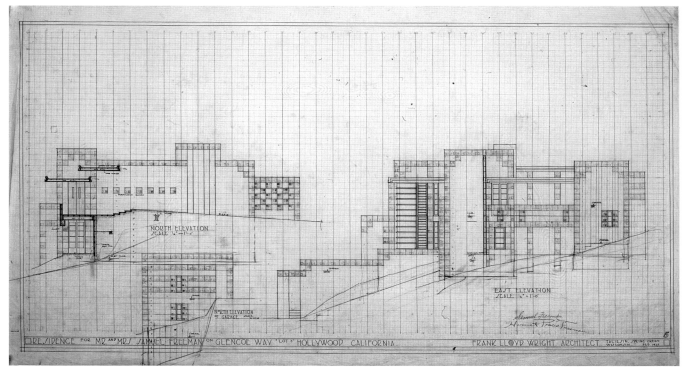

2-20. February working drawings set, Sheet 5: North Elevation and East Elevation, 1924.

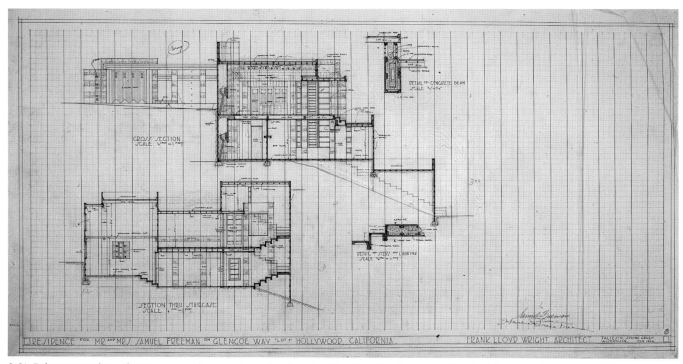

2-21. February working drawings set, Sheet 6: Cross Section, Section Thru the Staircase, Detail of Concrete Beam, and 1924.

A detail on the upper-floor plan (sheet 2) shows how to construct the south façade piers, which have blocks that step in and out along their length. *Another detail on Lloyd's copy shows how to frame the floor at the corners of the living room cantilevers, using paired 2 x 12s along the edges of the floor and 2 x 8 joists spaced 16" on center. The drawing includes the note, "Joist hangers for all joists." A hand drawing on the job set copy of sheet 7, near the Section Thru West Wall, indicates that in addition to wood framing, a small concrete beam should be placed at the edge of the floor between the columns.*

The south wall of the kitchen is moved inward by 16", to accommodate a planter outside a continuous ribbon window 15' off the ground. The new planter may have been imagined as an aerial herb garden (useless for the totally non-culinary Freemans). It never worked, however; opening the out-swinging casement windows would have decapitated anything growing there. And the planter had no drainage.

A low roof resting directly on the joists over the kitchen ceiling replaces the attic space already reconsidered on the January set. A dropped kitchen hood is still visible in the section.

The two versions of the kitchen (on the two sheets numbered 8) are neither dated nor signed by the Freemans, so it is not possible to know definitively when they were done, though the paper, layout, lettering, and other elements match the February sheets. In the one not built, which may or may not be the earlier, the wall between the kitchen and living room consists mostly of a continuous plane of alternating 1¾" vertical strips of glass and wood, strongly reminiscent of earlier Wright (and Stickley) furniture or the dense balusters of Wright's Prairie houses. It is also similar to a detail that shows up in some of the built-in furnishings in Lloyd Wright's Weber House of 1921. The image is strikingly modern: a continuous screen of light and dark vertical strips, with some parts operable panels and doors. From the living room at night, if the kitchen lights were on, the wall would have been a luminous plane, like a patterned laylight set on its side; if the lights were off, the alternating dark glass and wood screen might have seemed like a continuation of the glass walls to the south.

Why was this kitchen-wall design not built? It may have been abandoned because of cost or the difficulty of actually constructing it, or because it was rejected by the client. The other more conventional, and somewhat fussier, design for that wall consists of solid wood panels with recessed solid and glazed areas. It was the one adopted, then redrawn during construction by Lloyd's office, and built. Both versions include the freestanding table that straddles the two rooms, as well as a swinging door. (A similar design of solid doors with inset plywood panels is repeated for the wall of the pantry, set in the stair tower next to the kitchen.) Meanwhile, yet a third design of the kitchen wall can be seen in the Cross Section (sheet 6). It combines aspects of both other schemes, with five roughly equal panels that include a central area of strips of glass and wood capped by a larger square piece of glass. Above this runs a row of fixed glass panes that recall the glass panels of the wall downstairs between the bedrooms and the lounge. Inside the kitchen, the design of the cabinets remains essentially as drawn in January.

The word *wrong,* handwritten next to the Cross Section on sheet 6 points out that despite Lloyd's best efforts in January, the garage was still not at the correct elevation on the hillside. *The ground plane had to be raised yet one more block.* The inaccurate grades led to yet another alteration: *the two piers at the entry were supposed to have three lights each, set in bands of alternating perforated and plain blocks. However, as the garage and ground plane were raised, the*

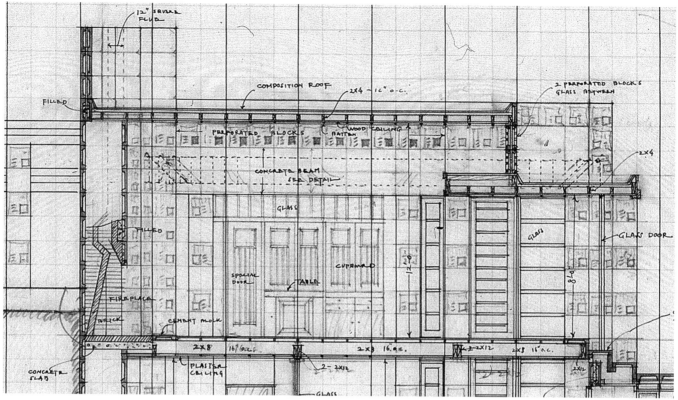

2-22. Detail view from Sheet 6, showing a design for the wall between kitchen and living room.

top of the pool effectively climbed up the northern column, burying the lowest light. Only two lights fit and were built.

The Cutler-Hammer brand electric resistance wall heaters that are intended to heat the house are shown on the drawings, along with refinements in the placement of the gas cocks and other electrical fixtures and outlets. The double sink in the laundry or storeroom is moved to the south wall (the January drawings had it first on the east, then on the north wall). In general, electrical outlets, plumbing, and other systems and finishes are more comprehensively described in the new set. *Lloyd's job set notes the locations of hose bibs on the exterior of the house.*

Doors and windows are dimensioned. *And re-dimensioned.* Framing members are called out, and dimensions are given to the rooms and major building elements. *The sizes and locations of steel reinforcing bars are also written on the sheets.* On sheet 7 is a Detail of the Bedroom Door, with both an elevation and a section, suggesting that it be built thinner at the edge, stepping up toward the center, with a plywood panel and square of glass in the middle.

The floors of the loggia, garage, and storeroom are all called out as "cement floor jointed 16" o. c.," in other words, poured slabs with a grid added.

Certain interior finishes of the final house are still not identified on the February drawings (although they are in the accompanying specifications). These include the wallboard finish on the walls in the three lower-floor closets and the plaster wall on the west side of the

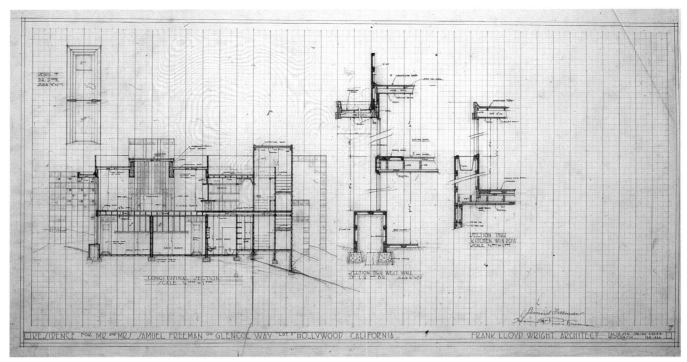

2-23. February working drawings set, Sheet 7: Longitudinal Section and Detail Sections, 1924.

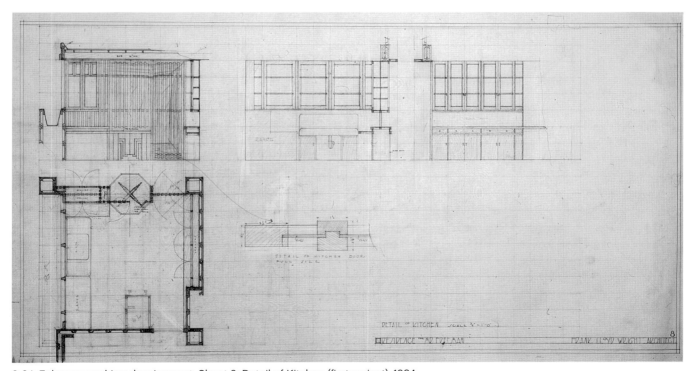

2-24. February working drawings set, Sheet 8: Detail of Kitchen (first variant), 1924.

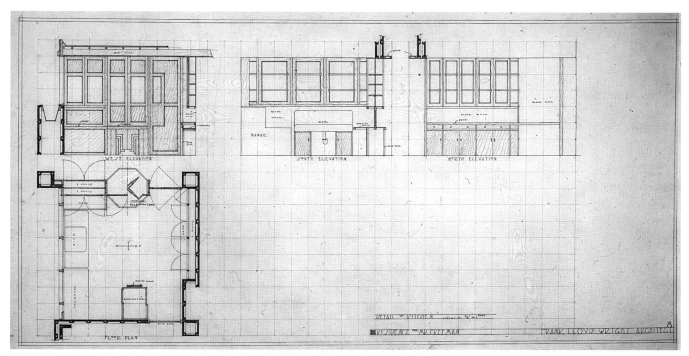

2-25. February working drawings set, Sheet 8: Detail of Kitchen (second variant), 1924.

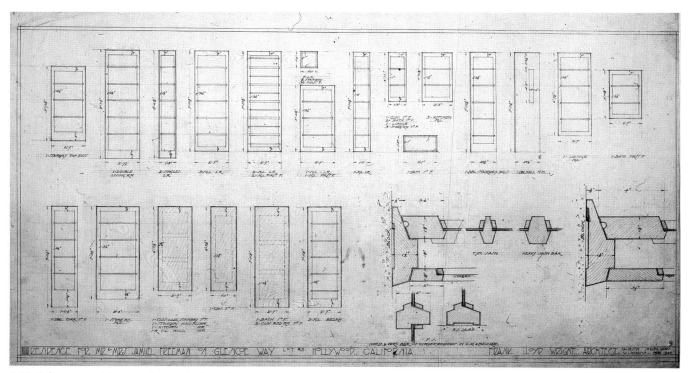

2-26. February working drawings set, Sheet 9.

stairwell. Wallboard appears to be drawn in the garage, but without any identifying note. A cross section of the overhang of the living room roof is added to sheet 7 of the February set.

The roof plan (sheet 3) shows the house with twelve separate roof areas, covered with composition roofing. Roof slopes and drainage are shown. *Revised dimensions for the roof members are given. The roof of the kitchen is pulled back 16", and the sets of steps added in January to provide access up and over the central raised area of the living room are crossed out.*

The decorative plaster soffits and fascias are gone from the garage and entry roofs, as well as from the cantilevered roof of the main house. Now of all-wood construction, the fascias have a tripartite design of horizontal strips, while the soffits are board-and-batten continuations of the system used to form the ceiling of the living room.

The cruciform block pattern of the January drawings is replaced in the February set with the pattern actually used, which is radically different. The final pattern is asymmetrical and suggests both organic forms and the site plan of the house; it is the only block pattern of Wright's Los Angeles work that has a figural design rather than a purely geometric one. When used as a perforated block, the complex cutouts evoke the patterns of dappled light cast by sunlight through trees. (The block patterns proposed for Wright's Arizona projects in the late 1920s seem to continue this exploration of more figural motifs.)

Unlike the patterned blocks at the other block houses, the Freeman House blocks can combine not just in sets of two but in sets of four to form a still larger pattern (although that actually happens only twice at the house). The Freeman pattern is also "weighted," that is, except when forming the groups of four, it is clearly more comfortable with the inset square positioned in one or the other lower corner of the block (that is, down), though in the actual construction of the house each of the two mirror-image pattern blocks were installed in both "up" and "down" positions. (Unlike the pattern of the blocks at the other houses, the Freeman pattern cannot be rotated 90 degrees.) All the patterned blocks are drawn on each sheet of the February set in enough detail to keep track of their orientation, especially the location of any perforated elements.

The mitered corner condition is now echoed in the design of the pattern on the block and provides a counterpoint to the highly rigorous square geometry of the rest of the house, but there are many other graphic elements in the composition as well: bars, squares, triangles, chevrons, parallelograms. Perhaps the liveliness of the pattern was intended to recapture some of the decorative quality of the patterned plaster ceiling and soffits that had been dropped from the design.

Just as the original block design held clues to the overall composition of the house, so does the new one. If the pattern represents the house on its site within a grove of eucalyptus, as the Freemans claimed repeatedly,[17] then perhaps it speaks of the way in which this house is different from Hollyhock, Storer, or Ennis. Rather than being placed on a platform, or within large terraces or formal landscapes, the Freeman House sits in nature. There is little mediation between inside and out. The french doors of the living room open directly into space, ten or more feet above the ground; the east balcony perches among the trees that preceded the house on the site; the main stair brings people to the dramatic roofscape that overlooks the world; and half the house is buried in the hillside.

A watercolor of the block pattern in Lloyd's files suggests that he was exploring its forms and figural content, perhaps as art-glass panels for the screen wall between the bedrooms and the "lounge" on the lower floor, or the transom above the well between the kitchen and the living room, or even as stencils for the soffits of the overhanging roof (see bottom image on page 6).

THE PRESENTATION DRAWINGS

Four additional drawings were produced during the course of the project: two elegant plans, an aerial perspective, and a worm's-eye perspective. These were presentation renderings for describing the house, possibly to the clients, certainly in publications, and include elements from both January and February working drawings. All four drawings, for example, have the most recent block pattern. However, the semicircular terrace remains in the plans, and vestigially in the aerial perspective (where it is partially hidden by a providential grove of eucalyptus).

Aside from that terrace, the plans are generally accurate, although the slumber terrace appears to be placed on the same level as the bedrooms, while upstairs the living room and balcony are shown without intervening steps as well. These plans have been widely reproduced in books that mention the Freeman House, starting with *In the Nature of Materials*, from 1942,[18] although the published versions often differ a bit from the originals. At some point, vegetation was added to the drawing at the parapet wall by the entry, although there was no planter in that wall. Interestingly, the Freemans later hung a shelf in that location and placed plants on it, unknowingly reproducing the effect from the drawing.

The worm's-eye perspective of the house, a view from the southwest, may have been done last of all the drawings because it does not include the lower terrace in any form but rather celebrates the relationship of the building to its natural site. The aerial perspective, however, was clearly contemporary with the other design drawings because it has some visible alterations that reflect the changes happening during the design process. The vantage point is the hillside just across Glencoe from the house. A main focus of the drawing is the roof, portrayed as a pleasant, habitable space. The block steps leading up to the central area of the living room roof, which were crossed out in February, are still shown. The garage roof is gridded, a possible holdover from when all the roof surfaces were to be covered with cement pavers, as on the balconies and terraces below. However, the main house roof is shown without pavers. The general elegance and finished quality of the roofs visible in the drawing was unrealizable. The drawing relies on a block for the parapets that was never made, a 16" x 16" x 3½" plain block without a coffer, and with a channel on only three sides. This block would have been the only way for Wright to achieve the look of the thin walls, finished on all sides. The perspective drawing raises the question of why such a block was not made. During construction, those walls were made of blocks with a channel at the top that required grouting, and with a coffer facing the inside that was painted with black, bituminous waterproofing.

Some of the roofs, such as that atop the stair tower, were set almost flush with the blocks at the top of the walls. In the drawing, these blocks are also shown with square edges, providing a crisp, clean line. The actual construction detail, however, called for mitered blocks at the tops of the walls so that roofing could be run up the angle. In the central area above the living

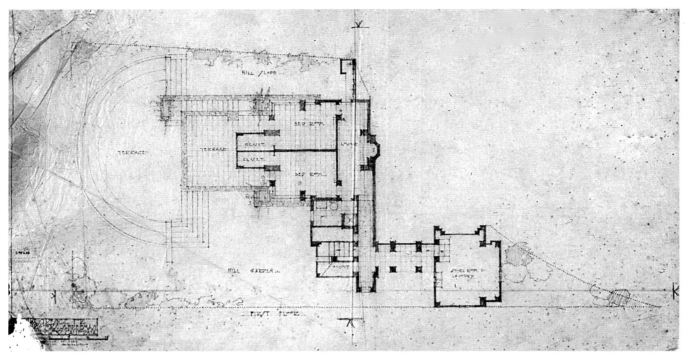

2-27. Presentation drawings: first-floor plan, 1924.

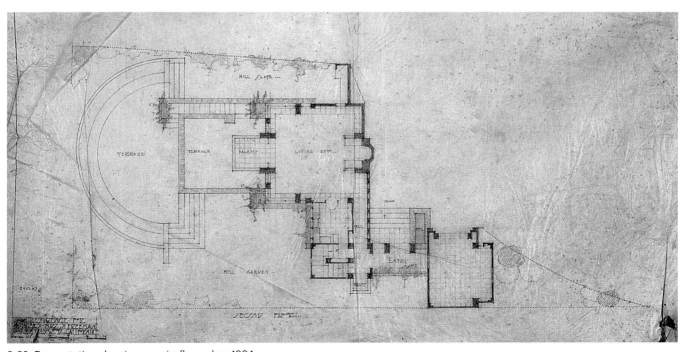

2-28. Presentation drawings: main-floor plan, 1924.

2-29. Presentation drawings: worm's-eye perspective, 1924. (See jacket for the image in color.)

2-30. Presentation drawings: aerial perspective, 1924. (See page 1 for image in color.)

room, the roofing is again shown set below the level of the block on all sides; as built it actually wraps over the edges of the roof on the east, south, and west. The perforated blocks, seen sitting directly on the lower roofs, are accurately depicted as vulnerable to long immersions in water. In fact, the clerestory blocks on the south side eventually melted away completely at the bottom because of this condition. The roofs seen in the perspective, with no slopes, drains, scuppers, cant strips, or flashing, do not even resemble the roofs from the working drawings, let alone their constructed reality.

The line of the street is not drawn correctly at the corner of the garage: it actually comes within a few inches of that corner of the building, bending quite sharply in front of the house. Also, the street in front of the garage is drawn at the elevation shown in the February set, before the revision raised it one more block, making it essentially level with the top of the pool.

As mentioned earlier, Glencoe Way rests on a retaining wall that projects almost a foot above the street along its southern edge and is visible even today, except where driveways cross it to access the garages of the houses on the downhill side. The perspective drawing does not show that construction, implying a much more dramatic condition to the west of the house than actually exists.

In the same drawing, the cantilevered roofs at the main house and garage are shown edged with a decorative fascia. Though plaster on the soffits or fascias disappears from the project in February, this drawing still depicts a design similar to that found in the first set of drawings from January. The lower of the two entry roofs is just visible as an extra line to the back (east), and it intersects a tree that predated it on the sheet. Another apparent holdout from January is the denser band of windows on the west elevation just south of the pier, which is shown 16" wide, rather than with 32"-wide french doors as in the later set. The drawing seems to show a two-story drapery hanging in the living room window. While the window was two stories tall, no interior space was.

The wall of the tool shed along the street shows most of the patterned block as perforated. None is. An inset row of perforated blocks to the left of the garage doors, where the smaller projection meets the north wall of the structure, is also shown in the working drawings, but is worth noting because it does not survive the construction process. Finally, the slumber terrace is shown with an 8"-wide wall along its south edge, which is how it appears in the section on sheet 6 in the February set, as opposed to the 16"-wide wall seen on sheet 1 and in the finished building. These discrepancies underscore how much of a moving target the design was.

The worms-eye perspective view from the southwest depicts the site as largely natural, with existing clumps of eucalyptus visible on three sides of the house; the steepness and drama of the hillside are somewhat exaggerated. The underside of the roof is shown white, which might imply the originally intended plaster but more likely was a technique to make the drawing read better. A faint remnant of the soffit decoration is also still in place. The window on the west side of the living room added in the February drawings is not shown, and the roofline over the kitchen does not reflect the correction on the plan that pushed it back from the face of the stair tower. The view of Whitley Heights to the east (the right side of the drawing) would actually have been blocked by the house seen in fig. 2-2, which still sits next door. The drawing itself is a tour de force; diagonal swaths of shadows, windblown foliage, and hillside slopes play against the thrusting cubic volumes of the house as the forms themselves step from soft shade into the glaring California sunshine.

THE CLIENTS' INPUT

What role did Harriet and Sam Freeman play in the initial design and the later changes, other than advocating for their budget and for the famously unrequited wishes of a two-car garage and bedrooms that allowed them to roll their beds outdoors? It is hard to imagine silence from Harriet, who was never at a loss for a strong opinion, forcefully communicated. But according to Sam Freeman's narrative of later years, "We told him, simply, the kind of life we thought we were going to live, and we left the house completely to him." And once the design began to be committed to paper? "Frankly, I wasn't capable of judging the drawings, and I accepted them in toto. I figured he was a very great man, a man who had much to give to the world, and I felt we were very fortunate to get his services. Because at that time we thought we were going to build a house for $10,000. So we did not put any restrictions, or favor him with any creative ideas, because we didn't have any. . . . We were so glad Mr. Wright agreed to do this modest house, we decided to stay out of it. And to this day, I think it was a very wise decision. Because I have run into so many people who want to build a house, and they say, 'I know exactly what I want.' I always felt that if a man were going to design a house for me, he had better know an awful lot more than I."[19]

Given the many changes the Freemans made to their house after it was built, and their oft-stated observation that Rudolph Schindler "made the house livable," it seems that they developed an alternative history of the house, abjuring any personal responsibility for the problems that they had, expressing pride in being part of an experimental and innovative period in a great architect's life, and, when memories stirred anger or resentment, blaming Lloyd Wright, who, Harriet would proclaim, "learned how to be an architect on my house."[20] In this, she was apparently reflecting some of the sentiments shared by at least one other block-house owner, Dr. Storer.[21] Sam, for his part, worked quietly and constantly on the house, fixing things. But the optimistic young couple of January 1924 expected something new, different, and exciting—and they were going to get it.

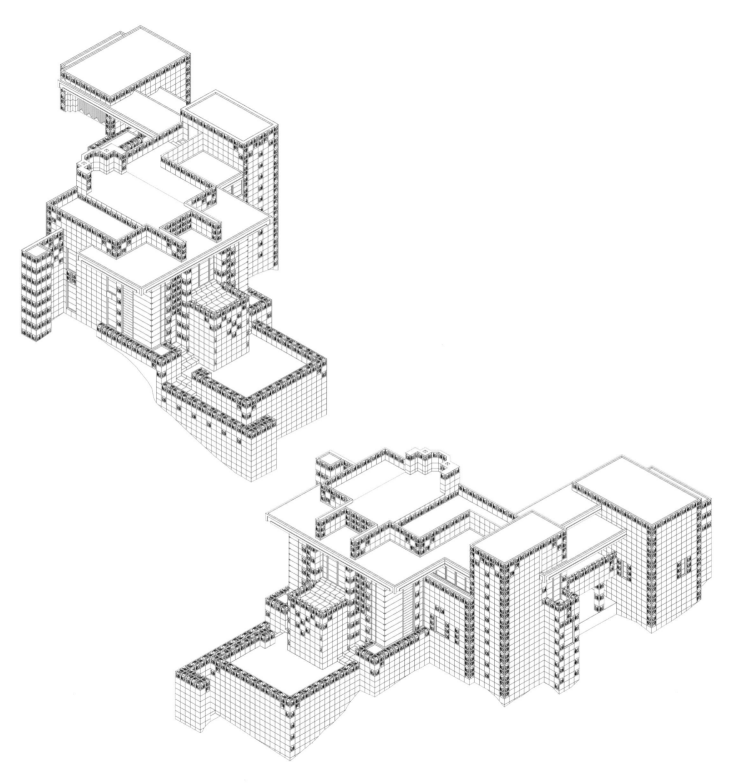

3-1. Computer model of the Freeman House as built in 1925. Above, viewed from the south west. Below, from the south east.

3

INTERPRETING THE DESIGN

What the site "wants to be," to adopt Louis Kahn's famous saying, is central to any preservation project. It is also an ambiguous concept. Hence, one of the first research projects I undertook at the Freeman House was a "thick description,"[1] an analysis that sought not only to describe physical appearances and phenomena but also to reveal the underlying deep structures (to use a term from cultural geography) of meaning and practice in Wright's work and in American building of the 1920s that either influenced the making of the house or could be said to be manifested in the house. The analysis was meant to help us understand and interpret the site and inform our work, to provide a context for what was really a continuous project that began in 1926 and was still under way: making the house "better." Here is one connection between the dual dilemmas of integrity and authorship described in Chapter 1. The many technical and functional problems at the house have given several generations of architects license to work over the design and, as a result, to destroy or cover up aspects of the original house and to ignore or discard important aspects of the house's history—while adding their own.

The textile-block houses demonstrated Wright's ideas for making a modern house: affordable for the middle class and appropriate for the climate, lifestyle, and landscape of Southern California. The Freeman House, as the smallest of his experiments, most clearly demonstrates these aims. It was the only one of the California houses designed without servants' quarters; it had the most flexible spaces; it and the Millard House were the only ones that fully explored the organic development of the square block in plan, section, and elevation; and its particular combination of mass and transparency made it comfortable in the sunny, temperate climate by providing discrete areas of sun, shade, and ventilation, while at the same time serving as a model for how to build in the hills, with the solid mass fronting the street and the transparent areas overlooking the city below.

SITING

Upon the opening of his Los Angeles office at the beginning of 1923, Wright stated his intention as "designing foothill properties between Hollywood and the sea."[2] He sought to take the lead in the rush of development flooding these areas, by defining both a new architectural language for the hillside homes and a better way for the projects to fit their sites.

Wright had precedents in his own work on which to draw, buildings in which cubic volumes of varying scales step down a hillside. Perhaps the first was the Hillside School of 1902 in Spring Green, Wisconsin; the closest to the Los Angeles projects, the Hardy House of Racine, Wisconsin (1905), perched on a bluff overlooking Lake Michigan. Like these two projects, the Freeman House has double-height windows facing down the slope, a cantilevered roof, a cubic main volume, projecting glass corners, and a hearth set opposite a glazed wall and view.

Wright was obviously fascinated by the sprawling, low-rise city of Los Angeles and by the automobile. He shared the ideas of regionalist planners such as Lewis Mumford and Clarence Stein who idealized "organized decentralization," and viewed roads as elemental features of the landscape—horizontal expressions of human freedom, the antidote to the tyranny of the vertical skyscraper. A striking feature of the Freeman House site is how the hearth of the living room becomes the implied termination of the axis of Highland Avenue, which is located at the bottom of the hill on which the house sits. The patterns of circulation within the house extend into the landscape via the movement of vehicles on that boulevard. For Wright, the automobile, not the tree, was the "natural" feature of the city. "Man is a fluid in metropolitan regions," he later wrote.[3] The same year that construction on the Freeman House began, Wright designed a cantilevered-roof car with long, horizontal windows, apparently intended to complement the contemporaneous block houses and transport their owners across the sprawling landscape of Southern California.

Wright's Los Angeles projects took his lifelong concern for a sympathetic and mutually reinforcing fit between house and site and transformed it into an exploration of the house as an outgrowth of the site itself. The walls of the house, together with the identically con-

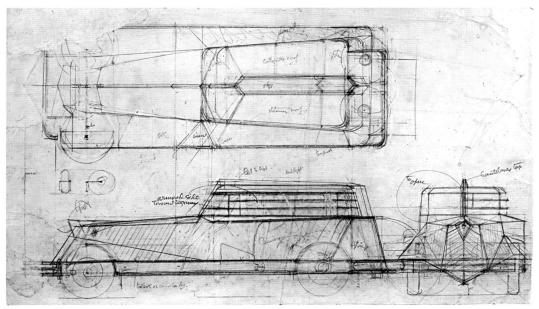

3-2. Wright's design for a car, ca. 1924, with a centilevered roof and window design evocative of the glass corners at the Freeman House.

structed terraces and landscape retaining walls, became rock outcroppings at least in part made from the same decomposed granite as the soils below them. The flat roofs were mesas from which the owners could occupy and command their precipitous site. The inclusion of local sand and soil in the block was an Arts and Crafts conceit, like using the stones of river channels to make the bungalow porches of the Arroyo architecture of Pasadena, or using local clays to make pottery. Wright himself described this sensibility in the opening paragraphs of his 1928 article on concrete for *Architectural Record*: "I am writing this on the Phoenix plain of Arizona. The ruddy granite mountain-heaps, grown 'old,' are decomposing and sliding down layer upon layer to further compose the soil of the plain. Granite in various stages of decay, sand, silt and gravel make the floor of the world here. . . . Buildings here could grow right up out of the 'ground' were this 'soil,' before it is too far 'rotted,' cemented in proper proportions and beaten into flasks or boxes—a few steel strands for reinforcement."[4]

The topography of the site has another consequence, one that Wright only fully exploited at the Freeman House (and to a lesser extent at La Miniatura and the Ennis House). The street façades of houses on the narrow roads of the Los Angeles hills are frequently different from the façades facing the rear yards, whether up or down the slope. As noted in the discussion of the early stages of the design, the south and north façades of the Freeman House could seem to be from two different structures. On the street side (the uphill, north, façade), the house has no setback, in accordance with Los Angeles hillside zoning allowances. That façade is developed almost as if it were a garden wall. It is largely blank, winding, and set with a few small openings that do not immediately reveal themselves as windows. Its anonymous character is a continuation of Wright's long-standing habit of hiding the entry of a house and providing a sense of protection against the street. At the same time, the façade's massing and location along the street recalls contemporary California architecture that found its influences in Mexican and Spanish colonial precedents, which also valued privacy and opacity. Another consequence of the long, folding entry wall is that the house seems lower than it really is, because of the proportion of height to length, and because it lacks any identifiable features from which one can scale its true size. By the time images of the house were published in *Architectural Record* just three years after its completion, the street façade had become a true garden wall, almost completely covered with ivy.

The downhill side radically shifts character. The south façade is a dramatic four-story composition that begins down the hill with a massive retaining wall for the slumber terrace, extends through the two-story principal living areas, and terminates in a stair-tower penthouse and a rooftop exedra formed by the chimney mass. While the windows on the street façade help to diminish the scale of the house, the two-story glass curtain walls on the city façade have the opposite effect. Seen from below, the tiny house becomes a sculptural object massive enough to carry out its responsibility as the visual terminus of a major urban boulevard. With its double-height glass screens and panels of perforated concrete, this façade is also much more open, as befits its location facing the city and the privacy of the vegetated slopes of its site.

Perched in the hills but overlooking the city, the Freeman House is a voyeur, with views (on a clear day) across fifteen miles or more of the Los Angeles Basin to Catalina Island to the south, Mt. Baldy to the east, and the Pacific Ocean to the west. At the same time, it is self-contained on its small lot, surrounded by the original eucalyptus and a profusion of other plants that postdate its completion. Its sense of both dignity and monumentality is vulnerable to the changes wrought by ongoing development nearby, especially from high-rise buildings, which effectively flatten the topography of the hills. Yet, the Freeman House seems to take little from the city of which it is a part, perhaps reflecting Wright's ambiguity about urbanism. It overlooks Hollywood, even dominates Highland Avenue, but does not share the form, materials, scale, or character of the buildings around it (see page 6).

Wright opened up his houses to the outdoors through several design devices: extending rooms onto terraces; arranging windows into bands instead of singular punched openings; floating the eaves of overhanging roofs out toward the garden; terminating axes of movement inside the house at a window or a door to the exterior; and bringing vegetation to the level of windows in raised urns and planters. This sense of freedom and connection to the landscape was even more important in California, where a benign climate attracted people who, like the Freemans, not only appreciated life outdoors but actively sought its benefits. The house sat on the only relatively flat part of the site, and the roof was meant to replace that flat area as an outdoor space. Wright wrote about the terraces of his California houses as helping to make the dwellings "half house and half garden." The house became an extension of the hill; its roof, the summit.

RESPONSE TO CLIMATE

The blocks provide respite from the glaring California sun in two ways. Their mass provides shade, and their dull, textured surfaces soak up light. Perforated blocks assembled into screens, which Wright referred to as "Persian faience,"[5] diffuse light entering the house, and the scattered spots of illumination soften the contrast between the bright outdoors and the dark interior. (Wright was exposed to North African and other Islamic models through examples displayed in Sullivan's office and through Lloyd, who studied those precedents in the office of Irving Gill.[6])

The screens are especially important for south-facing rooms, where bright light coming through a single window in a dark wall can create intense glare. In the bathroom, perforated blocks above the window help to scatter light around the room; in the kitchen, the light from the single band of windows spanning the south wall reflects off the side walls, helping to eliminate glare.

The broad overhang of the cantilevered roof almost completely shades the living room's expanse of south-facing windows in the summer, when such protection is most necessary; trees and the neighboring house to the west also help to shade the room from morning and evening sun during the warmest months. Rays of the lower winter sun can reach almost all the way to the hearth at the back of the room, bringing light and warmth when these are most desirable. The perforated blocks in the living room clerestory also admit daylight in the shape of elements of the block pattern that move around the room with the sun. From their positions along the walls, it is possible to tell what time of day it is and even the time of year.

Protection from the sun is provided in other ways as well. The lower-level bedrooms have no overhangs, but they are somewhat screened by surrounding vegetation and by the mass of the closets, which block most of their southern exposure. The east-facing terraces at both the entry and the lower-floor loggia are roofed and shaded by eucalyptus. The roof over the entry terrace also shades the front door, helping it to disappear from public view. The pool of darkness that surrounds the entry not only confers a psychological sense of coolness but, in the relative dryness of Los Angeles summers, usually cools the entryway appreciably in reality.

The large windows facing south, east, and west provide ample air movement and cooling breezes in the living room and the rooms downstairs. In 1924, the high central volume of the living room also could draw hot air away from the rest of the room because the clerestory windows were operable. The penthouse at the top of the stair tower also acts as a kind of wind scoop; facing west, it captures the ocean breezes.

On a day when the temperature outside reaches 95 degrees, the temperature of the lower level of the house can remain in the 70s because of the insulating properties of the concrete block and the air space between inner and outer wythes, which helps to provide a thermal break. Additional insulation comes from the below-grade location of the north side of the lower floor. Lower nighttime temperatures also help to cool the walls between consecutive warm days. The system has flaws: a prolonged period of hot or humid weather increases the temperature of the walls and floors; cooling then takes a similar length of time. In the winter, the temperature indoors often is not appreciably warmer than outdoors because of increased humidity and decreased solar heating when the days are shorter and the sun angle lower.

Initially, the house was heated by a series of thirteen electric resistance units set into the walls; these could warm not only the air but also the surrounding blocks. Their success cannot be determined except by inference from the fact that they were no longer in use within three years. Theoretically, a system that spread relatively high levels of heat to surrounding (nonflammable) concrete walls from which it could then radiate into the room would have been an efficient and clever way to exploit the material properties of the building. However, it is likely that given the extensive exterior areas of glass, the many open gaps between building elements such as windows and walls, the partial below-grade siting of the house, and the tendency of cold concrete to leach heat from a room, it was not easy to warm the house.

Wright's relative lack of concern about the winter climate in Southern California has occasioned some speculation. Indeed, early in the design of the Storer House, Wright proposed that the perforated block in the bedrooms not be glazed at all. When the client protested, Wright designed sliding glass panels on the interior. At least two factors seem to have been at work. Compared to the native climes of Wright and his clients, whether Wisconsin, New York, or Iowa, Los Angeles was a decidedly benign environment even in the wintertime. And many of the clients had come to California for their health. Though the custom of sleeping al fresco may have started with summer residences, in the 1920s sleeping outdoors, or in fresh-air environments indoors, was advocated year round by numerous Southern Californians, including the Freemans and many of their friends and family.

Even clothes were given fresh air. Recognizing the possibility of dampness, Wright placed an operable sash, a feature that can be found in closets at other homes of the period, in the three large closets on the lower floor. Unfortunately, the ventilation also made the clothes available to moths, which have voracious appetites in California.

AFFORDABILITY

In his lecture "The Art and Craft of the Machine," given in 1902 at Hull House in Chicago, Frank Lloyd Wright laid out a vision of how wedding the industrial revolution to good design could produce beautiful objects and places accessible to most Americans. In 1907, he designed "a Fireproof House for $5,000" for the *Ladies Home Journal*. It is his best-known early design addressing the Progressive ideal of affordable, universally available housing.

Years later Wright still maintained that he "would rather solve the small house problem than build anything else I can think of . . . ."[7] and that "[t]he house of moderate cost is not only America's major architectural problem but the problem most difficult for her major architects. . . . A pressing, needy, hungry, confused issue is the American 'small house' problem."[8] Throughout his career, Wright repeatedly undertook serious investigations of new construction technologies, motivated to a great extent by his interest in affordable housing. As mentioned in Chapter 1, the first attempt was the American System-Built Homes, several examples of which were built in Wisconsin and Illinois.[9] The textile-block houses were the second. Wright would later apply the term *Usonian* to the fruits of these efforts, a term that invented an adjective from the initials of the United States, and he applied it in retrospect to the textile-block houses of Los Angeles, referring to the Millard House as his first Usonian dwelling.

To house more people, especially those in the growing middle class, modernist architects (and others in the construction industries of the late nineteenth and early twentieth centuries worldwide) sought to build in ways that were cheaper, faster, and easier. They rejected redundancy, handcraft, and custom construction in favor of clean, simple, replicable designs using machine-made components that could be assembled by unskilled labor.[10] With the textile-block houses, Wright was leaving the architecture of individually crafted designs for this modernist ideal, however imperfectly realized. As noted earlier, the system was meant to be so simple to use that not only were skilled masons unnecessary but the homeowners could do the work themselves.

Finishes, or the lack thereof, were another way that Wright sought to move toward a more stripped-down, affordable, and essential way of building. He wrote, "In organic architecture there is little or no room for appliqué of any kind. I have never been fond of paints or of wallpaper or anything which must be applied *to* other things as a surface. . . .

3-3. Mono-material construction by the Maya at Uxmal: structure, skin, and ornament in stone.

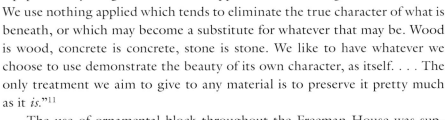

We use nothing applied which tends to eliminate the true character of what is beneath, or which may become a substitute for whatever that may be. Wood is wood, concrete is concrete, stone is stone. We like to have whatever we choose to use demonstrate the beauty of its own character, as itself. . . . The only treatment we aim to give to any material is to preserve it pretty much as it *is*."[11]

The use of ornamental block throughout the Freeman House was supposed to eliminate the need for painting walls or floors. Just the limited wood and plaster surfaces needed to be finished: oil and wax for the wood, a thin coat of paint for the plaster.

Another way in which the Freeman House was made both less expensive and more reflective of a democratic middle-class ideal was by eliminating servants from the design. There are no servants' quarters, and the kitchen, formerly the servants' realm, was easily seen and accessed from both the front door and the living room. The wall between the kitchen and the living room consisted of a series of operable panels and doors, a barrier intended to be as programmatically transparent as possible. Glass-fronted cabinets and multiple windows conferred literal transparency as well. The octagonal table, echoing the fireplace in plan, could be used as a sideboard in the living room and a work surface in the kitchen. With the panels open, people could sit on either side or use the table as a serving counter. And the table also could be removed completely and placed in the living room to serve as the main dining table.

This modern approach to the kitchen has precedents in the American System-Built houses.[12] However, the Freeman House's combination of the flexible space between kitchen and living area, its relatively small scale, and the single-loaded corridor plan presage the Usonian houses Wright designed between 1936 and 1959. The Freeman House is organized along a hallway that starts in the living room, winds past kitchen and entry, and then splits, leading upstairs to the roof terrace and downstairs to the laundry, bath, and bedrooms. The main corridors on both floors are dark tunnels that open toward their destinations, and light, at either end. Their placement along the inner wall at each level allows them to act as a barrier toward the street and toward the hillside. With the "head" made up of the major public space, and a succession of smaller rooms falling into place behind it, the plan forms the tadpole *parti* mentioned in Chapter 1.

Another programmatic feature worth noting is the lack of a master bedroom. Sam and Harriet each had a bedroom and closet (mirror images of each other) and shared a sitting area and bathroom as well as the slumber terrace.

AESTHETICS

The artistry of the Freeman House resides in both the composition of the building and how it serves as a setting for an aesthetic experience. While Wright had a great deal to say about his ideas, the contemporary condition, his and other architects' work, and his experiments in building technology, he was relatively silent on the techniques that he used to create form and space and pattern. Nor did he speak in any depth about precedents or the sources of his inspiration. But while his interest in social, political, and cultural issues informed and gave passion and purpose to his designs, in the end it was his skills as a composer of materials and spaces that keep his buildings alive for us today.

The block houses continue Wright's previous explorations into unit masonry construction and the integration of geometric patterns in all scales of building development, from plan to ornament. Louis Sullivan's influence can be seen in the use of repetitive, pre-cast, ornamental masonry units, which integrate ornament with a building's skin and structure. In most of Wright's work before 1930, certain symbolic elements, usually derived from plants or animals, become design motifs in various parts of the building, such as lights, windows, column capitals, and furniture. Pre-cast masonry first appears in his work as these thematic elements. Early examples include the column capitals on the windows of the 1904 Unity Temple and the stork panels at his own studio.

In Wright's words, "Integral ornament is simply structure-pattern made visibly articulate and seen in the building as it is seen in the structure of the trees or a lily of the field. It is the inner expression of Form. . . . It is founded upon the same organic simplicity as Beethoven's Fifth Symphony, that amazing revolution in tumult and splendor of sound built on four tones based upon a rhythm a child could play on the piano."[13]

The assembly of cubes and other simple geometric forms into a building can be found in Wright's work as early as his own Home and Studio. There, a semicircular terrace combines with an octagon, squares, and triangles in the plan and façades of the building. These platonic solids were still being combined in the design of the Freeman House, both in the block ornament and in the building, and Wright's interest in them helps to explain the persistence of the semicircular terrace in the drawings long after it was gone from the project.

The germ from which the Freeman House developed is the 16"-square block. Like a crystalline growth from a single molecule, or a fractal curve, the forms and character of the greater object are inherent within the individual component. The proportion, color, texture, and mass of the house all derive from the block. A three-dimensional 16" grid determines the size and placement of every element.

The principal openings in the living room facing south, east, and west are all squares: 6 blocks to a side, or 8' square. Other doors are generally either 2 blocks wide and 6 blocks tall (a triple square) or 4 blocks tall (a double square). Some openings, such as those in the kitchen, are 5 blocks tall with a special panel above to allow the opening to read as a triple square.

The plan of the living room is a square, 20 blocks x 20 blocks, or 26'8" on a side. The main volume of the house—the living room over the two bedrooms—is a cube 20 blocks x 20 blocks x 20 blocks, from the slumber terrace to the top of the parapets. Each of the remaining zones of the house essentially lies within its own quadrant on the site, forced into a Z shape by the bend of the road.

The octagon plays a secondary role. The chimney at the Freeman House forms five sides of an octagon both in the plan of the two hearths and as an engaged tower element on the exterior of the house at the street. This element is echoed by the octagonal dining table and by the design formed when the four rotations of the patterned block are set together.

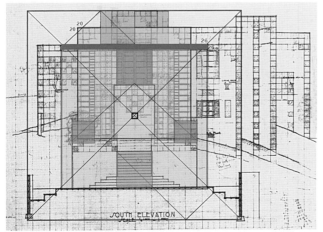

3-4. The location of squares on the south elevation. Diagram by author, overlaid on Wright drawings.

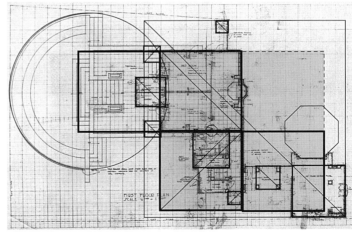

3-5. Geometries in the lower-level plan. Diagram by author, overlaid on Wright drawings.

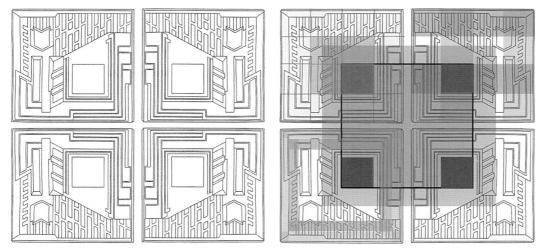

3-6. Analysis of the block pattern at the Freeman House, showing (left) the overall design created by the joining of the two different blocks in their two possible orientations; and (right) the proportions and geometries found in the pattern.

Placing a left- and right-patterned block above the same blocks set upside-down produces a whole new design, 32" x 32", dominated by an octagon. Octagons and squares have a strong mathematical relationship topologically: the two combine to form a "space-filling" geometry. In other words, a field of octagons requires squares to fill the gaps. (Squares and hexagons, on the other hand, can each fill fields by themselves.) Rudolph Schindler later continued the dialogue between square and octagon when he designed furnishings for Harriet's bedroom in the late 1920s.

The purity of the geometry was diluted by changes forced on the design during the process of fitting it to the site. Because of the inaccurate survey and other miscalculations, especially the curve of the street relative to the garage, parts of the house were shifted in both plan and section. And it seems that these ideal proportions were allowed free rein only where they did not compromise the necessities of program and construction.

Still, a system underlying and connecting the various elements within a work of art helps observers to comprehend it, and then to begin a dialogue with the work. To the extent that an ordering system successfully organizes the myriad ideas and physical constraints found within a building, it has power. Order also consists of a victory over chaos. The proportion and focus on the square and the 16" grid give the Freeman House much of its power.

EXPERIENCING THE HOUSE

The Freeman House is filled with experiences that Wright organizes by choreographing our movement through the building. Many of these experiences derive their power and drama from the tension that Wright created out of a series of oppositions. The underlying geometric order of the house is most easily read in the drawings, but these little dramas are revealed best by being in the building.

Wright's work has always deliberately exploited opposition, even to the point of a seeming willingness to elicit discomfort in the viewer (as in excessively low doorways or startlingly dark corridors). A long series of dualities makes his architecture continually challenging, dynamic, and assertive. (Similar qualities in the man produced a like result.) At least five of these can be found in the Freeman House: solidity versus transparency, light versus dark, compression versus expansion, inside versus outside, and the square versus the diagonal.

Wright's first sketches for the north and south façades of the house established a fundamental dichotomy between solidity and transparency, and between light and dark. The solidity of the concrete blocks makes the glazed openings welcome and dramatic, and the massiveness of the concrete around the hearth becomes a welcome, and literal, counterweight to the sense of floating generated by the cantilevered corners of the living room and roof terrace. In a building whose cubist concrete construction seems to represent the apotheosis of stasis, solidity, and stability, the choreography that Wright creates through his use of compression and expansion, light and dark, and opacity and transparency is all the more powerful. The visitor is drawn where Wright directs. At times, this movement seems to intensify the solidity of the concrete. In other instances, the concrete itself seems set loose.

Wright encourages movement by narrowing and darkening areas meant as passageways while brightening and expanding, both horizontally and vertically, the destinations. Like a branch floating in a stream, we are propelled faster through the narrow channels and then released to enjoy a pool of stillness. At the Freeman House, a sequence of these experiences begins at the street. When approaching the house, we move from the wide street onto the entry terrace, which is walled on one side, then down steps to another terrace, walled on two sides, walking first under a high roof, then under a lower one, and then through a still narrower doorway into the building. From the front door, we are squeezed down an almost windowless hallway toward the living room, the ceiling rising in steps as we go; then the walls open up, light floods in from three sides, and we can see through corner windows to the far horizon. Once in the living room, the highest volume is in the center, over the seating by the hearth, providing the spot of stillness. As we move toward the balcony, the ceiling lowers again, and the glass wall becomes two screens of perforated block on either side of the balcony door. But after we pass through the door and move outside, as the ceiling yields to sky and the walls to eucalyptus, the floor steps down to reinforce the expansion of space in every direction.

A similar experience occurs at the roof. The stairs leading to the public spaces on the roof are narrow and dark. Arriving at a small penthouse landing, we exit through a door that opens into a narrow, roofless passage framed by high parapet walls. Three more steps bring us to a 360-degree vista of the world.

In 1925, movement on the lower level proceeded in the same sequence as on the upper level. At the bottom of a dark, confining stair, one could turn right or left. To the right, a set of glass doors led to an exterior colonnade with a low ceiling (the loggia) from which the hillside dropped steeply and views extended eastward to the distant mountains and downtown Los Angeles. The colonnade ended in a short set of steps and a narrow door that opened to the high-ceilinged laundry/storeroom below the garage. If one turned to the left at the bottom of the main stairs, after several yards of dark, narrow passageway, the hallway floor stepped down while the wall to the left moved four feet further to the left and became part block, part frosted glass. This vertical and horizontal expansion created the "lounge." Straight ahead was a large casement window through which one could walk directly outside.

In the Freeman House, as in most homes, the plan dimensions of the rooms and corridors vary according to their function and importance. But unlike most homes, at the Freeman House the proportion of width to height is also different in every room, except for the paired bedrooms. The ceilings and floor levels constantly shift; in some areas, several times. This modulation of the section enlivens the spaces as one moves through the house and shapes one's reading of space, purpose, and meaning.

That every axis in the Freeman House terminated outdoors related back to Wright's ideas about the California house and the human attraction to light. His manipulation of light reinforces the movement induced by the compression and expansion of walls, floors, and ceilings. Walking toward the house from the street, one is attracted to the shadowed terrace outside the front door not just by the water in the pool and the coolness described earlier but also by the glimpse of light and city views visible over the parapet wall next to the front door. Inside the house, french doors mark either terminus of the curving axis that is the route of circulation from the front door to the living room balcony or, in reverse, from the living room to a small balcony by the front door and main stairs. In fact, the latter balcony exists primarily to provide a visible exterior space at the east end of the upper hallway.

As already mentioned, taking the stairs from the front door down to the bedroom level, you arrive at a hallway with a large window and french doors at the east end and a large window, usable as a door, at the west end. Along the lower hall, both bedroom doors included small windows that enticed the visitor to follow the light through those rooms to the french doors leading to the slumber terrace, set beside more corner windows.

Another layer of excitement is added by opposing the square and the diagonal. The rooms at the Freeman House are organized orthogonally, but you often move through them at an angle, having entered at a corner. As you move farther into a room, more and more of the space is revealed, and the direction of your gaze continually shifts toward the largest openings. On almost every surface, including the floor, the omnipresent grid records a transgressive diagonal motion. In the living room, where you walk at an angle under the massive beams supporting the roof, the feeling is especially illicit and exhilarating.

Diagonal movement was one of Wright's frequent strategies for freeing space from the confinement of traditional architecture, a concept he called "exploding the box." This effect could also be achieved by blurring distinctions between a room's planes or by the elimination of corners. Both of these strategies are employed at the Freeman House. The use of raw concrete block throughout the building blurs the distinctions between walls and floor, while the corners of the block cubes are themselves camouflaged or dissolved by becoming glass.

The drama of movement through the Freeman House is reinforced by additional elements in the architecture. The most powerful are the corner windows, joined by the broad cantilevers of the roof, the full-height french doors, and the horizontal mullions that mimic the horizon. All lead the eye from inside to out. In the living room, further impetus is given to this movement by the direction of the lines in the oak floor (ranged north to south), and by the same directionality of the roof beams and ceiling battens. Finally, depressing both the living room balcony and the slumber terrace down three steps so that their parapet walls are level with the interior floors prevents the walls from blocking the view.

One enters the house via a rocky defile and leaves it through a glass wall leading to a balcony high up in the trees; a progression from opaque to transparent. The architecture makes the transition as well. The only openings in the north wall at the street are the distinctively solid front doors and a row of seven perforated blocks with glass insets. Proceeding around the west façade of the house, however, the openings become steadily larger until they span two stories at the corners.

On the south façade, another kind of transition is observed, moving from the pair of massive vertical columns that appear to pin the structure to the hillside when seen from below to the floating bands of horizontal glass at the corners. The central opening between the columns on the upper level is a 6-block square. The transition proceeds from the columns themselves, which are encircled with alternating rows of plain and patterned block (in contrast to the columns on the north wall of the living room, which are patterned their entire height), outward to the two pierced screens of perforated block, each of which terminates in fingerlike extensions of block alternating with deep recesses. Thus, the tall, vertical shadow of a column is transformed into a vertical series of square shadows outboard of the screen. The final elements on the façade are the corner windows at each end. Even here, however, the part of the window next to the concrete screen is a 16" square of glass, recalling the concrete block but transparent. The entire transition terminates in the 32"-long bands of glass that reach to the corner.

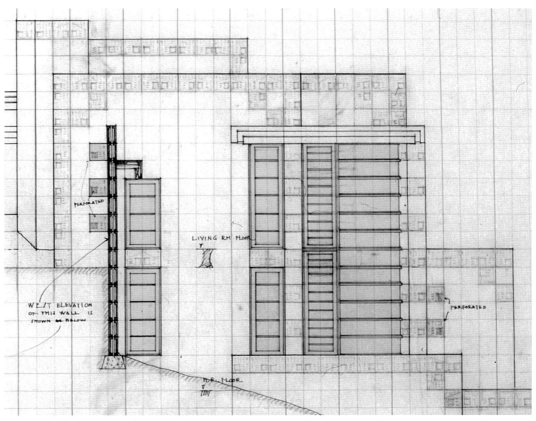

3-7. Openings on the west elevation become progressively larger moving from north to south; beginning with single perforated blocks, and stepping up in size to the 12-block-tall and 3½-block-wide corner curtain wall. Detail from working drawing manipulated by the author.

The cantilevered roof prevents the various compositional games being played with openings and block patterns from making the façades of the house feel chaotic or choppy. This horizontal element, visible on three sides of the main cubic volume, is a single, dominating datum line that literally overshadows all of the other elements on the façades. As strong as it is, however, Wright establishes a relationship of tension between the roof and the concrete cube by piercing the roof plane with piers and parapets.

METAPHOR

Many aspects of Wright's architecture comment on home, society, culture, place, even architecture itself. Most of the time, these added layers of meaning are clear, either visually or experientially—for example, the way the high backs of his Prairie-period dining chairs form a secure, inwardly focused enclosure around the assembled family. Sometimes, Wright added these layers of meaning after the fact, in writings or speeches, as guarantors bolstering a decision made primarily for other reasons, as when he proclaimed the sliding glass door "democratic." while discussing the Usonian house. Examples of especially important metaphor or iconography in the Freeman House are the eucalyptus pattern on the blocks, the two large hearths, the Mayan architectural style, the references to the four sacred elements (earth, air, fire, and water), and the massive beams in the living room.

Many of Wright's designs feature an interpretation of a plant that had, or was given, particular meaning for the project, a practice common among Arts and Crafts designers. In picking the eucalyptus for the Freeman house, as consensus claims he did, Wright chose the most distinctive tree in the Los Angeles landscape, even though it was an import from Australia. Standing above the grasses and chaparral, or scrub, the silvery eucalyptus was a distinctive vertical element in an otherwise fairly homogeneous dark and low vegetative cover. Wright wrote: "Curious tan-gold foothills rise from tattooed sand-stretches to join slopes spotted as the leopard-skin with grease-bush. This foreground spreads to distances so vast—human scale is utterly lost as all features recede, turn blue, recede and become bluer still to merge their blue mountain shapes, snow-capped, with the azure of the skies. The one harmonious note man has introduced into these vast perspectives, aside from the long, low plastered wall, is the eucalyptus tree. Tall, tattered ladies, these trees stand with careless feminine grace in the charming abandon appropriate to perpetual sunshine, adding beauty to the olive-green and ivory-white of an exotic symphony in silvered gold and rose-purple."[14] The presentation drawings of the proposed Freeman House prominently feature the eucalyptus. The "long, low plastered wall" was transformed by Wright into the long concrete-block wall along the street, and around the terraces. To this day, the Freeman House sits dappled beneath the clump of eucalyptus that preceded it on the site.

It is common in Wright's houses for the hearth, symbolizing shelter, to be set opposite a bank of windows or doors that open to the outside, setting up dialogues, or even another set of oppositions, between the home and the landscape, the family, and the community. At his Home and Studio, two seating areas bracket the living room. One is the inglenook by the fireplace; the other, a bay projecting toward the garden and the street. This duality serves several purposes. First, it provides a winter setting and a summer setting. Second, it allows the inhabitant to indulge the needs or whims of the moment, for womblike security or for engagement in the world passing by outside. Third, it establishes a fundamental principle for the form of a house: anchored at its core by the fireplace, which is also the most solid element in the home and is enclosed by an active perimeter that moves in and out to interact with or wall off the outside world.

The hearth contains fire, which not only provides heat but is the symbol of the life of the family. It is sacred, and its location in the home is sacred as well. Some writers have claimed that the concept of shelter originated along with fire as a means of protecting it. However one views this archetypal concept, it is clear that in Wright's architecture the hearth takes the form of a cave, the most primitive, secure, and grounded of shelters.

In his book *The Living City*, Wright himself sets up the dichotomy of the Cave Dweller and the nomad.[15] From the beginning of his career, the inglenook formed the cave within his domestic architecture. It only required the concept of "exploding the box" to complete the duality. With that in place, the exterior, itself often free to extend throughout the site, allowed the home's residents to wander visually through clerestories, laylights, skylights, and windows that ranged from opaque to transparent, and physically through porches, terraces, garden walls, and loggias stretching to the outside. Even ornament and decoration can be subordinated to the dual natures of these spaces. Patterns are usually more profuse and elaborate on the exterior walls, to encourage the mind to wander and to enhance visual delight, while the area containing the hearth is more severe, more regular, more substantial—relying on the flickering flames for animation.

In the Freeman House Wright intensified this duality. The hearth almost literally burrows into the hillside, while the walls of glass opposite it reveal not just a garden or street, but the world stretching to a distant horizon. (The hillside setting provides the opportunity to incorporate another iconic type of shelter, the tree house, which sets its inhabitants above it all, allowing them to see without being seen and to see farther and more than anyone else). Wright contrasts the two prototypes by setting the hearth and the opposing window wall in two different structural systems. The north wall of the living room is massive, unbroken by windows: a bearing wall in which pilasters frame the fire and patterned block forms a tapestry on the wall above it. The south wall is a post-and-beam construction of glass and cantilevered planes. Two large and two small columns support the floating roof, but they are set on either side of the balcony door, away from the corners. There is no vertical element, not even a mullion, within four feet of the corners, which seem to have been just taken away. The few blocks that remain at the south wall form elaborate perforated-block screens, obviating any similarity they might have to the opaque block at the hearth. These screens also provide a level of ornamentation similar to that formerly furnished by the art-glass windows of Arts and Crafts designers.

Central to Wright's physical and architectural wanderings between 1910 and 1924 was a search for an essential core to architecture. For him, and many others, that essence was found in the "primitive." It was thought of as both an ethnographic and a formal concept. It prompted a study of the works of simpler or older cultures to find a shared architectural grammar of ornament and form that was more meaningful, more "true," by virtue of being more universal. It encouraged a return to an architecture of platonic forms and solids: simple geometries that gave both order and a cosmological validation to the architecture. Theoretical underpinnings for this search came from the nineteenth-century German writer Gottfried Semper and his four components of the "primitive hut," the prototypical dwelling of the human race: the earthen mound, hearth, framework/roof, and lightweight enclosure.[16]

The search for architecture's universal, essential core on the one hand and for a national or regional design character on the other are contradictory impulses that underlie much of modern architecture, as well as other forms of modernist expression, including dance, music, and the fine arts. At the same time as Europeans were stripping history away from their architecture, the early California moderns—Gill, Schindler, and the two Wrights—were looking to historical precedents to give a sense of rootedness and place to their otherwise often radical works, and perhaps to please an American taste that had become enamored of exotic styles. One might argue that the Freeman House's evolution from the Mayan-influenced Romanza style of the early sketches to a less picturesque, more modern house as built, indicates the end of this experiment for Wright, and the integration of the important elements of his admittedly romantic experiments into more enduring polemical and architectonic concerns.

One last elemental gesture that survived at the Freeman House was the small pool by the entry, which offered an oasis from heat and sun. Situated partially under the entry canopy, the pool also reflected sunlight and ripples onto the soffit above it. Besides the obvious sense of refreshment, water had symbolic import. The Hollyhock, Millard, Storer, and Freeman houses all contained

3-8. Harriet in the east window seat of the living room, ca. 1925, in front of a screen formed from a panel of perforated blocks.

the four sacred elements: fire (the hearth), water (the pool or stream), earth (the site, and its extension, the concrete block), and air (the sky and views). At the entry to the Freeman House these four elements were represented by the courtyard: bounded to the northeast by the pool and to the southwest by the projecting tower of the hearth and chimney, framed in block that was made, at least in part, from the earth on which the house sat, the space was open to breezes that wafted through the open porch and views across the city and Hollywood Hills.

Even if the primitive style of the Maya had disappeared from the final design of the Freeman House, Gottfried Semper's four components were still very much in evidence. The earthen mound is expressed in the way the house is both cut into the hillside and (putatively), using the granite from the site, itself forms a new hilltop. Two hearths, one on each floor, dominate their associated interior space and are set into a distinctive tower that is the singular strong feature in the street façade. The main house's pair of massive concrete beams and column assemblies start in the earth and rise two stories to penetrate the plane of the roof. They are the framework, at least metaphorically, on which the rest of the building hangs. The lightweight enclosure is formed by the other great innovation of the house: the two-story glass curtain walls.

Frank Lloyd Wright first came to prominence as an architect of the Arts and Crafts movement, a period when, among other ideas, he investigated the expression of a building's structure through its ornament. In the octagonal drafting room of his Home and Studio, for example, massive chains of black iron connect a balcony to the beams of the roof above. While visually and aesthetically compelling, the chains perform no real structural function. They are ornament used in a structurally "logical" way. Wright represented the concept or idea of structure, as opposed to simply revealing the structure itself, as would architects of the Modern movement.

In the Freeman House, the massive concrete beams that span the living room from north to south appear to be part of a pair of great arches that support the entire house. In fact, the beams are massive in part because of the physical requirements of forming a beam out of both block and reinforced concrete, but mainly because each beam supports its own considerable weight as well as a row of perforated blocks that form the clerestory above. Because no continuous steel reinforcing runs from the beams into the pilasters at their north end or into the columns to the south, the beams actually do not establish a structural frame. The building's structure requires four additional concrete beams that span from east to west in the living room ceiling, and three more in the floor; but they are hidden from view because they would visually confuse our "understanding" of how the room is constructed, and because they would interfere with the more important aesthetic ideas of the north–south axiality of the room and the sense of lift and space created by the raising of the central section of the roof.

For all the inconsistency of the gesture, however, the house still represents a move toward a modernist revelation of structure, while the dominance of the structure visually connecting north and south, solid and transparent, dark and light, cave and tree house, inside and out, reinforces the dualities so central to Wright's vision.

Wright, writing two years after the Freeman House was completed, described the way the concrete blocks were standardized "unit-mass" elements woven together like an oriental carpet. He was conflating the idea of weaving and masonry, and connecting Semper's origin myth for architecture to modernist aspirations for the affordable house. But realizing Wright's rich vision for the Freeman House required that the building actually be built, which turned out to be not an easy thing.

4

CONSTRUCTION

If the design process for the Freeman House was difficult—with shifting topography, a disappearing architect, and myriad changes—its construction proved to be far more challenging. The consequences included the near bankruptcy of the clients and architects, multiple legal proceedings, an unfinished house, and a legacy of errors, omissions, hasty decisions, and botched details that would fester for decades, making the house increasingly vulnerable to the predations of time and the elements.

On February 19, 1924, a new agreement was drawn up between the Freemans and their contractor, now Holman, Wolff and Hackenschmidt, using the Uniform Contract form published by the American Institute of Architects and the National Association of Builders. The contract amount was still $9,100; the completion date, August 1. Article 1 states: "The contractors shall and will provide all the materials and perform all the work for the Erection and entire completion of a Pre-cast Concrete Slab Residence located on Glencoe Way." The contract continues:

> The dies, moulds and block-making apparatus proper are the property of the Architect and are all to be returned to him at the completion of the building or disposed of as may be directed by him. Dies for special pattern blocks such as may be peculiar to the building are to be paid for by this Contractor but to be the property of the Architect and returned to him at completion of work or upon demand. Other necessary dies, flasks, saddles, etc., are to be furnished by the Architect to the Contractor who will be held responsible for safe return of same in good order at completion of the job or when demanded by the Architect. This Contractor shall pay to the Architect a rental for the use of same to be agreed upon and a royalty of three cents per block for every block made and set in this work as compensation for the use of the System hereinafter specified in connection with patent sheet diagram [see fig. 1-18.].

This paragraph was based on the assumption that Wright owned the system. The royalty would have yielded Wright an additional $330 (plus any rental fee for the equipment) over and above the architectural fees. However, there was no patent (despite the "patent diagram" referred to in the contract), and no royalty was collected from the Freemans and, ultimately, few if any fees.

A week later the project took on a completely different complexion. Holman and Wolff disappeared as contractors and Lloyd Wright took over (Hackenschmidt continued to be involved for some time as foreman).[1] The reason for the change may have been to put the person most familiar with the block system in charge of the project, and Lloyd Wright was already in charge of the Storer House. Perhaps the complexities of the arrangement were too much for the contractors. No information survives about what caused the change. But the new contract for construction with Lloyd Wright, signed on February 26, was significantly different from the previous one: it drops any reference to project cost or completion date . At the same time, the Freemans and Frank Lloyd Wright signed a new side agreement in which the architect pledged to pay for any project costs that exceed $10,000, for a proportionate ownership of the building. (A similar arrangement had been executed between Wright and Mrs. Millard, and it evidently turned into a long-term debt for the architect.) The agreement between Lloyd Wright and the Freemans had its ironies as well. For example, "Should any matter arise as to the interpretation of, and the nature of the work to be done and the method of it's [sic] execution, the Architect shall be the sole arbiter and the Builder will co-operate with said Architect solely and in accordance with Plans, Details or such instructions of the Architect as may be given from time to time."

4-1. Building permit for the Freeman House describing a "pre-cast slab" construction, two-story residence, with 2 x 8 floor and roof joists, and a composition roof. Also listing Frank Lloyd Wright, architect, and Lloyd Wright, contractor, and giving an estimated price of $10,000. The permit itself cost $20.

These new documents were signed the day after the contracts were signed for the Ennis House. Now all three block houses were being built with Lloyd Wright as both contractor and supervising architect. Only the Freemans signed the February set of working drawings. Their new builder did not.

Site work on the house seems to have started almost immediately after the agreements were signed, even while the drawings and building permit were under review by the City of Los Angeles. (In Los Angeles, grading is done under a separate permit.) No one recalled a ceremony to celebrate the commencement of construction.

Lloyd Wright's first responsibility as contractor was to assemble a crew. "Several carpenters actually walked off the job, because they didn't like the look of it," Sam Freeman later recalled. "No one understood what Wright was trying to do."[2] However, construction began in earnest with the appearance of a team of mules yoked to a Fresno Scraper to grade the site for $10 per day; the animals spent much of March walking back and forth across the property, carving a flat spot on which to place the building.[3] Emil Hackenschmidt, the erstwhile contractor, oversaw six laborers who did "pick and shovel" work. Only two people, Talma Tanner (who worked in Lloyd Wright's office) and Hackenschmidt, were paid hourly ($1 per hour); most other workers received $4.50 or $5 per day.[4] Tanner began the work of designing and ordering the molds and dies for the blocks.

The Lloyd Wright job files contain numerous payroll records for the project. These were written on a 5½" x 8½" voucher form, with Lloyd Wright's name and phone number at the top. Spaces were provided for the job name, for a number to be stamped so that each voucher was numbered individually, for the date, for "purchased from" information, and to record hours worked per day and a description of the work. In another column, materials and equipment were to be noted in case the voucher was not for wages but rather for nails, sharpening picks, and so forth. The bottom third of the form contained space for the total hours, rate, total amount due, and check number, as well as for the recipient to sign that he had received payment. Because the forms were filled out sometimes by individuals, sometimes by the foreman, and sometimes even by Lloyd Wright (whose printing style is distinctive), the names of the crew morphed from week to week: W. A. Dixon became W. A. Hixon; G. Hamilton became G. Harmtin; Carl Steensen became Charles Steensen. The records were kept better at the beginning and end of the project than in the middle. Different foremen seem to have had different styles, and Lloyd himself was not always punctilious about the records. There was no clear or consistent accounting for the labor costs. Most of the forms lacked any description of the actual work performed, a potential problem because workman's compensation insurance rates were based on labor categories. Only after the project started experiencing serious financial difficulties did the accounting become more comprehensive.

By the end of March, the work was shifting from excavation to foundation. Sam Freeman noticed that the work started to slow down and seemed to be getting harder. Still, construction proceeded relatively smoothly for several months. The Freemans came by the job site almost every day. Sam said, "My own friends thought my wife, Harriet, and I were crazy when we started building this house."[5]

Wood was purchased to build a construction shack and to make formwork and other simple frame structures that were used to support the blocks as they were assembled, necessary so the grout poured into the channels between the blocks could cure for some days before a block assembly was self-supporting. The two carpenters who worked on building the frames were paid $9 per day, twice as much as the laborers.

During March, Lloyd Wright also began the process of obtaining bids for specialized aspects of the project to be done by subcontractors—roofing, plumbing, electrical wiring, and millwork.

Meanwhile, work on the drawings continued. As described in Chapter 2, pencil and ink sketches and notes were regularly added to a copy of the February working drawings at the job site. These additions included details that had been inadequately described, addressed unanticipated conditions encountered on the site, and responded to changes in the design that resulted from the construction process itself. Among the features resolved on the job site were such major questions as how to frame the cantilevered corners of the living room floor, as well as minor modifications such as moving the light fixtures from the top to the bottom of the living room clerestories. Over the course of the next year, Lloyd Wright and Talma Tanner prepared several sheets of drawings in the office for doors, windows, and other elements. And more drawings, notes, and telegrammed directives came from Taliesin to Los Angeles, either in response to specific requests or to correct something seen in the photographs that were apparently sent from Los Angeles to Taliesin to allow Frank Lloyd Wright to monitor the progress on the three houses that were under construction.

For example, a construction photograph (fig. 4-16) shows a block pilaster extending up the south face of the stair tower from the planter outside the kitchen window. The pilaster was an error; it appears on the west elevation of the January working drawings set, where

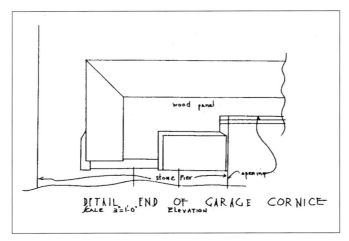

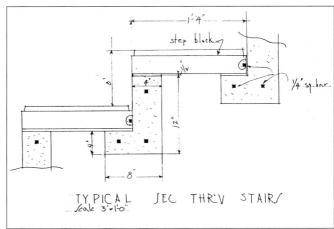

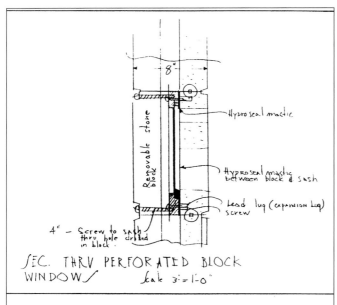

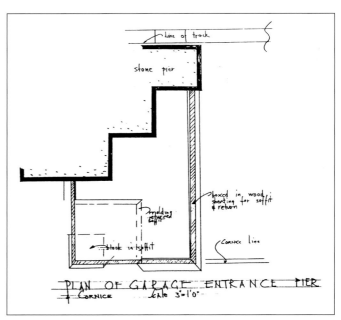

4-2. Details drawn during construction in Lloyd Wright's office, 1924.

it is also faintly crossed out. It is gone in the final house (see figs 4-23 and 4-32). Other photographs show an early version of the entry fascia, built according to the drawings but without the step detail that would characterize the finished roofline (see figs. 4-19 and 4-20; for the finished roofline, see fig. 4-33). Hazel Roy, a long-time friend of Harriet's, commented, "Oh yes, Harriet said they would often tear down as much each day as they built."[6] The photos proved confusing a half-century later, because they seemed to show an original vision compromised by later interventions, until it became clear that they were records of construction errors or revisions.

On April 8, the Freemans took out a $12,000 mortgage for a four-year term from Sam's father, Adolf Friedman, at 7 percent interest, to finance the construction.[7] That should have been sufficient to cover the $10,000 estimate, plus architects' fees and other expenses. Just three weeks later, on April 30, Friedman "release[d] the property in payment of the debt secured by the mortgage," thus canceling the debt. (Friedman also transferred the deed at the same time, for $10.) The Freemans could now start paying the monthly bills.

Once the site was prepared, footings and foundations (such as they were) were poured. Various parts of the block mold were delivered by the Aluminum Castings Company: one ornamental die, one top die, one flask, and 60 "plates" (the lightweight $3/16$"-thick sheet-metal coffers on which each block was made inside the mold, then used to remove the block from the mold). Several months into the process a half plate was delivered to the site, presumably for an ornamental top plate. One worker's receipts mentions setting up miters, evidently to help with the production of corner blocks. Bags of "plaster sand," "plain sand," Riverside Cement, and Mt. Diablo Cement were delivered to the site—or to the corner of Glencoe Way and Hillcrest Road, some 75 yards down the hill, or even farther away at the base of the hill, whence they were carried on the backs of the laborers up the steep slope to the site. With all the elements in place, the crew set up a block press and production began.

April also saw the delivery of 5 cubic yards of decomposed granite, probably used mostly as fill to bolster the southeast corner of the site. (As imprecise as they are, the records for the actual materials used in the house, still extant in Lloyd Wright's archives, became useful for understanding the properties and behavior of the block over the years.) Finally, 2,000 feet of $1/4$" reinforcing steel (rebar) were delivered to the site that month, along with more lumber. The rebar would be used to assemble the new blocks into a building. The crew shrank, evidently because of the completion of the site work and footings, and a number of those who had been laborers graduated to more demanding tasks, at higher pay.

MAKING THE BLOCKS

Byron Vandegrift, a young laborer on the job site, described the process of making the blocks:

A heavy table with an iron top $1/2$" thick and 4' wide by 6' long was set up on the hillside west of the house. Sand and cement for the job was left on Hillcrest, because Glencoe was not yet paved. I would carry the sacks to the site. In a wooden box, the sand and cement were mixed (4 to 1 mix) 2 times dry with a hoe. Then just enough water was added so that the material held its shape.

The [block-making mold] would be put on the table. It was filled with a shovelful of mix. The top was wiped off with a stick. The top plate was put on the form. A 2x4 was placed on top of the form. The 2x4 was hit with a 6 lb sledgehammer several times. Then the form was slid to the end of the table where the block was removed from the form. Then the block was watered 2 or 3 times every day for 21 days, checking at 7 and 14 days for strength. There would always be 2 or 3 rows of blocks drying in the sun. We worked six days a week, 7:20 to noon, and 12:30 to 4:30 Monday through Friday, and 7:20 to noon on Saturday. I also worked some Sundays.[8]

This description does not mention various pieces of equipment that were part of the block-making process in the early months. One was a press, a device essential for minimizing the

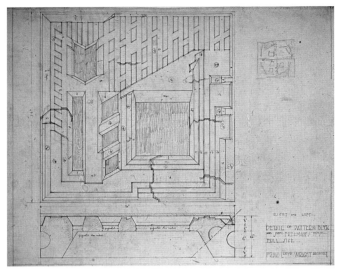

4-3. Pattern block detail created to prepare the aluminum face plates required to mold the blocks. The drawing depicts both patterned and perforated blocks and both field and corner blocks. In the manufactured blocks the sides of the coffer were more vertical, while the channel for the mitered block changed to an oval from the circular form seen at the bottom; corner blocks were made without a coffer. The perimeter reinforcing channels for corner and field blocks do not align (see fig. 4-5)—a construction challenge. Faintly visible in the upper right corner of the sheet is a crude sketch of four blocks rotated and assembled into the larger pattern shown in fig. 3-6.

4-4. Construction photo, detail. Block making on the hillside next to the street. The table on which the blocks were made is visible to the right of center. To the left of the tree, sacks of cement are stacked in front of a crew member. At right, newly molded blocks appear to be curing flat on small tables next to the house, prior to being stacked on end on wooden boards, as on the left.

problems caused by the dry mix, for which Sam Freeman began to be billed $75 per month[9] in March; by the time Vandegrift came on the job in September it was gone. A Blystone concrete mixer, rented for $85 per month, was also at the site in March, but it was gone after a few months, evidently being shared among the three houses under construction. A survey instrument, not further identified in the job records, but rented for $25 per month for many months, would have been used to establish the heights of the different levels of the lower floor, and to ensure that the rows of block stayed level.

Lloyd Wright estimated that 9,000 blocks would be required and identified the different types needed to build the house. The main block was a plain 16" x 16" block. There were two patterned blocks (sometimes called "fancy" or "decorated" by the crew), a left-hand version and a right-hand version. Variations of these three basic blocks needed to be made with one or more edges mitered at a 45-degree angle. If the block was to be placed at the edge of a wall, usually only one miter was required. If the block was to be set in a column or along the top of a wall, two sides were mitered. And if the block was at the top of a pier or column or on the top of a parapet at a corner, three sides had to be mitered. Five blocks, part of the stepped piers on the south façade, are mitered on all four sides.

This meant that five varieties of the plain block were required (unmitered, one side mitered, two adjacent sides mitered, two opposite sides mitered, three sides mitered), but the patterned-block requirements were more complicated. These were oriented on the façades according to how their asymmetrical face design combined with other patterned blocks. To accommodate all of the possible configurations, patterned blocks had to be made so that one, two, or three miters could occur in any combination of the four sides. Thus, the patterned blocks potentially had to be made in four variations of the single-miter type, whereas the plain blocks needed only one.

None of the mitered blocks in the house are coffered; they are all flat across the back, and therefore much heavier than other blocks. This was not the intention, as the detail of the pattern block (fig 4-3) shows; however, the mitered channel as drawn was evidently unfeasible, because it required thin projecting sides that would not have survived the molding and curing process. This was likely not realized until production started. At that point, the coffer was dropped, and the channel was elongated into an oval so that it could achieve the required depth without any sharp or thin projections.

The mitered blocks for the Freeman House had another problem not posed by the U- and L-shaped blocks at the other two houses. The channel formed by the intersection of two mitered blocks is not aligned with the channels formed by the regular blocks that meet in a row or column. It is an inch or more off to the side, so vertical reinforcing cannot go continuously from one block type to the other, as should happen at an opening in a wall. Again, it is not clear whether that consequence of the miter was fully appreciated prior to construction.

The decision to make mitered-block corners may have been intended to save money by avoiding the more complex casting process required for corner and column blocks at the other houses, but it led to durability problems as well as to the difficulties in filling the grout channels and the need for many more block types.

4-5. Corner patterned half blocks at a pilaster. These are mitered along one side (the missing block along two sides), and not coffered. The reinforcing and grout tubes from the flat block at the top have to jog in the bottom channel in order to align with the mitered blocks below.

Many conditions required a half block—8" x 16": the coping at the tops of parapets, steps and inside corners, and horizontal or vertical strips around the house where a half module was necessary to shift back to the dominant grid. As many as nine varieties of these half blocks were needed: plain, the left hand of a left-pattern block, the right hand of a left-pattern block, the left hand of a right-pattern block, the right hand of a right-pattern block, the top half of a left-pattern block, the bottom half of a left-pattern block, the top half of a right-pattern block, and the bottom half of a right-pattern block. For each of these nine varieties, subvariants were needed for different corner conditions: either square on all four sides or mitered on one, two, or three sides. Again, each of the miter variations could occur on any combination of the four sides.

Another set of blocks—8" x 8" quarters—was needed in a few locations, such as the top of a column of half blocks. Permutations of these quarter blocks included a plain variety and four possible quadrants of the left- and right-pattern blocks, for a total of nine variations that could require between zero and three miters. Neither half blocks nor quarter blocks were coffered.

Several sets of blocks on the roof, especially around the south elevation of the living room clerestory, are approximately 12" x 16". These blocks are shorter than the others to accommodate framing and roofing. It is not clear whether they were made by cutting blocks or by casting in an altered mold. There are four varieties of these blocks.

Finally, there are perforated blocks of both left and right pattern that make up the dramatic screens on the south façade and decorative openings elsewhere. They do not come in half or quarter versions, but some are used in corners, which suggests that they may be mitered on one or two sides; however, their actual shape is unknown. Noncoffered blocks seemingly cannot be perforated as they would be too thick to cut; yet, all of the other mitered blocks in the house lack a coffer. Because of their location, it has not been possible to determine exactly

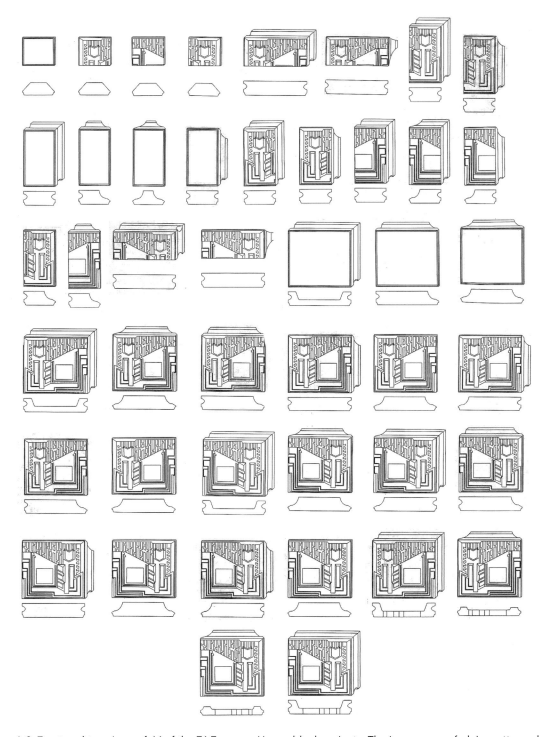

4-6. Front and top views of 44 of the 74 Freeman House block variants. The images are of plain, patterned, and perforated block; with top, bottom, and/or side miters; in quarter, half, and full sizes.

how the corner perforated blocks were handled. An additional group of six perforated blocks are among those that are short by approximately four inches at the bottom.

Still other variations include blocks with square edges but no coffer, apparently used as a kind of bond beam (a beam set into a wall to reinforce it or tie it to other elements) where structural strength was felt to be important. Blocks with no coffer but with square edges and no perimeter channel for reinforcing steel were used throughout the house as floor pavers; some were mitered (at the edges of stairs, for example). Blocks cast using wooden back plates, which produced plain blocks with sharp-edged coffers, were used in the lower-floor closets (fig. 4-12). A block mitered on one edge and cut on the opposite was used where a square pilaster terminated a wall, such as at either side of the entry doors. While two of the three blocks in each row of the pilaster were mitered, the one that abutted the face of the wall had to be cut or cast short.

The huge number of possible varieties of block meant that the crew had to determine as best they could the actual type and position of every block in the house. Patterned blocks used upside down had to be mentally reversed to see if they were a possible match for another pattern. Making multiple copies of all the potential block types on the chance that some of them would show up in the house was unreasonable and inherently inimical to the low-cost concept of construction. Still, construction records identified twenty-one different block types being made as late as the period September 2 through November 1, 1924, when masonry work should have been essentially complete using blocks made months earlier.

By careful examination of the house, seventy-four variants have been identified—seventy-four different sizes, shapes, and designs of a unit intended to be a simple, easily replicable alternative to the complexities of traditional construction. (Nine blocks remain unidentified because their location makes them impossible to inspect and categorize.[10]) Of the seventy-four types, forty are represented by fewer than ten blocks, thirteen are singular examples. Over half of the blocks in the house are of one type: the plain, coffered block with square edges and a perimeter channel on all four sides for the reinforcing steel.

Because making and curing the blocks was a lengthy process, a crew member who encountered a condition that required a block type not found in the piles of blocks accumulating around the site couldn't just make one up on the spot and install it. Work would have to halt in that area and proceed somewhere else until the required blocks were ready. Complicating this process was the constant revision and modification taking place: the blocks being installed were not necessarily those shown on the drawings. Were these revisions due to rethinking the design, to structural exigencies, or to the blocks that happened to be available that day?

An even larger problem seems to have developed early on that must have greatly complicated the remainder of the construction process. Almost all of the block dimensions just enumerated depend on the walls of the house having a consistent thickness, which, as described in the drawings, was equal to a half module, or 8". That is how the system was supposed to work: two wythes of 3½"-thick block set 1" apart. However, for whatever reason, many walls were not built that way. They vary, and are often 9" or 9½" thick. That means that adjacent blocks in the walls and floor pavers have to be 7" or less wide, in order to bring the system back to the 16" grid. In general, the thicker walls form the perimeter of the house, while parapets and interior walls are more likely to conform to the 8" dimension.

BUILDING CONTINUES

While work at the Freeman House seemed to be moving along, the other projects were not going so smoothly. In early April, Lloyd Wright sent a telegram to his father: "Storer stops work searches funds Ennis pattern face not here yet must stop work unless forwarded immediately post by airplane." [11]

Lloyd Wright's urgency was not returned by his father. A few weeks later, two more telegrams issued from Los Angeles: "Call Mr Wrights attentions to wires vital." "Give immediate attention wire 28 unanswered matter important wire."

Nevertheless, construction at the Freeman House continued unimpeded in May. The mixer and press were generating blocks full time, at the rate of several hundred a week (by the fall, when the process was being done entirely by hand, around seventy-five per day were being produced). Another 6,000 feet of rebar were delivered, and over 1,000 feet of Oregon pine lumber. Framing for the first floor had begun (see fig. 4-14).

A new estimate for electrical work arrived at $355, and one for plumbing and heating at $655. These were not much different than the cost estimate handwritten on the January roof plan, which was $300 for "wiring," and $750 for plumbing. Still, certain items went out for bidding repeatedly, either to lower the cost or because the design or the requirements were changing. The electrical system, the very first item bid, was among the last items completed.

By the end of May, construction was catching up with the working drawings, which, as we have seen, described the building only in the most general way. More information was needed. Lloyd's first request was telegraphed on May 24: "All well, Office address 5417½ Hollywood Blvd. Please forward sash and door details for Ennis and Freeman—need immediately."

After the textile-block system itself, the design of the doors and windows required the greatest number of post-working-drawing sketches and redesigns. The original dimensions on the plans called out the (assumed) rough openings. Thus, a window two blocks wide and four blocks tall was identified as 2'8" x 5'4" (2 times 16" by 4 times 16"). However, as the crew soon discovered, even the rough openings did not follow the block module, in part because that dimension is taken at the joint and fails to account for the projection into the space of the face of the block set at 90 degrees to the opening, and in part because the joints are irregular, despite (or because of) being mortarless. Thus the opening for the door of the west bedroom leading to the slumber terrace is actually 2'7" wide, while the opening for the door of the east bedroom is only 2'5½". After the frames were inserted, the actual dimensions of the openings were even narrower. The complexities of the real versus actual sizes of the fifty-five different doors and windows were reflected not only in the annotated plans but in three different complete sets of door and window details that were issued, two by Frank Lloyd Wright and one by Lloyd Wright (fig. 4-11). The difficulties also showed up in the estimating, manufacturing, and purchasing of these items: some had to be returned to the millwork shops for further work. (Eric Wright believes that, in the end, all the french windows in the living room were actually installed upside down.)

In June, a "left hand ornamental die" was furnished. Given the punishing use of the mold described by Vandegrift and similar stress likely caused by the press, it was not surprising that the dies began to fail after several thousand blocks. A later accounting from Aluminum Castings mentioned three dies and a flask purchased by the Freemans through June. At this

4-7. The lower walls of the first floor, and the slumber terrace, are visible in this construction photograph taken from the street looking south.

4-8. Blocks quickly filled the site. Note the moisture patterns on the block: the tops were drying out in the sun while the bottom of the blocks would retain the water needed for curing longer. Blocks are stacked three to four rows high, resting on pairs of boards laid flat. The frames used to hold the stair-tower walls together as they set are visible to the rear (east), the slumber terrace to the right (south).

4-9. Half blocks, mitered blocks, plain blocks, patterned blocks, and perforated blocks are all visible in this photograph taken while the slumber terrace and first floor were under construction.

4-10. East wall of the lower level nearing completion.

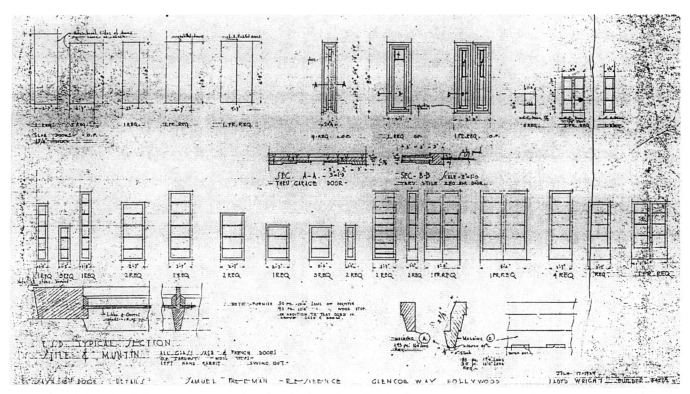

4-11. Sash and door detail sheet. Drawings produced in Lloyd Wright's office for the Freeman House, supplementing sheet 9 of the February working drawings set.

point, the Freemans had spent $284 on molds. (At the Ennis House, in contrast, $823 had been spent for the much more complicated molds for the L- and U-shaped blocks used there. A standard cast-stone mold and press purchased through the Sears catalogue would have run between $60 and $100.)

Also in June, another 2,000 feet of ¼" rebar were delivered, along with 480 feet of ½" square bar destined for poured-in-place structural members.

Mox Lumber was already delivering hundreds of pieces of jamb and screen molding of clear Oregon pine to be used in constructing the frames for the doors and windows, even though Lloyd's telegrams implied uncertainty about their final design and dimensions. Mox also shipped more framing lumber. A new plumbing estimate came in at $885, which was trimmed to $765. Another electrical estimate of $285 was revised to $228. These revisions of the original estimates, which had been based on the drawings, were noted to be "more accurate," implying that a combination of negotiation and some site visits to the growing house allowed the prices to be reduced.

On June 25, Frank Lloyd Wright finally replied to the May telegram: "Ennis garage wall straight, no break. Storer fixtures, Freeman Sash and kitchen details mailed today. Here's hoping and will write in few days. Father."

Construction continued apace in July. The clay liner for the chimneys was installed, and joist hangers were delivered for framing the second floor and roof. The hangers were intended

4-12. In this construction photo, the bedroom closets show the disparity in condition and appearance between the front and back of the blocks. A connection between two walls at right angles led to a crude reinforcing detail. The retaining wall for Glencoe Way is behind the partially completed wall of the hearth.

4-13. The retaining wall at the east side of the slumber terrace. As the slumber terrace was backfilled with dirt and construction debris, the wall bowed and cracked. The same phenomenon was besetting the Ennis House.

4-14. West wall of Sam's bedroom. The living room framing is being installed.

4-15. View of slumber terrace and bedroom under construction from the west, showing the same area of the building seen in detail above, left.

4-16. Construction photo showing the upper floor completed and roof framing under way. The circle marks the location of a pilaster rising alongside the kitchen planter that will later be removed.

4-17. Living room and west bedroom. At the top in this photo is the formwork used to pour the small concrete beams in the living room ceiling and the framing used to support the large, block-formed arches until they set.

to supplement the rather direct method of connection between concrete and wood outlined in the specifications: each joist was to be stapled to the bent top of the rebar coming out of the grout tubes between the blocks. Since both joists and block joints occurred at 16" on center, this presumably provided regular connections between the walls and the floors and the roofs. The joist hangers were used to attach to ledgers or other pieces of wood framing at windows, gaps in the block walls, and other locations where there were no walls on which to rest the joists.

The door and window details drawn at Taliesin were sent out for estimates. Another 1,000 feet of rebar were purchased. More framing lumber and cement arrived, along with brackets and other hardware for framing. Four more block dies were delivered, although it is not clear whether they were for the Freeman or Ennis projects, or both.

In August, six months into construction, Sam Freeman still felt comfortable talking to Lloyd about having Frank Lloyd Wright design "a cottage" for his father.[12] (Nothing came of this project; Schindler took it on later.) Lloyd was also trying on his own to develop additional projects for the father/son team. But Frank Lloyd Wright fell silent and Lloyd's attempts to get responses to his queries were unrequited. Panic appears in his telegram to his father on August 19: "Where are you? A gift to one powerless to receive it is no gift at all but a bitter joke. Either assistance requested is immediately forwarded or irreparably injure our opportunities here."

Block making from April through July had used up the initial deliveries of sand and cement. August brought 20 more yards of sand, 10 more yards of decomposed granite, 250 more sacks of Riverside Cement, 10 yards of a 50/50 ¾" mix (most likely a sand and gravel mix for the footings and other poured-concrete elements), and another left-hand die for the blocks. A new block-making campaign of significant scale was under way. The construction photographs make it clear that the small site could accommodate only a limited number of blocks and supplies (for example, fig. 4-8); as blocks were incorporated into the building, the space around the house was freed up for more.

Trucks that in March took loads of dirt and rock away from the site now brought loads of stone and dirt back—more fill for the lowest part of the stair tower and the slumber terrace, as well as for the gap between the retaining wall for Glencoe Way and the lower-floor interior walls of the house and garage. Most of these areas were not completely filled in until the end of the construction process. Before then, the fill was set down in 4-foot-deep layers, with a row of concrete deadmen, 4 feet on center, cast in trenches on top of each layer. Meanwhile, wood plank bridges spanned from the street to the upper level of the house and garage. (Most of the retaining walls bowed and cracked when they were backfilled later—see fig. 4-13—as might have been anticipated from the experience at the Ennis House.)

Another 2,100 feet of lumber were purchased in August, half for roof sheathing, the rest for the roof framing. (Among the charges for lumber is $89.60 for Martha Taggart. Taggart was Lloyd Wright's mother-in-law, and her house was an important early commission for him. Although it had supposedly been finished several years earlier, charges for various types of work there show up several times in the Freeman House records.) Firebrick for the Freeman House fireplaces arrived as well. Three different thicknesses of rebar—⅜", ½", and ¾"—were delivered to the site for use in the various concrete beams, as well as another 7,000 feet of ¼" rebar for the block assemblies. By now there were well over three miles of steel in the building. An unusual invoice arrived for 200 pounds of dry modeling clay, which was used to fill gaps between the blocks where the joints did not close completely, either because the rows were uneven or the blocks were not square. The clay prevented the grout poured into the perimeter channels from leaking out. Another invoice listed seven electric heaters.

August's bills must have been a shock for Sam Freeman. They came to over $3,500, more than twice the charges in any previous month. With thirteen men working on site, labor costs jumped as well, to $1,617.01.[13]

In early September, Lloyd received three estimates for roofing the house. Another 600 feet of roof sheathing, 20 yards more of fill dirt, miscellaneous framing hardware, and more cement, sand, and steel for block production and poured-in-place concrete elements were delivered. Fifty-eight decorative 1" x 16" panels of Oregon pine, 12 to 16 feet long and finished on all four sides, for the living room, kitchen, and hallway ceilings arrived as well.

A half-block die, 7¹⁵⁄₁₆" x 15¹⁵⁄₁₆", made by Harrison Machine Shop for Aluminum Castings, was delivered on September 9. It was likely the top half of a patterned design for the copings on the top of the roof parapets.

Union Hardware and Metal Company began shipping door, cabinet, and window hardware, bathroom furnishings, and the track system required for the garage doors. Many of these items have survived to the present day.[14]

Work started on the plumbing and the lower bath-

4-18. Building the garage and beginning the upper roof. Note the gap between the street and the house, and the temporary bridge connecting the street to the garage.

4-19. West elevation seen from Glencoe Way. Both upper and lower roofs now connect the garage to house.

4-20. North elevation from across Glencoe Way.

room. A water heater purchased for $100 was destined for the hallway closet behind the bathroom. (This was a change from the original specification, which called for small electric instant-use water heaters to be located in the kitchen, bathroom, and laundry room.) However, if it actually arrived on site, it seems to have disappeared almost immediately. Four months later there was still no water in the house. Sam Freeman later claimed that no water heater had been installed. Eventually, one was placed outside in a shed attached to the corner of the stair tower; pipes from it snaked along the face of the building, plunging through crudely made holes in the blocks to reach the fixtures. The source of water before that, however, remains a mystery.

At this point it became clear that the project was slipping out of control. The house might have appeared nearly complete: some roofing was in place, plumbing and electrical work was under way, and carpenters were installing the finished decorative ceilings upstairs. The estimated six-month construction period had ended. September's bills brought the total project costs to $10,787.98 (as noted on Lloyd Wright's Distribution Sheet), some 10 percent more than the finished house was supposed to cost in the first place.[15] The Freemans' budget for the project was used up. Per the agreement, from this point forward any expenses were to be the architect's responsibility.

Lloyd Wright's job files for the Freeman House contain about a dozen pages of notes, calculations, and expense breakdowns from the end of September and early October that indicate a fairly serious discussion between the Freemans and their contractor. Several sheets are devoted to an analysis of the cost of the blocks, first calculating them at 68 cents each, then at 64 cents each, installed.[16] According to Lloyd, by September 30 10,563 blocks had been made and 9,770 blocks installed. (The 2004 block survey of the house, arrived at a total of 9,784 for blocks installed. However, not every block below grade or inside a column was located or identified, so the real number is probably about 100 higher. Still, Lloyd's numbers are intriguing, because block production continued for several more months.)

Another calculation listed the material and labor costs for the project through October 1,[17] totaling $11,169.26, or $400 more than the Distribution Sheet. (On an accounting dated September 28, the cost to date had been higher still—$12,757.08—but that included a number of items contracted but not yet completed, such as plumbing and electrical work.) Yet another calculation attempted to break down the labor costs into work related to masonry and work related to "carpentry etc." According to this exercise, by September 1 the labor expenses for the blocks totaled $1,947, while the remainder of the labor came to $3,874.59. Adding $1,200 of labor for the month of September, the total for the project by October 1 was $7,021.59. (Only $5,903 was reported to Aetna Insurance for the purpose of workman's compensation coverage.) In short, there were several accountings, all different and all over budget.[18] The confusion effectively poisoned the relationship between Lloyd Wright and the Freemans at a time when trust was sorely needed. Most of the calculations seem intended to prove that the textile-block system was not a mistake rather than to accurately record expenses. (The apparent fudging of labor costs in order to minimize workman's compensation insurance payments, which continued through the remainder of the project, ended with Lloyd Wright and Sam Freeman in court.)

Despite the mounting troubles, blocks were still being made and installed at a rapid rate. As of September, no doors or windows, including the great double-height walls of glass on the

Style	Size	Miter	Number	Notes
Left	16 x 16	-	2	nc
Left	16 x 16	lrtb	4	4 miters
Left	16 x 16	lt	5	
Left	16 x 16	lrt	7	
Left	16 x 16	l	18	
Left	16 x 16	rt	38	
Left	16 x 16	lr	142	
Left	16 x 16	-	162	
Left	16 x 16	t	181	
Left	16 x 16	r	221	
Left	8 x 16	-	1	
Left	8 x 16	t	10	
Left	8 x 16	r	23	
Left	12 x 16	r	1	
Left	8 x 16 bottom	t	1	
Left	8 x 16 left	-	3	
Left	8 x 16 left	t	4	
Left	8 x 16 right	t	2	
Left	8 x 16 right	r	3	
Left	8 x 16 right	rt	3	
Left	8 x 16 top	rtb	1	
Left	8 x 16 top	-	1	
Left	8 x 16 top	tb	18	
Left	8 x 8 left top	tb	2	
Plain	16 x 16	ses	7	
Plain	16 x 16	se	9	
Plain	16 x 16	-	42	wood coffer
Plain	16 x 16	ss	488	
Plain	16 x 16	s	922	
Plain	16 x 16	-	4496	
Plain	8 x 16	ses	1	
Plain	8 x 16	-	4	cc
Plain	8 x 16	ee	10	
Plain	8 x 16	e	12	
Plain	8 x 16	ss	42	
Plain	8 x 16	s	105	
Plain	8 x 16	-	496	
Plain	12 x 16	-	3	3/4 roof
Plain	8 x 8	s	1	
Plain	8 x 8	-	12	
Right	16 x 16	lrtb	2	
Right	16 x 16	-	2	nc
Right	16 x 16	rt	5	
Right	16 x 16	lrt	20	
Right	16 x 16	lt	39	
Right	16 x 16	r	44	
Right	16 x 16	lr	147	
Right	16 x 16	-	166	
Right	16 x 16	t	186	
Right	16 x 16	l	238	
Right	8 x 16 bottom	t	2	
Right	8 x 16 left	l	1	
Right	8 x 16 left	t	1	
Right	8 x 16 left	tb	1	
Right	8 x 16 left	lt	5	
Right	8 x 16 right	rt	2	
Right	8 x 16 right	t	4	
Right	8 x 16 top	ltb	1	
Right	8 x 16 top	-	1	
Right	8 x 16 top	tb	17	
Right	8 x 8 left top	tb	1	
Right	8 x 8 right top	tb	2	
Paver	8 x 16	-	200	
Paver	8 x 8	-	50	
Paver	16 x 16	s	100	
Paver	16 x 16	-	800	
X-Left	16 x 16	lrb	2	Perforated
X-Left	16 x 16	r	4	"
X-Left	16 x 16	-	104	"
X-Left	12 x 16	-	3	"
X-Right	16 x 16	lrb	2	Perforated
X-Right	16 x 16	l	4	"
X-Right	16 x 16	-	114	"
X-Right	12 x 16	-	3	"
Unknown			9	estimate
		TOTAL	9785	

4-21. Inventory of blocks used in the Freeman House.

Key:

Style

Left = a patterned block with the 'tree trunk' to the left as viewed
Plain = a block with a smooth face
Right = a patterned block with the 'tree trunk' to the right
Paver = a block used as flooring without a perimeter channel or coffer
X-Left = a left-patterned block, with elements cut out to form a screen
X-Right = a right-patterned block, with elements cut out to form a screen

Size

bottom = the bottom half of a patterned block
left = the left half of a patterned block
right = the right half of a patterned block
top = the top half of a patterned block
left top = upper left quadrant of patterned block
right top = upper right quadrant of patterned block

Miter

l = left mitered
r = right mitered
t = top mitered
b = bottom mitered
s = one side (left or right) mitered
ss = two opposite sides mitered
se = a side and end (top or bottom) mitered, or two adjoining sides
ses = an end and two sides mitered, or three adjoining sides
ee = two ends mitered
e = one end (top or bottom) mitered

Notes

nc = no coffer
4 miters = blocks on the lower south façade mitered on all sides
3/4 roof = hand cut on site to fit roof conditions
cc = used as chimney cap, cut for flue

south façade, had been installed, nor had any electricity, gas, or water started to flow. Lloyd Wright made a list of items not yet completed:

Electric Contract	285.00
Electric Heaters	168.00
Plumbing Contract	765.00
Roofing Contract	127.00
Sash and Doors Contract	1,179.49
Dirt for Back Fill	40.00
Eastman [construction supplies]	150.00
Finish Hardware	319.00
Painting	200.00
Carpentry (Finish)	500.00
Flooring	100.00
Masonry	288.00
Cleanup	60.00

He then took the figure of $10,787.98 for the work done to date from the Distribution Sheet, added the erroneous total of $3,181.49 for the outstanding items, along with his 10 percent fee, and arrived at a new total project budget of $14,287.61. He gave this figure to the Freemans at the end of September, one month after the house was supposed to have been completed. It was 50 percent greater than the estimate contained in the January agreements. Worse, if the correct sum for the missing items had been used, the projected cost would have been $15,387.62. And Lloyd omitted or forgot some critical items, such as plastering the lower-floor ceilings and stairwell, and the glass for the doors and windows. His calculation also did not allow for price increases: painting, for example, would cost $340, not $200.

Lloyd Wright and his clients understood that costs were spiraling inexorably. Early in September, Lloyd apparently wrote a long letter to his father, explaining what was going on with the Storer, Freeman, and Ennis projects. On September 15, Frank Lloyd Wright responded with his own lengthy missive.[19] He expressed surprise that the work was not as advanced as he had imagined it would be and that Storer would turn to him for $3,000 to finish that project; dismay at how the Ennis House looked; and incredulity about the survey problems at the Freeman and Ennis houses. He even suggested a lawsuit against the surveyor. That concern with the surveys came nine months after the problem had been discovered suggests that Wright may not have been involved enough in the working drawings to realize the full impact of the errors before—or that he was searching for a scapegoat. Wright also advised Lloyd on how to deal with Mabel Ennis, an ultimately fruitless endeavor because the Ennises ended up firing them both. Wright then blamed an unnamed "them" for trying to put obstacles in front of pioneers and, with a comment about "deficit mentality," anticipated that the "profit in the schemes" will be small. "Freeman, Hackenschmidt et al.—are the usual difficulties, no more. Do not chafe too much. The stake is large for which you are playing."

It seems a pretty safe bet that no one, not Lloyd, and certainly not the Freemans, would have disagreed with that last remark. All four textile-block houses would eventually require Wright to spend his own money in order to complete them. In full pursuit of his experiment,

4-22. Construction photo of the house and the hillside taken from the west, with roof framing almost complete.

4-23. The south façade, with the roof complete. Compare this to fig. 4-16: the pilaster has been brought all the way to the top of the penthouse at this stage.

4-24. Construction photo view from the southwest corner of the property. The perforated-block screens are not yet all the way to the roof.

4-25. View from a bungalow court at the corner of Highland and Franklin. The masonry is largely complete, but no glazing has yet been installed.

he would have to pay a price. He was in no financial position to step up to the plate. He proceeded to lay the facts of the situation out to his son. He had no new work, was $47,000 in debt, and his second wife, Miriam Noel, had appeared with a lawyer to demand more money. He had just made a payment toward what he owed Alice Millard on La Miniatura, and he was engaged in a battle with Aline Barnsdall over the projects on Olive Hill. He told Lloyd that he would try to send some money on September 15, but not to expect any before then. (As that is the date of the letter, September 15 may have been a mistake.) Wright offered to send Lloyd a block of Japanese prints to sell, and ended the letter with some financial advice (which might have struck Lloyd as presumptuous coming from a man who rarely lived within his means) and a final comment about his son's temper.

Little in the letter actually helped the projects. Another exchange of telegrams included this from Wright: "Suggest you had better come at once. In any case, let work rest until you return, if necessary. Draw on me one hundred fifty expenses. Bring detail figures Storer, Freeman, Ennis." However, Lloyd did not leave immediately. Instead, he stayed in Los Angeles to meet with A. M. Johnson, the potential client for both a house in Death Valley and the National Life Insurance building, and to show him the block houses.[20]

Faced with an unexpected $5,000 jump in the cost of his home and mounting uncertainty that the figures being quoted had any validity, Sam Freeman had been attempting unsuccessfully to contact his architect himself. On October 4 Lloyd wired his father: "Freeman keeps his end of contract. Wants and deserves answer his letter. Wire."

Five days later, he wired again: "J[ohnson] . . . says you are coming out soon. Looks over buildings. Indifferent. Makes no move to finance. Storer and Freeman upset. Shall I approach J tomorrow before he leaves and attempt to get action?"

Frank Lloyd Wright was not only courting Johnson as a client but trying to entice him to invest money in the block houses, evidently going so far as to promise such an investment to his desperate clients. He replied to Lloyd the next day: "No action expected until Johnson sees me. All you can do is to show work to advantage, then come on here. Tell Storer to draw on me for two thousand, Freeman for enough to keep going."

Here we have the first indication that Frank Lloyd Wright might actually have put money into the Freeman House, as he was committed to do by the agreement he and the Freemans had executed in February. Sam's later comment, "with all the aid he gave us . . ." seems to confirm that Wright contributed.[21] The first record of a payment by Frank Lloyd Wright showed up in his son's job records in November.

In mid-October, Lloyd Wright finally left for Taliesin. Talma Tanner wired him there on October 18 to explain that one of the sash and door details sent the previous month didn't work: "Details for hinged windows next glass screen do not allow them to open under ceiling moulding."

The problem concerned the only two in-swinging windows in the house, located on the inside of the perforated-block screens that flank the doors to the living room balcony. Because the line of the ceiling is at a block module, and the moldings, or battens, that cover the joints between the wood panels descend three inches from the module, they blocked the windows from opening, as all the windows were drawn, essentially, in multiples of a block in height and width.

Lloyd solved the problem by adding additional wood to the head of the window frame, thus shortening the opening. A few days later, from Chicago, he wrote an angry and exasperated letter to his father at Taliesin. He began with a list of drawings required immediately, including the "fireplace benches" at the Freeman House, and other items at the Storer and Ennis houses. He then launched into a furious exposition of what he had done on these projects for his father, what he was losing financially, and how he felt he had been treated.

Frank Lloyd Wright's reply is not known. He was supposed to come to Los Angeles at the beginning of December, and may have responded then in person. His summary of the experience, written six months later, in June 1925, attempted to put a somewhat positive spin on both the work and his relationship with his son:

> You are eminently fair, degenerating I should say to utter absolute generosity—the unpardonable crime of the American fool. Enclosed is tardy response. I think the "publicity" achieved has been mostly on a shoestring and rather wild. I hope it won't react unfavorably some day. There is some solid work we might do if I could get down to anything like that—and I may soon. Fate is a dirty fighter, as you see in my case,— And it is because, character is fate and therefore on the ground first in any event. I think you write well, dance divinely and lie with charm but are not convincing when you lie. No Welshman ever is. So let's go to it with the bald and naked truth and swing a wicked damn into all this shoddy and sham that passes for civilization in the E Pluribus Unam of the U. S. A.
>
> Yours nevertheless and notwithstanding,
> In other words, [22]

Yet work continued. In fact, it seems to have moved to a higher level of intensity. For October, Lloyd attempted his only known project schedule, listing all of the ongoing work and the actual or anticipated completion dates.[23] Though some items were completed by the dates Lloyd set, others, such as the sash and doors, would take several more months to manufacture and install. Lack of funds may have hampered progress in part, but as it turned out, still more drawings and details were required to fit various elements, such as the windows, to the house as it was actually being constructed.

Newton Electric Company completed the rough wiring and installed switches for the wall heaters. Pioneer Lumber Co. ("We put the wood in Hollywood") delivered the Schumacker plasterboard that lined the hall and the bedroom closets downstairs, along with more finished lumber, both Oregon pine and clear oak. E. K. Wood Lumber Co. delivered more framing lumber and finished ceiling panels. Lloyd ordered landscape materials and a gardener to install them. More sacks of cement and sand and another 400 feet of rebar arrived.

Atlas Roofing was contracted to supply the gravel roof, for which it had submitted a bid of $127 in August, but because there are no surviving images of the roof from any of the sixty years that the Freemans resided there, no confirmation exists that this work was completed as described. (Over the years, at least five different re-roofing projects were carried out, each installed on top of previous work; none included gravel.) Lloyd's crew returned 423 empty cement sacks to the supplier for a credit of $42.30 on October 14, which helped defray the cost of a rush order for 100 sacks two days later, which cost the project $80.

On October 21 Lloyd Wright received a letter from Simons Brick, the first of many letters to come on the same theme, "We shall greatly appreciate payment . . ." Soon, every dollar mattered. Orders were still going out, but none of the bills for materials, supplies, or subcontractors had been paid since the end of September.

Labor costs were high again in October, because twelve crew members were working six days a week and were entitled to overtime rates for Saturday afternoons. A few even worked on Sundays. According to Lloyd's records, Sam Freeman kept up with the labor costs through October. By November 1 the project had cost Sam Freeman $12,733.11, not including the outstanding bills or work not yet completed. The labor issues must have been especially galling for the clients if Harriet's later recollection was at all true: "Sam and I would come up at the end of the day to see what had been accomplished and the workmen would just laugh."[24]

On November 14, 115 sacks of Riverside Cement were returned to Eastman; a plain die was returned to Aluminum Casting; and 538 feet of finished lumber went back to E. K. Wood Lumber Co.—almost half of what had been delivered to the Freeman House the previous month. Correspondence reveals the gathering financial crisis. On November 1, the LA Decomposed Granite Company wrote Lloyd, "We are still looking . . . for a remittance to cover your past due account. A check by return mail will make us both happy!" There was a balance of $2.10 from September 30. On November 4, Hopper's Blacksmith Shop wrote, "While we try to be accommodating . . ." for an outstanding amount of $4.25. On November 11, Lloyd wrote to Mox, Pacific Clay, Pioneer Lumber, and Geo Eastman. He promised Eastman that Sam would pay his bill. He claimed that Mox had delivered eight more slab doors and three more sash than ordered. He asked Pacific Clay to provide an explanation and itemization. He requested itemization from Pioneer (but promised money from Dr. Storer). The Geo Eastman company responded on November 18: "Dear Sir, Your letter of November 11th was duly received, and in answer advise that we are willing to wait until early December for Mr. Freeman to arrange settlement of his account." On November 19, Pioneer wrote, "Dear Sir: Dr. Storer gave us a check in settlement of his account. Kindly favor us with a settlement of the Taggart and Freeman jobs, and oblige . . ." Two days later, Simons Brick Company wrote, "Will you please let us have check for $11.50 by return in settlement of overdue account." Atlas Roofing wrote on November 30: "May we please be favored with your remittance."

On November 19, Lloyd Wright telegraphed his father: "Freeman can't meet payroll. Am held responsible to Labor Commission five hundred. Can Taliesin please wire seven hundred A. B. code or Western Union without fail."

Six days later, Frank Lloyd Wright replied: "Have wired Ennis to pay you seven

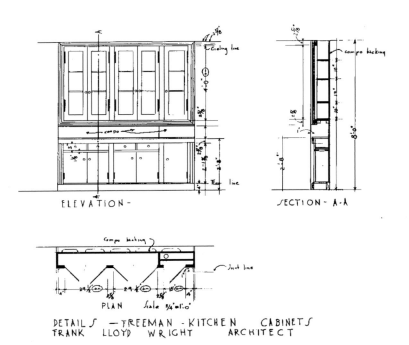

ELEVATION-

SECTION- A-A

PLAN   Scale ¾"=1'-0"

DETAILS —FREEMAN - KITCHEN CABINETS
FRANK LLOYD WRIGHT   ARCHITECT

4-26. Kitchen cabinet detail drawings, produced during construction in Lloyd Wright's office.

fifty, being five hundred for Freeman, two fifty for you. Charge to me pending settlement. Go and see them and wire me results. Arriving about December fourth. Father."

Sure enough, Lloyd Wright noted on a Distribution sheet: "Nov. Received on [account]. FRANK LLOYD WRIGHT $500." Just below that, another entry for the same month credits Wright with an additional $166.20.

Work continued. Lloyd turned to new, unsuspecting suppliers and subcontractors for the plastering and other finishes. Toward the end of November, however, he started laying off workers. In part this could be attributed to progress on the building and changes in the nature of the work, but the reason was mostly economic. Blocks were still being made on site, so evidently even the exterior of the building was not yet completed. The workers would be lucky to get paid.

On December 1, Lloyd calculated a new project total based on the costs incurred to date, and a revised estimate of the outstanding work. It now came to $16,839.56, to which he then added his fee, for a grand total of $18,523.51. In two months, Lloyd's estimate had increased by $4,000, an amount that in itself was almost half of the original estimated cost for the entire project. The suppliers continued to dun: "Portions of this account 60 days past due. Would appreciate remittance by 12/10/24" (Pacific Clay). "While we wish to be accommodating . . ." (Hopper's).

After some eight months of construction, the crew now was ready to turn from the complexities of the block to the complexities of installing the dramatic windows and glass screens. On December 8 Sunset Sash Door and Mill Co. forwarded a three-page list of custom doors and windows "to be reviewed by customer." As noted earlier, the construction of the many doors and windows at the Freeman House was complicated by the difference between the intended and actual sizes of all the openings, as well as by the variability of the block lines relative to the sills and lintels. During construction, the material had also changed from the

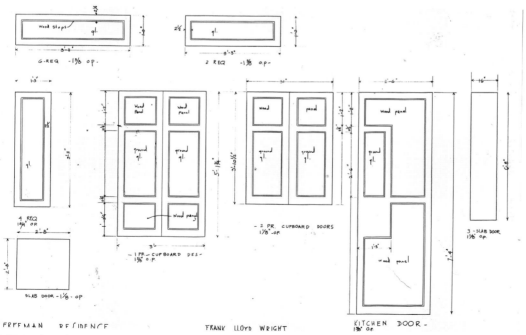

4-27. Kitchen door and panel details, produced in Lloyd Wright's office during construction.

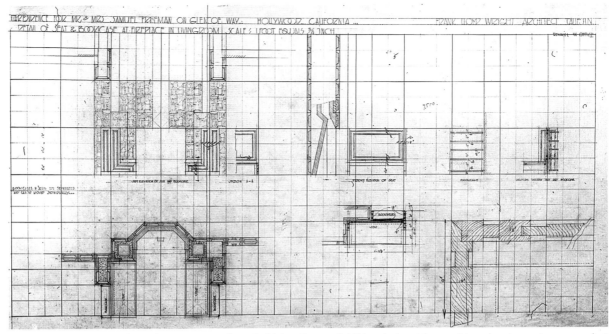

4-28. Detail of Seat and Bookcase at Fireplace in Living Room. Additional sheet for working drawing set prepared at Taliesin during construction, 1925.

4-29. Left, drawing showing how the furniture group was to be installed on either side of the fireplace, inboard of the pilasters, and spanning from block pavers to oak floor. Right, drawing envisioning as-built condition in 1925, showing the final location of furniture on the wood floor and in line with the pilasters. Also shown is a re-creation of the original door, cabinetry, and movable table in the wall between the living room and kitchen, and cube lighting attached directly to ceiling (at upper right).

4-30. Living room furniture, 1925. Because the benches are shorter in height and length than the book-cases, it appears that the benches were indeed built to go next to the fireplace as shown in figs. 4-28 and 4-29, but were then modified to sit where they are in this picture either during construction or shortly thereafter. The floor pavers are already grouted and painted.

intended redwood to more affordable Oregon pine, and the system of copper screens that would have served as an important element of protection for the full-height openings at the second floor was abandoned.

A week later, another list of custom items was forwarded by Sunset Sash Door and Mill for review. It included the windows with mullions 8" apart, and the living room furniture: the bookcases, benches, and dining table (with a note: "hold for detail"). The price for the furniture was $80, "plus $11 for changes."

December 15 saw a shift in focus from rough construction to interior finishes—with an agreement between Sam Freeman and the painter William Haase to "properly execute and complete the interior and exterior painting herein mentioned and specified." The work requested was fairly minimal. Haase was to apply one coat of water-based paint to the plaster ceilings, one coat of shellac to "all wood work"—not much of a coating for either protection or appearance—and bronze powder to the lower band of the wood cornices at the entry and around the living room. He had already painted the cornices with a gray-green oil-based paint, so the bronzing made the lower part of the cornices appear gold-leafed.

On December 29, John Johnson installed a 21' x 21' "carpet" of select white oak in the living room, as well as a 9' x 5' rectangle on the stair landing at the roof level. For $125, he furnished 54 yards of ½" x 1½" strips, installed them, and then sanded the wood and applied four finish coats (one of filler, two of shellac, one of wax).

Lloyd's crew was in flux. Some who had received notice in November were still working, as were a number of other long-term crew members. But six new men, half of them glaziers, were hired as well; Fuller and Company had won the bid for the glass for the windows and doors ($89.70). The glass order consisted of twelve lites (panes) 12" x 16", ten lites 6" x 16", twelve lites 16" x 16", 24 lites 16" x 28", twenty-four lites 16" x 58", one lite 16" x 26", and twelve lites 11" x 40" ground glass. (The losing bidder, American Glass, had specifically called out double-strength glass for the corner windows, which would have been a better choice given the way the panes rest on top of each other.)

Two days after Christmas 1924, Newbery Electric quoted $145 for "4 special square lanterns on rods," and "8 special square lanterns to fit close to ceiling." Three days later, they sent a revised estimate of $167.50 for those items plus numerous porcelain light sockets, including four for the columns outside the front door and eight for the clerestories in the living room. (Another estimate in January slightly amended the last item: "2 16-foot cords of 4 lites each with plug attachment." The price dropped 50 cents, to $167.)

Just ten days after Lloyd's estimate of December 1 he prepared a new estimate, and the price to finish the house jumped another $3,000 to $21,888.17, including workman's compensation insurance, contractor's fee, and architect's fee, almost two-and-a-half times the original estimate. Around Christmas, Lloyd tried his calculations again. Because Sam Freeman had kept up with the payroll through October, Lloyd used labor costs from November 1, but material costs and subcontracts from October 1. He totaled everything, added 10 percent on the labor and materials for his fee since October 1, and arrived at a new total of $20,316.80 (the math does not work in these calculations).

Then Lloyd added another 10 percent, apparently for the architect's fee, to arrive at a figure of $22,348.48. In another calculation, starting again with $20,316.80 but this time subtracting 10 percent, as if he not only refunds the architect's fee but his own as well, the new total is $18,275. Then he adds and subtracts two more figures to arrive at a total of $17,097. How he arrived at this number is a mystery. Elsewhere on the sheet, he noted monies paid in since November 1, including $666.29 from his father in November and another $633.00, presumably from Sam Freeman, in November and December. But this income of $1,299.29 would not have altered the actual cost of the project, and does not fit into the calculations.

The day before Christmas 1924 the last four of Lloyd's workers were off the job, according to the papers filed with Aetna Insurance Company, which handled the workman's compensation insurance. In truth, at least Byron Vandegrift continued to be employed on the job for some weeks or months. (Vandegrift later claimed in various interviews that he worked for several months on the project after the rest of the crew had been let go. The paperwork is ambiguous.) The nature of the atmosphere at the job site is exemplified by the foreman's final letter to Lloyd on January 3.

Dear Sir:

. . . I expect to leave here tomorrow or Monday morning. I have made arrangements with the WE Cooper Lumber Co to take care of my act [account]. I have prepared a lien which they will hold for a week or 10 days and if this act. is not paid they will be compelled to file same. I have been compelled to send home for money to get back home. I trust this will be settled up promptly, and that the future will be brighter for all concerned. Yours truly,

Arthur Judevine

416 – 6 Str. Baraboo Wis.

4-31. The west façade with glazing installed. Plants have been set in the bedroom planters and in select locations around the house. Excavation for the foundations of the Schaeffer House, which would become the neighboring house on Glencoe Way, is just visible at the lower left of the photo. A small Christmas tree faintly discernable in the living room window helps date the image to the end of 1924. Note the only exterior location for the four-fold block pattern, in between the two windows just right of the tool wall.

Sam Freeman owed Judevine $574 for November and December. He paid $234. The balance due was $340. Alongside that figure is the encircled note: "Offered to settle for 300.00." It is not clear whether Sam or Lloyd made the offer.

The unhappy Freemans contacted Frank Lloyd Wright, who telegraphed his son on January 8, 1925 : "Bad reports from Freeman. Can't you get plumbing and hardware installed. Are you on the job or not. Why paint blocks inside and how bad is color of wood work. Barnsdall writes to settle and can soon. Settled Freeman bills. Will remit architect fee and your superintendence fee if Freeman can finance building as own home. Seems only fair. Father."

The tension is obvious. Wright implies that he has paid all the outstanding bills on the project; Lloyd Wright's records do not reflect that, but they are not clear enough for us to know how much Wright put into the Freeman House. Sam Freeman's later remark, "I think he [Frank] was probably out of pocket," suggests a contribution of not much more than the architectural fees. We do know that Sam Freeman could not finance the project, as Lloyd wired his father the next day: "Freeman must have five hundred to get him into house. Sub contractors require payments on account to finish. Work at a stand still. Nevertheless, attend job daily. Freemans absolutely unable to meet any obligations. Toned blocks bedrooms and lower hall only. OK when finished. Woodwork same."

Three days later, both suppliers and laborers started filing mechanic's liens against the Freeman House with the County of Los Angeles. Between January 12 and April 4, Sam and Harriet were hit with sixteen liens, ranging from $45.50 to $636.28 and totaling $3,388.56. Byron Vandegrift also reported both Sam Freeman and Lloyd Wright to the Labor Commission for nonpayment of insurance.[25] He recalled later that Sam Freeman paid off a large sum of money to him over the next ten years.

And still work on the house continued. On January 16, the plumbing work inside was completed, and billed at $765. A week later, the plumbing and controls for the "fish pond" by the front door were completed. Among the many bills and dunning letters pouring in, some suppliers noted that both the Freeman House and the Ennis House accounts were now delinquent. This suggests that Lloyd had diverted some of the money paid by Ennis to the Freeman House project.

The painting contract ended badly. Lloyd wrote to William Haase: "After carefully going over the work done, that left undone, and the work that will have to be done over again such as the shellacing [sic] of all wood work, recoloring unfinished stone floors and walls, etc., it is my opinion that the sum of one hundred and forty five dollars is ample allowance and pay for the work done . . ."

Haase also filed a lien. (The most interesting detail in the letter, however, is the reference to coloring the stone floors. This is the only known written documentation that a thin layer of ochre paint found on the floor blocks during an investigation in 1989 was applied during the original construction of the house.)

In many cases, cost overruns were either the consequence of, or the cause of, alterations to the design. Sometime in early 1925, the most visible of these changes was undertaken: the revision of the fascia over the garage mentioned earlier. This was another casualty of the surveying errors. The floor of the garage had to be raised during construction to accommodate the actual level of the street, as was noted in the final hand revisions on the working drawings. This left the fascia so oppressively low in appearance that it was redesigned to introduce

4-32. The house, completed, with the pilaster shown in figs. 4-16 and 4-23, a construction error, removed. In this view, probably from late 1925, plants can be seen growing up the walls, apparently according to the wishes of both Lloyd Wright and Harriet Freeman.

a step that visually lifted it in the middle. At about the same time, as the two-story windows were finally under construction, the 8" x 16" panes depicted on the working drawings for the area next to the concrete screens on the south façade of the house were changed to 16" x 16" panes. While the change to the garage fascia cost money, the window alteration was probably an attempt at cost savings.

Only a few areas in the house remained unfinished in February, but work had slowed to a crawl. The Freemans were facing the loss of their home before they had even moved in if they could not find a way to cover the mounting legal judgments. Even the Bureau of Power and

4-33. The garage and entry, 1930s. Note the pool and the tripartite fascia, with its lower band of gold (see fig. 5-1).

Light was threatening suspension of gas and electric service. Meanwhile, Lloyd was distracted by the fact that the Ennises had taken control of their project and were no longer building their house as his father had designed it.[26]

At the end of the month, five weeks after the plumbing was installed, Sunset Tile provided an estimate for work in the bathroom. It suggested a rather traditional installation of white hexagonal tile for the shower floor plus white glazed wall tile and a 16" curb to the shower. The incorporation of tile was necessary to protect the porous, gritty block from moisture and erosion. Whether any part of the proposal was implemented is unknown, because the bathroom was later altered.

On March 23, 1925, the Freemans filed a Notice of Completion with the Los Angeles County Recorder, which said work on their "4 room house known as and numbered 1962 Glencoe Way" had been finished on March 12.[27] An exhausting and unhappy process was nearing its conclusion. Or at least the first phase was ending. After little more than a year, work on the house would resume, and continue largely nonstop until Sam Freeman died in 1981.

Harriet's recollection was scathing and, at least in hindsight, unfair: "Lloyd Wright was a landscape architect who learned to be an architect at our expense. His father put him in charge here, and that's why it took so long."[28] For some time, Sam had actually joined the crew in an attempt to help get the house completed. Decades later, he would point to some of the construction photographs, which could be found in a bowl on the living room coffee table, and identify himself working. Sam apparently was rather proud of his involvement.

Harriet said: "Our house took 13 months to build, instead of the three months Wright assured us it would take. If it came in over $10,000, he told us he would take care of the difference. It cost over $25,000, paid totally by my wonderful husband Sam, who also paid for the nine liens against it."[29]

"The house did cost more than the estimate," Sam would later say, "but this is a handmade house. An experimental airplane also costs more than one in production. But it is a house whose value has increased and it is worth more today than houses of comparable price built in 1924 whose cost did not exceed the estimates."[30]

Several friends of the Freemans later recounted how "they were in an empty house for a year and a half, living out of cardboard boxes,"[31] demonstrating just how devastating the construction process had been to the young couple's finances and how badly Wright and Lloyd had repaid the Freemans' trust and enthusiasm. However, Sam's version of the story turned the anecdote around: "Now the thing that I think is interesting, when the house was finished enough for us to move in, we did not have a stick of furniture. We sat on boxes, and the house never seemed bare."[32]

He said, "If you go to an architect like Wright for a house, you don't tell him what you want. You let him tell you. As a result we got a house which has never been monotonous. Most houses are exhausted as soon as you move into them. Ours wasn't. For the first months we had very little furniture, for we found that it was not a house that we cared to turn over to a furniture store to 'load.' Most empty rooms are cold cubicles, but our sparsely furnished living room came alive for us with space forms. A Wright house is not one that depends upon furnishings for its beauty."[33]

Still, Sam would also admit, "Knowing Mr. Schindler made living here much easier."[34] But that part of the story is told in Chapter 6.

5-1. The southwest corner of the living room and bedroom, 1925, after the Freemans moved in. The two-story curtain walls run independently of the intermediate floor; they are self-supporting and play no role in the building's structure. The horizontal mullions connect at the corner by means of an L-shaped block, reproducing a detail from the Imperial Hotel in which thin horizontal lines thicken at the end, and those elements in turn form a dotted line at the juncture of building and sky.

5

MATERIAL REALITIES

It took some time for Sam and Harriet Freeman to recover from the tumultuous and costly ordeal that was the construction of their new home. For a year the building sat in essentially the same state as when the workmen departed, while the Freemans lived as best they could in the largely unfurnished structure. Change came—slowly at first, with the painting of some wood trim and other elements, and then more rapidly, with a series of major projects throughout the house starting in 1928. But before chronicling how the Freeman House was transformed, let us examine the house as it was built and consider the integrity, durability, and significance of the textile-block construction system.

Wright was well aware of the chaos, inaccuracy, and material uncertainties besetting the textile-block houses, as he wrote in *Architectural Record* in 1927:

> None of the advantages, which the system was designed to have were had in the construction of these models. We had no organization. Prepared the molds experimentally. Picked up "Moyana" [mañana?] men in the Los Angeles street, and started them making and setting blocks—The work consequently was roughly done and wasteful.
>
> None of the accuracy which is essential to economy in manufacture nor any benefit of organization was achieved in these models. And yet the cost of the building was not more than that of the usual Los Angeles type, of that same plan, with a good "Spanish" exterior.
>
> The blocks were made of various combinations of decayed granite and sand and gravel of the sites. The mixture was not rich. Nor was it possible to cure the blocks in sufficient moisture. The blocks might well have been of better quality.
>
> Some unnecessary trouble was experienced in making the buildings waterproof. All the difficulties were due to poor workmanship and not to the nature of the scheme.
>
> But it is seldom that buildings of a new type are built out-right as experimental models with less trouble than were these, notwithstanding our lack of organization and our concentration on invention."[1]

How fair is this evaluation? For one thing, few members of the block-making crew had Hispanic surnames.[2] The accuracy of the blocks was not bad, although disorganization on site was clearly an issue. Most problems arose from the system. And many of the impromptu techniques developed by Lloyd Wright and his crew to address the gap between the architect's vision and the realities of construction described in this chapter not only made the project possible but also continued to be used in other Wright block projects for another two decades. Wright tinkered with the system for the rest of his life. By the 1940s he was designing block houses that were somewhat easier to build, leaked less, cost less, and still held many of the aesthetic and polemical ideals of the initial experiments. However, the problems that arose during the design and construction of the Freeman House had substantial implications not only at the time but for decades, and thus for conservation efforts. Sixty years of jury-rigged solutions never really solved the problems; they either postponed the inevitable or made things worse.

Assessing a historic site's condition starts with a careful, methodical perusal of the building from top to bottom. The problems or issues encountered can be grouped into several categories. Some have less to do with the building per se than with the demands of contemporary life—problems with the functionality of the site for the owner's purposes, for example, or with deficiencies in performance relative to current life-safety codes or disabled-access regulations. Another set of problems arises from inadequacies in systems that perform essentially as designed, but the design itself proves deficient. A third set of problems is the failure of elements to do what was expected of them in the first place.

When construction materials are chosen for a building, there are expectations about the job they will do. How well the materials perform is an indicator of the appropriateness of their selection. In other words, the *performance* of a material is the result of its *behavior* over *time*. Time is important because we expect buildings to last, and because time introduces different conditions under which the materials have to perform. The behavior of a material, in turn, is a product of a number of factors: its *properties* (both chemical and physical), its *manufacture* (how well made, whether on- or off-site), its place within an *assembly* of other materials aimed at a particular function (how it is detailed), its *installation* (how well the construction crew did their job), and, finally, the environmental *stresses* to which the material is exposed from manufacture to the present, and the consistency and appropriateness of any required *maintenance*. Considering each of these factors during the design process enables the architect to create a durable building. For the preservationist or materials conservator, a study of the materials, assemblies, and systems of a building in terms of those factors can help identify what has gone wrong and what needs to be addressed.

A brief survey of each of these factors, illustrated by their impact on the Freeman House, is followed by a more in-depth discussion of the primary material used in the textile-block houses, concrete.

PROPERTIES. The chemistry of a material and its associated physical properties are the basis for its response to the world. The tendency of steel to rust in the presence of water, air, and acidity is an example of chemistry at work: the metal takes on hydrogen and oxygen ions and converts to various ferric oxides. As corrosion progresses, the sheets of rust rise up from the surface of the steel, greatly expanding the total volume of the material and providing passage for more water to reach fresh metal, potentially perpetuating the process until no more steel is left. In turn, this expansive process applies significant pressure against surrounding materials, in a mechanical process called rust-jacking.

Steel reinforcing bars buried several inches in concrete, a highly alkaline material, are protected from corrosion both by distance from water and air and by the alkalinity of the concrete. If the steel is exposed to the elements because of problems with the concrete such as cracks, porosity, loss of alkalinity (carbonation), or incomplete cover due to poor placement of the steel, then rust-jacking can occur, further cracking the concrete, dislodging chunks (a phenomenon known as spalling), and exposing more steel—which continues the vicious cycle. This phenomenon is one of the most common sources of damage at the Freeman House.

MANUFACTURE. The very process of making the material used in a building can introduce flaws that may be exacerbated by the conditions on the site. Though a press was used for making some blocks, many, if not most, were made using a six-pound sledgehammer. Hitting the block mold and the damp concrete with a sledgehammer introduced a hairline crack along the centerline of the channels ringing the blocks. When moisture entered the joints between the blocks, the perimeter reinforcing steel, and the crack, expanded over time, until part or all of a block face popped off the building This form of spalling, distinctive to the textile-block houses, I call "ring fracture." It was especially insidious because its presence was unknown until a catastrophic failure occurred, most noticeably in response to shaking from an earthquake.

The pounding also caused other cracks elsewhere in the block, smaller but just as problematic from the point of view of water infiltration and structural weakness. An associated problem was that the molds were evidently pounded on a somewhat bouncy table. When they were struck, vibrations caused the concrete to shake inside the mold and lose some crispness of detail. To maintain the pattern, some blocks required several passes in which more material was added to the mold and/or hand-patched after the block left the molds.

ASSEMBLY. Building materials are typically combined into an assembly to perform a particular function. How this is done affects the performance, as well

5-2. Ring fracture at exterior parapet wall. This wall was made up of coffered and noncoffered blocks. Crossties are visible between the wythes. While not a typical condition (the planes enclose a larger volume in the parapet than a 1" air cavity), the image provides a good view of a phenomenon that plagues all the block houses.

5-3. Damage at the juncture of three mitered, patterned full blocks caused by rust-jacking (expansion of the steel reinforcing). Exterior block joints provided ready access to water. An area where the grout failed to form a complete tube is visible at the bottom. These blocks, part of an exterior planter, were also under pressure from deformation of the planter over time, caused by pressure from the dirt inside and settlement.

as the durability, of the assembly. A typical wall at the Freeman House comprises two wythes of concrete blocks interwoven with steel bars encased in grout tubes, all sitting on a small, poured foundation. The blocks were dry-stacked, so to achieve a true vertical or horizontal joint, they would have had to be made perfectly: without a mortar bed, the assembly could not accommodate error. However, because the blocks were handmade in forms repeatedly pounded with sledgehammers, slight imperfections were to be expected. But a variation of $\frac{1}{16}$" in a block meant that the wall made from such blocks would be off by an inch every 16 feet. In order to fix these offsets, in some places the workmen used wooden shims to position the blocks properly. The shims left small gaps in the joints between the blocks, so, as mentioned earlier, many joints had to be sealed with clay before the grout was poured into the channels between the blocks.

Another flaw in the block assembly came from the need to tie the two wythes together to form double-wythe walls; here were two parallel (generally), very wobbly planes one inch apart, each made of 16"-tall, roughly rectilinear tiles stacked directly on top of one another without any mortar. According to the specifications, the wythes were "to be tied together across the air-spaces by $\frac{1}{4}$" steel rods hooked to vertical rods at every intersection of every joint and the rods asphalted or covered with a thickness of Portland cement mortar—equivalent to 2" in thickness."[3] However, once the blocks were assembled there was no ready place for the ties. The blocks encased the grout tube from each side, and the grout tube completely encased the reinforcing, at least theoretically. So, as the walls went up, the corners of the backs of the blocks on both sides of the cavity were broken off wherever it was decided to place a tie, thereby creating space for a workman to wrap a round bar around the vertical reinforcing on each side. Then the channels were filled with grout, the next blocks set on top, and the process repeated. This crude ad hoc solution not only risked damaging the blocks but made the process of pouring the grout and protecting the rebar almost impossible. In fact, the wythes were connected much less frequently than specified (perhaps 10 percent of what was called for). None of the connecting rods encountered during later work had been waterproofed in any manner. The fact that the exterior walls were actually wider than they had been drawn may have in part been a consequence of the need for some additional space in which to effectuate the ties.

INSTALLATION. The construction process at the Freeman House was difficult, as has been described. The grout tubes were a challenge; for the system to work, the grout, introduced at the top of a vertical channel between two blocks, had to flow down the channel and spread left and right at the bottom of the block to encase the rebar laid in the horizontal channels. This happened only imperfectly. Made from a dry-tamped mix and cured in the hot sun for an indefinite period, the blocks were thirsty. Though Wright specified "saturating" them before pouring the grout, the grout, which could not be made too liquid or it would flow out of all the gaps between the blocks, quickly became viscous and essentially stopped flowing after only a modest amount had reached the bottom of the tube and begun to spread. In addition, the channels were sized to hold a single $\frac{1}{4}$"-diameter rebar in a $1\frac{1}{2}$"-diameter tube of grout. However, in many instances two reinforcing bars were placed in a channel to overlap bars near their ends. And at many corners ties were wrapped around the bars to hold the wythes together. Thus, as many as six bars could be jammed into a tube at the corner of a block—two lapped vertical bars, two lapped horizontal bars, and the two sides of the tie wrap. Grout was thus blocked from moving through the tube, leaving the bars exposed.

At the top of the building, some stretches of parapet show no attempt to grout the

5-4. Chimney tower on roof after Northridge earthquake. Theoretically, joining a mitered block to a regular square-edged block should have provided the angle necessary to construct the octagonal chimney. However, doing that for both wythes of the wall turned out to be beyond the capacity of the system because either the interior or exterior wythe was off the module. The blocks cut to fit lacked a continuous channel for grouting, and the system was not capable of forming the required angle, so the reinforcing was simply laid without any cover in between the blocks, which were effectively then largely dry-stacked in place.

system because of another problem: blocks meeting at angles that didn't allow for a grout channel. Two mitered blocks formed a 90-degree angle; connecting a square-edged block to a mitered block yielded a 135-degree angle—one of the angles required for an octagon. However, the interior wythe of the octagonal chimney parapet had to bend in the opposite direction, creating an angle of 225 degrees, which resulted in a large gap at the intersection and therefore no enclosed vertical channel between the blocks. In those areas, neither the vertical nor horizontal channels were grouted, as there was no way to contain a liquid grout within the system.

STRESSES. The stresses affecting a building can be categorized by their origin, duration, and severity. There are long-term, relatively consistent impacts such as wear and tear from the occupants, biological growth, and gravity. Other long-term impacts are cyclical, such as those that are climate related. Short-term impacts include earthquakes, high winds, and fire. Numerous other stresses fall somewhere between these in duration and periodicity. All other factors being equal, environmental stressors can make a building fail; their absence can make a building a success. Had the Freeman House been located in a climate with freeze-thaw cycles, it might have long since collapsed. Conversely, located in an area without earthquakes, it would not have been structurally under-designed and, of course, not suffered seismic damage.

The Freeman House had termites, both dry-wood and subterranean—a function of its construction and its location in a region with both pests. The subterranean termites exploited the cavities between the block wythes to construct mud tubes that accessed wood moldings and trim pieces. The dry-wood termites lived happily in the wood ceilings.

Southern California's consistent bright sun and alternating seasons of rain and drought took a toll on the woodwork, especially the shellac finishes on doors, windows, and soffits. After the shellac failed, these items were painted, in various colors over the years, yet still continued to deteriorate. Ultimately, the most vulnerable fascias were held together with cloth tape.

Los Angeles' acid fog, running a pH of between 1.7 and 4,[4] and a daily phenomenon for much of the spring and summer, is particularly damaging for the textile-block houses. When it rolls in at dusk, the fog hits the warm blocks, vaporizes, and passes through the outer wythe of the walls, aided by the highly porous nature of the blocks. The water vapor recondenses when it reaches the air cavity and the colder inner wythe; it runs down the cavity and soaks

5-5. Deterioration of the block due to acid rain, carbonation, and rust-jacking. Exposure to weather and sunlight resulted in extremely porous, friable blocks, especially on the south façade. Corner blocks are particularly susceptible to water penetration at the joints.

the blocks at ties and at the bottom. By morning, the outer wythe has cooled and become damp. Then the rising sun burns away the fog and cooks the acid in the blocks, leading over time to carbonation and decomposition of the cement matrix. Having lost their alkalinity, the blocks no longer protect the reinforcing steel.

Another example of periodic stress occurred because the terra-cotta chimney flues were grouted to the surrounding blocks. As the flues expanded whenever a fire burned in the hearths, they would push against the chimney blocks, causing both the terra-cotta and the blocks to fracture.

Short-term or singular stresses at the Freeman House have taken many forms, from damage inflicted during alterations to holes made in the roofing by an inadvertent footstep. More dramatically, sometime during the 1940s a car missed the turn on Glencoe Way and plowed into part of the house. The damage was repaired with newly cast replacement blocks, and a low block wall was built in front of the house.

CONCRETE

Concrete is itself a complex combination of materials—or perhaps, more accurately, four classes of materials. Today, its composition and properties are highly regulated because it is a manufactured product subject to both building codes and industry standards; it is also highly variable because it comes in a range of types designed for different uses and conditions, and is typically made fresh for every installation.

Concrete is a mixture of cement, sand, gravel, and water. Cement and water form a paste that holds together the sand and gravel, or fine and coarse aggregates. The coarse aggregates provide most of concrete's compressive strength and much of its color and texture. The cement used by Frank Lloyd Wright at the Freeman House, and most commonly used today, is Portland cement, which became the dominant form of cement in the United States at the beginning of the twentieth century.

Portland cement describes both a product and a process. Powdered lime (calcium carbonate) is mixed with water and ash or other materials in a paste, which is heated in large kilns until it forms a clinker—a burnt, hardened ball. The clinker is ground into a powder, which is either packaged for sale as is; sent on to ready-mix plants, where it is placed into the familiar concrete trucks for delivery to a construction site; or sent to concrete-block plants. The clinker stage and the high heat required to produce it are the primary features that differentiate Portland cements from earlier varieties and make the material so energy intensive. The composition of the original paste, the temperature of the kilns, the speed of cooling, the size of the final powder particles all affect the performance of the concrete. Some variations in these factors are deliberate, resulting in different cements for different applications, such as cold-weather construction or underwater use. Some variations are not significant; others can be accidental and problematic. Much of the development of concrete technology over the past century has focused on regularizing the product and defining, through industry standards and local ordinances, the chemical composition and performance expected from the various forms of the material made today. Thus, somewhat paradoxically, concrete is both the world's most common commercial building material and a refined product dependent on sophisticated research and technology. As the material of choice for Wright's do-it-yourself kit house experiment, it made sense. Concrete was inexpensive, seemed easy to use, and could mimic or replace virtually any traditional material. For early modern architects, this widely available, highly mutable and plastic product of the industrial revolution symbolized progress and the future.

Sand, the fine aggregate in concrete, is itself made up of a number of minerals. Quartz, the most common, is benign. But other elements can harm cement. Some impurities can reduce the alkalinity of the concrete or dissolve, leaving cavities that weaken the material and make it porous and susceptible to water infiltration. Other impurities can react with the cement to form new compounds that expand and crack the concrete. Wright, whose primary interest in the sand was the color and texture it gave to the textile block, seems not to have known about or considered many of these other concerns. At the Ennis House, he used decomposed granite from the site, which gave the blocks a particular reddish tone and tied the block conceptually to the earth. At the Freeman House, where there was little or no decomposed granite on site, 20 cubic yards were purchased for the project, and used both for fill and as an admixture in the blocks.[5] Dirt, bark, and other organic material also show up in the mix, either because they accompanied poorly cleaned decomposed granite or as part of a separate attempt to warm up the color of the block and give it some variation in appearance. While coarse aggregate provides the bulk of the compressive resistance in most concrete, a range of aggregate sizes allows an even distribution of cement and aggregate throughout the mass of the final concrete member. The aggregate in the Freeman House blocks, though, was kept small and homogeneous in order to maintain a crisp, even texture, thus robbing the blocks of strength. Fortunately, in many locations around the house, the block was not required to do much more than support itself and a few others around it, as both poured-in-place concrete members and wood framing did much of the structural work.

Technically, a material composed of cement, water, and fine aggregate is a mortar, not a concrete; however, Wright's textile blocks did not function like a mortar, as a binder or filler. In fact, he used the terms *cement blocks* and *cement tiles* in the specifications for the Freeman house, and called the wythes *shells*. In a sense, because they were made in molds, the textile blocks came out of the tradition of cast stone, a popular concrete building product of the late nineteenth and early twentieth century, although unlike those, Wright's blocks were not meant to resemble natural or carved stone. Many others were developing similar cement-based masonry construction units, under various names such as Nel-Stone (developed by William Nelson, and arguably the model for Wright's system) and Knit-lock or Segmental (the terms used by Walter Burley Griffin).[6] In 1934, at least forty types of cement-based masonry construction were in production in the United States.[7] Many blocks were produced by small-scale entrepreneurs using widely available and inexpensive machines—a popular cottage industry. Over time these materials have been most widely identified as concrete blocks, based primarily on how they were used, so we will continue using that term.

Though well-made concrete has good compressive strength, it has little capacity to resist bending or tensile forces; that is why it is combined in modern construction with steel. The textile-block system has an interwoven network of steel bars intended to take those forces. However, the blocks used at the Freeman House were so large in area and so thin in section that they developed bending forces internally for which there was little structural capacity and no reinforcing such as the metal mesh later embedded in the blocks at Florida Southern College. Using a single wythe of blocks as a retaining wall, which was done in all of the Los Angeles block houses, exposed the thinnest part of the block—the area in the center over the coffer, where the face is only 1½" thick—to the horizontal thrust of the hillside. Numerous failures resulted, especially at the Ennis and Freeman houses.

When cement and water mix, a chemical reaction converts the concrete paste into a solid material. This process, hydration, is complex and takes time to develop. Even after working strength is reached, typically around three to four weeks after a pour, hydration continues for years, even decades.

Hydration produces heat, which can be substantial enough to drive out moisture by evaporation, thus stopping the process. For this reason, while concrete is curing, especially in dry climates, it is either covered to keep the moisture inside or kept moist by spraying water on the surface, or both. The blocks at the Freeman House started off as a dry-tamp, already short on water, and then were stored on the site, exposed to the sun, for varying periods of time. Though the specifications called for keeping the curing blocks moist, and a few photographs of the site show blocks moist at the bottom, most photographs show dry blocks stacked in ways that would make successful wetting difficult. The porosity, softness, and friability of the blocks were caused in part by inadequate hydration.

The mix itself was another reason for the poor quality of the block. Wright specified one part cement to four parts "clean sand or other suitable aggregate . . . thoroughly mixed in a mechanical mixer to the consistency that will stand up when squeezed by the hand."[8] This proportion doesn't work. For the Portland cement used by Wright, the correct mix to create a strong block would have been closer to one part cement to two parts sand.[9] With low amounts of both water and cement, there is not enough paste to make a strong, durable block.

This error has raised questions in the conservation community as to why Wright thought that he could make block with such a lean mix. One answer, proposed by materials conservator Norman Weiss, is that a widely used concrete manual of the time described a good mix as one part cement to two parts sand and two parts gravel, suggesting that only a fifth of the mix needed to be cement. However, the gravel takes up considerable volume in finished concrete, so the active paste is really the cement, water, and sand mixture that sits between the pieces of coarse aggregate. Discarding the gravel in order to arrive at a finer mix does not mean the volume of coarse aggregate can simply be replaced with sand. The cement cannot absorb twice as much sand and hold together. Why not increase the amount of cement? Two reasons. First, it is expensive to do so. Second, Wright did not want a block with a smooth cementitious appearance; he wanted a sandy, varied, primitive look, in which the decomposed granite and other materials recalled the natural color and character of the site. He was also visually recalling the texturally interesting sand-float finishes he specified for the walls and ceilings of his houses from that era, including the nonblock walls and lower-floor ceilings at the Freeman House.

The second part of Wright's specification, that the mix should be dry enough to "stand up when squeezed by the hand," flies in the face of industry publications that, at least as early as 1912, clearly warned against making block with a dry mix:

> It is highly important that an abundant amount of water be used in the concrete for blocks. The cement requires it, and in no other way can dense, damp-proof blocks be made. The quantity of water necessary to a given amount of dry materials varies. If the block is made by tamping, there should be at least sufficient water that liquid cement will flush to the surface when the concrete is rammed into the block mold. Frequently block manufacturers, in their efforts to turn out quantities of blocks with a minimum number of molds, have made the very serious mistake of mixing the concrete too dry, so that the blocks might be stripped of the molds more quickly. No amount of tamping will produce density in a concrete lacking sufficient water.[10]

The statement could not be clearer or more accurate in its description of the failure characteristic of the blocks at the Freeman, Storer, Millard, and Ennis houses. Wright not only wanted speed but likely resisted a wetter mix to avoid the resultant thin coating of "liquid cement," which would have required cleaning the blocks with acid afterward, especially tricky on the pattern blocks. (However, a considerable amount of muriatic acid was used on the site, so cleaning the block of cement scum may still have been part of the process.) Finally, the more water and cement used, the less visible the sand would have been, and the grayer the blocks.

The American building industry at the time had another technique for achieving both strength and a finely detailed surface in a patterned block: using two different concrete mixes during its manufacture. A wetter, coarser mix formed most of the block, while a layer of a finer mix, often with pigments or sands of a specific color, was placed directly against the patterned or plain face plate. Walter Burley Griffin undertook something similar during the construction of his 1924 block houses in Australia. He rolled the newly formed damp blocks in ground sandstone, coating them with the color and texture he wanted. Another technique utilized by some block manufacturers in Elgin, Illinois, where there was a substantial block industry, was to place a waterproofing compound into the mold before filling it with concrete. Meanwhile, to address the potential problems resulting from inadequate hydration, William Nelson steam-cured his blocks after transporting them on a train with eccentric wheels so that the blocks were well vibrated.[11] Such subtleties are missing from Wright's textile-block system in 1924. (Interestingly, many of the blocks at Florida Southern College, on which Wright started work in the 1930s, were made with two different mixes in the same mold because the pigments required to make the blocks the color he sought were so expensive. Only the first inch or so of the block was made from the pigmented mix.)

ADDITIONAL CHALLENGES AND PROBLEMS

Another problem arose from the mixing process. Though a small Blystone commercial mixer was used for several months early on, much of the concrete was prepared by hand in a wheelbarrow. Every few blocks, a new batch of cement, water, and sand was mixed from scratch, undoubtedly with variable results. As the mix sat in the wheelbarrow, it would start to harden, and lumps of concrete would begin to form in the initial "false set" process. These lumps would occasionally be incorporated into a block. Add to this the differing skills and inclinations of the many crew members responsible for making blocks over the course of nine months, and it is easy to understand the high variability in the blocks' characteristics.

The complex shape of the mold was also problematic. As in making the concrete mix, the molding of the blocks was supposed to be machine assisted, in this case by using a press. During the process, the mold was to be set with the intricate face pattern on the bottom to ensure maximum penetration of the concrete into all the details. However, the press seems to have vanished from the job site fairly early, and the hand-powered manufacturing process meant that most blocks were made face up because of the coffer on the back. Post-press block making involved laying a board across the face of the mold and hitting it with a sledgehammer; the relatively large, flat area of the face plate was needed to absorb the blows. Then it was necessary to squeeze the mix under the partial obstruction of the perimeter channel and all the way down into the projecting lower part of the block that ringed the coffer. But, as the pounding pushed the concrete down into the deeper parts of the mold, gaps could be left on the face. The gaps needed to be filled in, the top plate replaced, and the block hit again. And as noted above, using a sledgehammer had its own deleterious effects on the integrity of the final product.

In sum, the Freeman House blocks are weak because they lack sufficient cement and coarse aggregate, often include dirt or other non-beneficial ingredients in the mix, were inadequately cured, and often developed cracks during manufacture. Moreover, the porous blocks, which can absorb as much as 15 percent of their weight in water, are frequently subjected to an acid soup of rain and fog, so most of the exterior blocks are fully carbonated and the cement is disintegrating; as a result, the concrete decomposes and the blocks crumble. A concrete block produced in a commercial plant typically can resist compressive stresses of 5,000 pounds per square inch. One block from the Freeman House crushed at 50 pounds.

Further damage to the blocks is caused by their placement in the textile-block assembly. Each block is surrounded by grout tubes, which are harder and denser than the block, because they were made from a much wetter and richer mix. They are also often at a different temperature from the block faces because of their interior location. As the walls expand in the warm sun or move in response to settlement or minor seismic tremors, the tube system, wherever it has remained intact, exerts a crushing force on the soft block. Perhaps fortunately, the grout tubes are often noncontinuous. However, that means that in those areas the grout does a poor job of protecting the steel reinforcing, which then rusts and jacks first the grout tubes and then the blocks, or dissolves completely, making the system incapable of resisting any lateral forces.

Finally, the house required some seventy-four different sizes and shapes of block. Clearly, this complexity greatly aggravated what was already a difficult process, in terms of both the logistical issues of making and keeping track of so many different blocks and the problem of designing and manufacturing the appropriate molds.

5-6. Blocks at the base of the south face of the slumber terrace. These show the effect of rust-jacking due to the lack of cover in the horizontal joints, exacerbated by the horizontal pressure from the dirt behind the wall. The stiff vertical grout tubes break through the soft blocks where the wall has bowed. The lower blocks are in worse shape because they are most saturated with water from both the ground and the fill behind.

A total of 889 sacks of Riverside cement, 200 sacks of Mt. Diablo cement, 100 cubic yards of clean, or plain, sand, 35 cubic yards of 50/50 ¾" mix (a sand and gravel mix used for poured-concrete elements), and 20 cubic yards of decomposed granite went into the construction of the Freeman House.[12] These materials went into the making of blocks, footings and slabs, beams and columns, and fill to build up the hillside.

It is interesting to note that the poured-concrete elements at the house, unlike the blocks, used the industry standard for gravel. The poured-in-place elements are stronger, more conventional in their manufacture and composition, and more durable than the blocks. Generally, these elements were also better protected from the weather, though in a few places where building leaks allowed water to reach them, they also suffered deterioration.

The poured-in-place beams were made two ways: either poured into wooden forms or poured into cavities between blocks. The two great north–south beams that span the living room ceiling are examples of the latter. Assuming that a good bond between the poured-in-place concrete and the pre-cast blocks was achieved during construction, the result was effectively a pair of beams 16" wide by 32" deep, an appropriate size for the span of 21'4". The working drawings showed appropriate locations for steel reinforcing in the poured elements, and included notes about the sizes of reinforcing bars necessary to handle the loads. However, attempts in the 1980s to ascertain whether the building was actually constructed with the proper amount of steel in the right locations were ultimately unsuccessful. As it turns out, the concern behind the inquiry was warranted.

COLOR

The question of color is an interesting one in the context of a "mono-material" house. Of course, the design always included at least two other finishes: wood (in the ceiling paneling, doors and windows, and floors of the living room and penthouse) and plaster (ceilings and stairwell walls). But the color of the blocks was always central to the appearance and character of spaces and surfaces at the house.

Because the blocks on the interior are protected from the effects of climate, especially sunlight and acid rain (except where exposed to leaks), it seems reasonable to expect that they would give us a good sense of Wright's intentions regarding block texture and color. However, the matter turns out not to be so straightforward. As we saw in Chapter 4, problems with block color became an issue toward the end of the project.

The "toning of the blocks" that Frank and Lloyd discussed in January 1925 and that was carried out only "in the bedrooms and lower hallway," was evidently an attempt to remedy the flat, cold appearance of the blocks downstairs, which had been caused by an excess of surface cement, leaving them slick in texture and a bright, unmodulated shade of gray. Lloyd addressed this with a green stain, so subtly applied that it is only detectable through the faintest of brush marks on some blocks and by a slight difference in color between the faces of the blocks and the depressed joints where the brush did not reach. The stain likely included some muriatic acid as well, to help dissolve the cement scum. The success of the treatment can be seen by contrasting the treated blocks with those inside the closets off the two bedrooms, which retained their original appearance. Interestingly, the weathered exterior face of those same closet blocks matches the remainder of the façade well, which indicates that the mix was not the primary source of the problem.

At least as significant as the toning of the downstairs walls was Lloyd's painting of the block floors, an application of color that showed up in neither the plans nor the specifications. It entailed applying an oil-based ochre paint to the face of the block pavers, followed by an ochre-pigmented grout for the depressed joints. The only written evidence for this work is the 1925 letter from Lloyd Wright to painter William Haase, in which Lloyd mentions "recoloring the unfinished stone floors and walls." Paint analysis of the surface of the blocks confirms the color, and the absence of a dirt layer on the block beneath the ochre paint indicates that it was an original finish. Lloyd was matching the floors to the yellow ochre finish on the plaster ceilings, and to yellow-pigmented magnesite flooring in the bathroom and kitchen. Based on the photographs of the living room from 1925 (fig. 5-8 and see fig. 4-30), the floor paint was relatively transparent; but it clearly darkens the block. The floor treatment was not consistent: the block risers in the main staircase have gray grout and were not painted; the treads have pigmented grout and were painted.[13]

It seems unlikely that Frank Lloyd Wright would have approved the floor treatment, as it so radically altered the visual coherence of the mono-material house and inserted an edge between planes that was meant to disappear as part of the concept of "exploding the box." However, over time, more and more color would be applied to the blocks inside.

OTHER MATERIALS

Plaster, another cementitious material, was the finish used for the ceilings of the penthouse and lower floor and for the west wall of the main stairs. Wright specified three coats of plaster on wood lath with a sand-float finish. The very thin oil-based yellow paint that was applied over the surfaces left the sand grains exposed, making a clear connection aesthetically and materially between the yellowish, sandy plaster and the yellow-green, sandy textile blocks.

The block floors in both the kitchen and bathroom were covered with a thin layer of magnesite, a flooring material invented in Germany in the mid-1800s and popular in Southern California from the 1920s to the 1950s.[14] Composed of magnesium oxychloride cement mixed with sawdust, ground quartz, or silica, along with pigments or dyes, it can be installed over wood, cement, or other subfloors, and is relatively flexible, impervious to grease, oil, and solvents, and easy to keep clean. It is often advertised as antibacterial. Because of its wood content, it is comfortable to walk on, although it looks like poured concrete. Wright frequently specified it.

The magnesite was tinted yellow in both locations, matching the light yellow paint on the plaster ceilings. (Later, the kitchen floor was painted red.) Because the block floor is a continuous plane (except for the joints) from room to room and there are no thresholds to mediate between differing floor levels, the magnesite had to be poured relatively thinly and tapered at the doorways or room entries. As a result, it chipped at those locations over time, and it also sustained a few cracks because of settlement. However, it was still essentially intact and in good condition in both rooms in the 1980s, with a wonderful patinated appearance.

A considerable amount of wood was used at the Freeman House: structurally, for floor and roof framing, sheathing, and roof crickets (angled pieces that help roofing transition between horizontal and vertical surfaces); for doors and windows; for finishes such as the ceilings in the living room and kitchen, and the south wall of the lower hallway; for flooring in the living room and the penthouse; and for cabinetry, furnishings, and fixtures. The two sections of wood flooring are oak; all the rest is Oregon pine—although the original intention was for all the wood except for the flooring to be redwood. The less expensive wood was, however, stained to resemble the missing redwood. It appears that this was done by applying an umber-colored stain followed by several coats of shellac.

Shellac was also applied to the roof soffits outside the living room—to maintain visual continuity with the interior, in the same way that the original design called for the plaster of the living room ceilings to continue onto the soffits—and to both the interior and exterior of doors and windows. The shellac was not, however, a durable choice on the outside of the building.

As noted in Chapter 4, the fascias all around the building and the soffits at the entry were painted a soft gray green—not shellacked—from the beginning. The application of bronze powder to the lowest of the three bands on the fascias established a thin shimmering gold line all around the house at the edge of the roof.

5-7. The main stairs at the entry. This photo shows colored floors, painted block walls at the lower level, and painted plaster wall (at right). The block floors were colored during construction by the insertion of an ochre grout in the joints and then a layer of ochre wash on the face. They were painted dark brown later, when other areas of the house downstairs were also painted to hide efflorescence and staining due to water movement. The sand-float plaster surfaces were covered with a thin coating of light yellow paint.

GLASS

The textile-block system, with all its visual impact and attendant technological and economic trauma, must dominate any discussion of the Freeman House. The relatively late date for the manufacture and installation of the windows during the construction of the house (ten months into the project), and the bitter problems besetting the project at the time, can cause us to overlook the contribution of the system of openings—doors, windows, and screens—to the design and character of the house. But the transparent elements of the house deserve at least as much appreciation as those that are solid and opaque.

At the Freeman House, Wright attempted to free the glass from the visible structure necessary to realize these transparent elements, creating a two-story curtain wall with no support from the intervening floor. Furthermore, he took this wall of glass around the corner, still without visible vertical support, creating one of the most dramatic moments in modern architecture to that date. He achieved this largely by ignoring the material reality of both the glass and the wood involved.

All of the exterior doors and windows, with the exception of the front door, are constructed of glass and narrow strips of wood running horizontally every 16" (or 8" in four windows), and set into thin wood frames. Individual fixed or operable units are meant to disappear within the larger system of the curtain wall. Wright's description of the National Life Insurance Company skyscraper, which he was designing essentially contemporaneously with the Freeman House (although it was never built), could just as well have been written for the house:

> [T]hin pendant wall-screens to be carried by the outer edges of cantilever floor slabs. . . . Exterior walls as such may disappear—instead see suspended, standardized . . . screens only slightly engaged with the edges of the floors. . . . Windows in this fabrication are a matter of units in the screen fabric, opening singly or in groups at the will of the occupant. . . .
>
> The edge of the various floors are beveled to the same section used between the windows where engaged with the wall screen. So these appear in the screen as one of the horizontal divisions occurring naturally on the . . . unit lines. The floors themselves however do appear at intervals in the recessions of the screens: this in order to bring the concrete structure itself into relief, seen in relation to the screen as well as in connection with it, thus weaving the two elements of structure together.[15]

One important difference between the curtain walls of the two projects is that the National Life Insurance Company window mullions run vertically. Wright's description added: "There is no emphasis needed on the horizontal units. They would catch water or dust." He is correct, of course. While Wright removed the vertical mullions from the glass screen in the Freeman House, he did away with the horizontals in the skyscraper. Besides stressing the vertical nature of the tower, the absence of horizontals would have prevented water from running into the mullions, causing leaks and damage to the mullions, both of which happened at the Freeman House. The horizontal line of the glass at the house, however, was necessary aesthetically. From the inside, the lines repeat the horizon and minimally disrupt the broad view. From outside, the horizontal mullions balance the concrete verticals of the living room columns and the stair tower, and echo the strong band of the roof. Wright underscored the importance he placed on the corner window at the Freeman House by including a picture of it in his 1928 essay, "The Meaning of Materials—Glass."[16]

The wood door and window frames, thin to begin with, became even more tenuous structurally when they were shaved down on site to fit into the openings. While these almost invisible frames reinforced the idea of space flowing freely between inside and out, some were ultimately too thin to survive operation. The bedroom doors had no space in the jambs for locksets, and

5-8. The southeast corner of the living room, ca. 1925. The corner window is built without a vertical mullion at the intersection of the south and east planes of glass, with the horizontal mullions echoing the distant flat horizon line. Cantilevered roofs shade the openings; a window opening inwards in front of the screen allows ventilation through the room.

those had to be added during construction by cutting into the glazing. An equally tenuous situation was found at the two-story corner windows. The horizontal mullions were too thin to make a connection at the corner, necessary to keep the glass curtain wall from bowing away from the building. Although the detail is found in none of the drawings, the corner problem was solved by placing a thicker, L-shaped block of oak, approximately 3 inches long in each direction, at the intersection of every pair of horizontal mullions to receive the two pieces of wood as they came together. The result was beautiful, not unlike the detail found on a number of the corner windows at the Imperial Hotel, where the masonry lintels thicken to form a block at the corner.

However, over the years the system failed to hold. The sheets of glass tended to slice into the mullions, especially as they rotted from exposure. The weight of the glass panes in the two-story windows, pressing on top of one another, caused some to crack. By the 1950s, wind and water were blowing into the corners of the living room through the gaps.

These and other problems with the materials and assemblies at the Freeman House would trigger a new round of projects only a year after construction finished. And they continue to provide challenges to this day.

6-1. View of the Freeman House from the southwest, in the eucalyptus trees, a few years after construction finished.

INHABITATION AND CHANGE

In March 1925, the Freemans were in tenuous possession of their new home, pending the outcome of the multiple liens and law suits. Although a certificate of occupancy had been issued by the city, the actual level of completion at that point is not clear. Harriet and Sam slept on metal bedsteads, and cardboard boxes served as bedroom furniture. Five pieces of Wright-designed furniture sat in the living room: the two benches and the pair of bookcases that formed the inglenook by the fireplace, and the dining table set into the kitchen wall—Wright clearly viewed these as part of the architecture. Four Wright-designed standing lamps lit the room. Were the two matching ceiling-mounted light fixtures ever manufactured or installed? Wiring to the area suggests that they were, but there is no other proof. Was the bathroom tiled? What was the source of hot water, if any? Were there kitchen appliances? Was the downstairs hallway ever used as such? We don't know the answers.

The building will never again be so clearly a work by Frank Lloyd Wright (and son Lloyd) as it was in the spring and summer of 1925. For many Wright devotees, this chapter chronicles a prolonged attack on a great work of architecture, a series of alterations and emendations that compromised the architect's original vision. However, it is also true that the house as it was in 1925 provided the Freemans with much of their incentive for change; they might even have argued that what they did over the next six decades only improved their home.

During those years, six different architects would make changes to accommodate the wishes of the couple who had hired Frank Lloyd Wright with such high expectations. As for Lloyd, once he and Sam finished their joint appearances before the Labor Commission, explaining why they were delinquent in paying the crew's salary and the insurance, the Freemans seem to have had no further contact with him.

The Freemans moved into their new home only three years into their marriage. The relationship survived, but apparently it had not been an ordinary relationship to start with. It was a subject of endless speculation and amusement among friends and family. Harriet's nephews Gary and Hap Lovell recalled: "The strange thing was that as far back as we can remember they were two separate families really. Sam and Harriet. They just went their own ways. They coexisted in the same house. They were afraid of change. They loved the house and they wanted to die in the house. I guess they had respect for one another; they got along well."[1]

A major impetus for changes to the house, therefore, was to accommodate the couple's distinctive relationship. Ken Burns's 1998 documentary *Frank Lloyd Wright* alludes to a couple who lived together in a house long after their marriage was over because neither wanted to give up their Wright-designed home. That couple was the Freemans, but despite reports to the contrary (as in *Many Masks* by Brendan Gill),[2] they never divorced. Neither left the house or each other; both died in the living room, just five years apart.

The Freemans had no children, but they shared friends who had the same interests in art and politics. Each also had a circle of close friends and mentored numerous young people. A constant stream of guests visited, some moving in for weeks or months at a time. The Lovells and other members of Harriet's family came frequently and stayed over. The Freemans also had paying tenants, many of whom were or became close friends. They were a source of income during the late 1920s and 1930s, but even after money was no longer an issue, in the late 1930s, the Freemans continued to welcome tenants, as much for the company as the cash. The lodgers introduced another set of requirements not anticipated or considered when the house was designed.

A few photographs from their first year at the house focus on Sam and Harriet (separately) in characteristic poses—Harriet dancing in and near the building, even before it was finished, and Sam sitting in a chair in a corner window, gazing out contemplatively. A bond was forming between the house and its owners. Still, problems arose early on, and in August 1926 the couple asked Rudolph Schindler to fix them. In retrospect, it seems inevitable that Schindler would be drawn into the drama of the Freeman House. His first project was to arrange for all the exterior woodwork to be painted green, likely because the original shellac finish was already failing. At the same time, it appears that a coat of brown paint was applied to the lower hallway walls and to

6-2. Sam in the living room, ca. 1925.

6-3. Harriet dancing in the unfinished house. One way we can date this image to early 1925 is that while the windows are installed, the floor pavers are not yet grouted; doing so was evidently a late decision during construction.

the block floors throughout the house.[3] Outside, a hot-water heater was installed in a shed next to the stair tower and connected to the various rooms requiring hot water by pipes across the face of the building.[4] And Schindler planned to rework one or more of the four standing lamps in the living room. Harriet's dislike of the Wright lamps can be inferred from her lifelong insistence that Lloyd had designed them. (She eventually gave two away.) Schindler sketched a hanging "Reading Lamp" attachment, using the same square tubing and frosted glass as in the original, but the alterations were not realized.

The same year, Schindler prepared a design for "Mr. Sam Freeman," which apparently was a remodel of an existing house on Romaine Street, just around the corner from Schindler's own house. This was likely the project for his parents that Sam had offered to Wright the year before. Schindler would continue to do work there over the years.[5]

During the next twenty-seven years, Schindler undertook forty design projects at the Freeman House, including almost all the furniture, lighting fixtures, picture rails and picture frames, a fireplace, outside trellises and stairways, a new kitchen wall, and two apartments. The work took place in four major campaigns—1928–29, 1932, 1937–39, and 1952—with numerous smaller interventions in between.[6]

Even before the changes began, though, Harriet was ready to make her

6-4. Edward Weston's portrait of Schindler, owned by the Freemans.

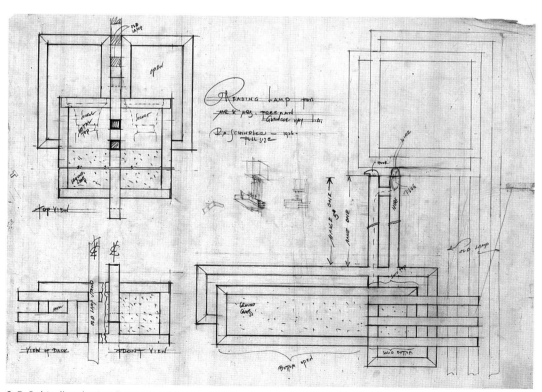

6-5. Schindler design for a reading lamp, 1926, not executed. Probably the first project Schindler designed for the Freeman House, it was for a hanging extension to the standing lamps designed by Wright, in an attempt to make them more useful to Harriet.

house a salon. One early event, a dance performance in 1928, was described by Wyn Ritchie Evans (the daughter of silent-screen actor Billie Ritchie and wife of award-winning songwriter Ray Evans):[7]

> I was introduced to the house and the Freemans by a poet friend from the Oceano Dunes [artists' community]. . . . One day he said a wonderful eastern dancer was performing at this Frank Lloyd Wright house, and would I like to come along. This was first time I met Harriet and Sam. The dancer, John Bovingdon, was actually from Harvard, and just returned from Bali, and had the gamelan gongs and described and showed the system of dance done there. . . . The house overwhelmed me. I felt such an immediate response. Although it had a temple-like feeling about it, whether it was because of the architecture or the creative dance or what, it felt very alive. Then Harriet and I became very friendly. We'd exercise together. I became part of the gang. [The artist Gjura] Stojano hung out there, although he didn't live there.[8] Also another young sculptor, Benny Bufano.[9]

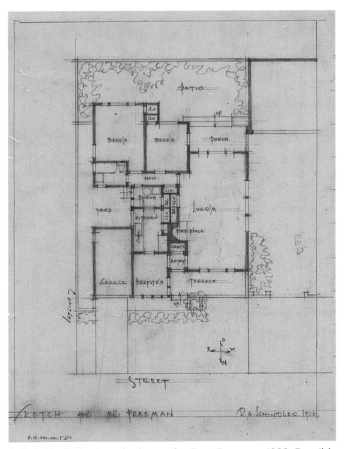

6-6. Schindler's plan of a house for Sam Freeman, 1926. Possibly designed as an alternative to fixing the Freeman House, this house plan was more likely intended for Sam's parents, for a site in West Hollywood.

That same year, the Freemans commissioned Schindler to convert the west bedroom into what would be called "Sam's" apartment. Schindler had just been "fired" from the Health House project by Philip Lovell. The source of funding for the work is not clear: the Freemans were still paying off the initial construction cost, and Sam's income was modest. Perhaps Harriet contributed some of her own family money. And perhaps it was meant to be self-financing through rentals. The work was certainly done economically.

The new "apartment" (sans bathroom) combined Sam's bedroom with part of the lounge—the area in front of the fireplace in the lower hall.[10] Schindler removed the intervening wall, discarding the blocks, and built a new one of wood turned 90 degrees and repositioned so it made the fireplace part of an enlarged L-shaped room. Two closets were placed on the east side of the new wall, flanking the door into the new apartment—essentially re-creating the two closets that had been in that area in the schematic design. To the west of the fireplace, along the north wall, Schindler installed a Pullman-type kitchen with a tiny oven, two-burner range, cold-water sink, and shelves for food storage. He concealed it behind two doors within the left half of a wood cabinet; the right half contained more shelves. Opposite the kitchenette he added another cabinet where the former door to the bedroom had been. A new bookshelf was built against the original east wall, at the corner where the wall had been removed.

Using an architectural device he employed in much of his work, Schindler united all of the new elements with a band of wood that encircled much of the room 5'4" off the floor. This established a datum, a line partway up the walls from which cabinetry, doors, and windows either rose or dropped, and that visually organized the elements of the room. Here he picked the sill line of the frosted-glass windows set atop the wall between the lounge and the bedrooms, the datum already established by Wright.

Wright's drawings depict that wall as a single wythe of block up to a height of 5'4", topped by vertical strips of frosted glass. The face of the block was inside the bedrooms, so the back of the textile-block wall, with all the defects of the manufacturing and installation process visible, was exposed to the lounge. Schindler faced the exposed back side of the blocks with wood planks trimmed with horizontal battens in both the new apartment and in what was left of the hall.

Schindler also attached a wood desk and reading lamp to the window wall at one of the block columns, using a leg made of a dense series of vertical slats to support the desk on the interior side. He added an armchair with a matching slatted back. All the new woodwork—walls, cabinetry, and furniture—was pine, finished on the apartment side with a green/yellow stain. The kitchenette interior was finished with aluminum paint. On the outside of the new wall to the apartment, facing the east bedroom and bathroom, the finish was a redwood stain intended to match the other woodwork in the house.

6-7. Entry to Sam's apartment from the west. The wall containing the door was relocated to transect the lounge from its original position, where it had been an extension of the wall seen at the right in the photo.

6-8. Entry to Sam's apartment from the east. This view from the lower hall shows one of the two closets set on either side of the entry door.

As soon as it was completed, the apartment was available for rental or loan to friends. It had its own street address, 1960 Glencoe Way. It was accessed from the street by a flight of brick steps, probably constructed by Sam, who loved to build things in brick. (He would often volunteer to lay patios for friends, and later had to be persuaded not to pave the slumber terrace in brick.) When the apartment was occupied, Harriet and Sam lived together in "Harriet's" bedroom. The first visitor-in-residence was apparently the Latin bandleader Xavier Cugat, who was just getting established at the Cocoanut Grove in 1928. Cugat's friendship with the Freemans was later commemorated in the name of the Freemans' fox terrier, Rhumba, who lived at the house in the 1930s.

The only surviving drawing of Schindler's for Sam's apartment is a small notebook sketch. Several sheets of formal drawings were executed the next year for a much more elaborate set of furnishings for the living room and Harriet's bedroom. This round of projects may actually have been partially funded by Philip Lovell, without his knowledge. Leah, who maintained her close friendship with the Schindlers, somewhat illicitly had Schindler make the furniture for her rooms at the Health House. The furniture he designed for the Freemans was close in appearance and materials to those pieces, which would have allowed the two furniture projects to share a budget.[11]

The first priority in 1929 was to replace the inglenook in the living room, which Harriet hated for its formality and almost religious asceticism. Schindler designed a large suite of furniture— storage, seating, and horizontal surfaces surfaced with a figured-gum veneer and finished with orange shellac—for the northwest corner of the room. Along the north wall, he placed a set of open shelves and a cabinet with a wonderful painting by Gjura Stojano of a woman playing a koto attached to one of its two doors. The trim that ran along the top of the storage unit extended in a block joint along the west wall, crossing above the casement window. At right angles to this cabinetry Schindler set a large seat constructed from a queen-sized mattress and an angled backboard consisting of long horizontal tubes originally covered in a teal fabric and later reupholstered in gold. This daybed was "home" for a number of guests over the years, some for months at a time. Harriet's friends recalled her inviting guests to "Come flop down with me." Half sitting, half lying down, in a pile of pillows and bodies, visitors could watch her or other guests dance.

Initially, the mattress was designed to slide part way under the backboard to make it more like a sofa seat; sometime later the mattress was fixed in place. A small end table with a sliding top, just four inches above the floor, sat between the north side of the seating and the block pilaster by the fireplace. At the opposite end of the seat was a movable kneeler of the same height, upholstered like the couch. At some point between 1929 and 1938, a large console table with a black linoleum top edged in wood was built behind the couch, enclosing the back. (Eventually, the Wright dining table and the new Schindler dining table that replaced it would be surfaced the same way.) Schindler designed a remarkable little cantilevered lamp, with two lights, to sit on the table.

The two Wright-designed high-backed benches seem to have been discarded immediately, while the two bookcases that backed them were placed side by side on the east side of the fireplace—as seen in the photograph of the interior of the Freeman House published in *In the Nature of Materials*.[12] At some later date, an elegant upholstered couch was placed beside the bookcase (see fig 6-29).

6-9. Kitchenette and pantry, Sam's apartment. Left, these three panels, with battens to match the wall opposite, enclose a kitchen and pantry. Right, the two panels open to reveal a cold-water sink, two-burner stove, oven, shelving, towel bars, and wire baskets next to the floor to keep their contents cool.

6-10. Desk, lamp, and shelf combination, Sam's apartment.

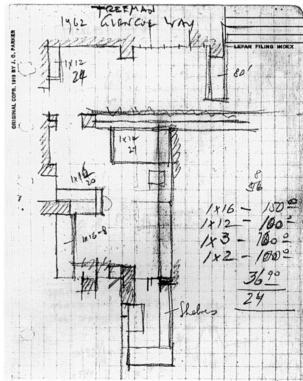

6-11. Preliminary sketch for Sam's apartment, 1928. This early version retains the wall between the lounge and Sam's bedroom, effectively creating a two-room suite. As built, it became a single L-shaped room.

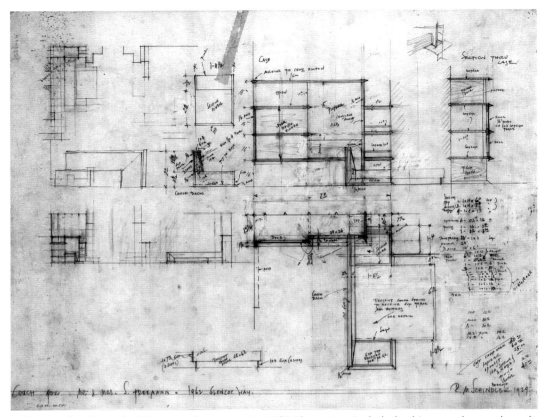

6-12. Schindler design for living room furniture suite, 1929. The project included cabinets and a couch made from a queen-sized mattress.

6-13. Living room furniture suite, ca. 1986. Schindler's design for this ensemble also included a little kneeling bench seen to the left of the couch. The cabinet door is faced with a painting by Gjura Stojano. The armchair was designed by Schindler later, probably around 1938, and includes rotating metal trays under each arm, one for a drink and one containing an ashtray.

Downstairs, in Harriet's, bedroom, Schindler constructed two complex storage units with attached beds. The one in the northwest corner consisted of a rectangular chest with two built-in lights, a bench, and, behind a folding door, a series of slide-out shelves. It was set directly in front of one of the electric wall heaters—an indication that the heaters were not in use by then. A twin bed in a matching wood box projected from underneath the chest, serving either as a seat or, if rolled away from the chest, a bed.

Opposite this, on the east wall, wrapping around a narrow window and block column, Schindler placed another dresser with three mirrored front panels that formed a partial octagon in plan. Inside was an elaborate system of shelves and storage. Two bare lamps on either side of the unit provided illumination for Harriet to apply her makeup, sitting on a Schindler-designed stool. Yet another cantilevered wood lamp hung from the south face of the column. A second twin bed in a wood box fit between the column and the southeast corner of the room. Like the furniture in the living room, the pieces in Harriet's bedroom were veneered with figured gum and shellacked.

In his designs for the two bedrooms and the living room, Schindler employed the 16" module for both overall dimensions and formal geometries, although like the blocks themselves, the furniture also used 8" and 4" divisions. The ornamentation was a variation of the tripartite batten Wright had designed for the living room ceiling; Schindler changed the three equal steps of the original to one long and two short steps. With the battens he created

6-14. Sam on the slumber terrace, 1930s. One of the terriers is Rhumba, the Freeman's dog named in honor of their friend and tenant Xavier Cugat.

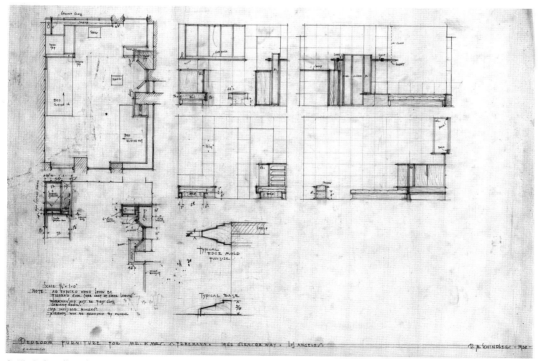

6-15. Schindler design for Harriet's bedroom, 1928. The design includes two suites of furniture—each with cabinetry, lighting, and a bed—along the east and west walls of the room.

16" horizontal bands on larger pieces, such as the cabinet doors in the living room and the bedrooms, the new wood wall in the lounge, and the trim along the edges of light fixtures, picture rails, and furniture.

After Xavier Cugat, a young Romanian artist, Jean Negulesco, a painter and set decorator for the Parisian stage before he came to America, occupied Sam's apartment. Upon his arrival in Los Angeles in 1930, he stayed with the Freemans while looking for work in the movie industry; he subsequently became a director (among his films were *Johnny Belinda* and *How to Marry a Millionaire*) and remained a close, lifelong friend of the Freemans. Two important works of art at the house were by him, gifts to Sam: a line drawing of a group of women danc-

6-16. Harriet's bedroom. East furniture suite, consisting of a dresser with sliding drawers, two lamps, and a sliding bed on wheels.

6-17. Detail of lamp over Harriet's bed.

6-18. Harriet's bedroom, showing the west furniture suite closed.

6-19. The west furniture suite with cabinet doors open.

ing in a circle, which hung in Harriet's bedroom, and a watercolor of a horse's head, which is visible in a number of the images of the living room.

Five years after the completion of the Freeman House and the street on which it sat, the Hollywood Heights neighborhood was largely built out. The community of less than a thousand people included an astonishing number of artists, actors, dancers, musicians, and others associated with the movie industry: close to half of the working population of the neighborhood were employed in either entertainment or design.[13] Dance schools, actors' co-ops, studios, and rehearsal spaces were among the institutions that lined Highland Avenue and Hollywood Boulevard, all a few minutes' walk from the Freeman House. Residents socialized with each other and collaborated on projects, and "Everyone knew everyone else."[14]

In 1932 the Freemans decided they needed a second apartment. This one seems to have been aimed at generating income: the tenants, though interesting, were less likely to be long-time friends. Schindler created the new unit out of the east end of the lower hall, the loggia, and the laundry/storeroom. He transformed he laundry room into the main living space, and created a bedroom of the loggia by pouring a new floor that extended the space four feet to the east and adding a wood roof and glass window wall. A second round of work in 1937–38 added built-in dressers, a mirror, and two closets between the pilasters on the west wall of the former loggia.

The new bathroom was located in the main house, in the part of the lower hall that extended under the balcony by the front door. It was accessible from both the "laundry" apartment and the main house. The wood wall constructed at the base of the stairs to cre-

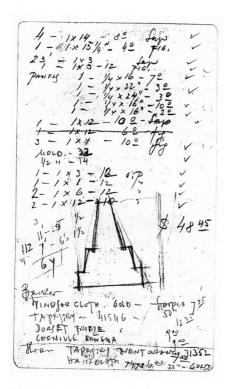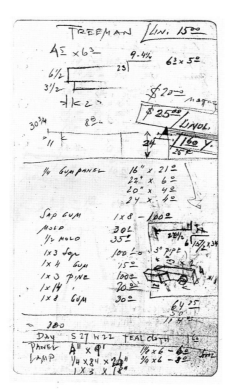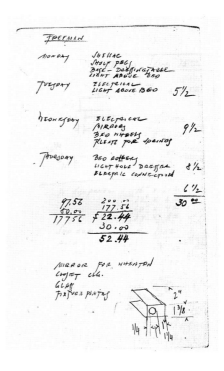

6-20. Miscellaneous Schindler notes for Freeman House projects. Over twenty-six years, Schindler did dozens of projects for the Freemans, large and small, and had myriad pages in his small notebooks filled with sketches and calculations dedicated to these.

6-21. Entry to apartment under garage, 1930s. This was the "street" entrance to the apartment under the garage and entry terrace designed by Schindler. The small block and wood structure contained the refrigerator for an adjacent kitchen, and the steps lead to Glencoe Way.

ate the bathroom bisected the original pair of French doors that had led out to the loggia. The formerly operable west leaf was fixed in place and the glass covered with plywood, while the other leaf served as the door to the new bathroom. A simple slab door was installed in the new wall, which was otherwise articulated into 16" horizontal bands—the same treatment Schindler used on the walls of the first apartment. Above door height, a frosted-glass transom ran the width of the hall, allowing a little light from the window at the end of the hall to illuminate the area at the bottom of the stairs. In addition, two light fixtures were set between the transom's sheets of frosted glass. In the closet to the east of the stairs, Schindler first placed a cast-iron tub, almost the same size as the closet itself; he later replaced it with a shower. Curiously, when the door from the hallway into the bathroom was open, it covered the door from the bathroom into the new apartment; various family friends speculated that this feature was designed to hide the apartment, but from whom was never specified.

The original bathroom shower was refinished at the time the new bathroom was installed; both were covered with the same rectangular tile. Schindler also installed a cleverly designed medicine cabinet for the wall above the sink in the main bathroom. It contained two light bulbs set behind squares of frosted glass etched in the mirrored doors. Small holes were drilled in the sides of the cabinet to vent the heat. Above the cabinet, a single piece of frosted glass

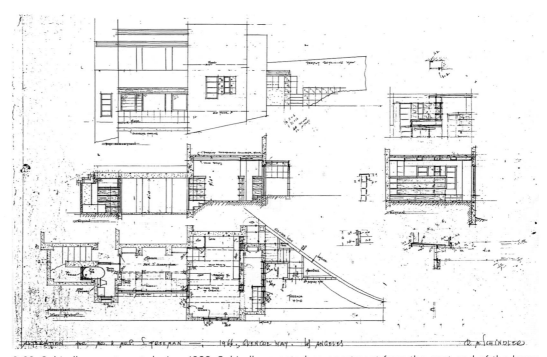

6-22. Schindler apartment design, 1932. Schindler created an apartment from the east end of the lower hallway, the loggia under the entry terrace, and the laundry/storeroom under the garage. Those spaces became the bathroom, bedroom, and living area and kitchen, respectively. The unit had its own street entrance via a new set of steps.

was set at right angles to the wall in a block joint, masking another light bulb that hung from the ceiling.

Tenants of the new apartment during the 1930s included the Swiss physicist and mathematician Fritz Zwicky, an acquaintance of both V. I. Lenin and Albert Einstein, who taught at Cal Tech; dancer Dorothy Wagner, "an exotic creature with long blond hair," who was a member of Lester Horton's earliest dance company;[15] Clark Gable's publicist Ivy Wilson, and the actor Claude Rains, who remained a close friend of Harriet and her dance circle for years.[16]

Sam found Schindler's economy appealing, especially after his experience with Wright. "Schindler's genius was that he could make a house for people with very little money,"[17] he said. Schindler not only watched the costs but frequently included income-producing units in his residential designs. In part, perhaps, because his practice matured during the Depression, but even more likely because of his and his clients' attraction to a dense social environment, these apartments were an integral aspect of his architecture. Three years after completing the laundry apartment, Schindler took on two more projects immediately to the east of the Freeman House. One was an important example of his explorations in inexpensive construction: a "double-residence" with a rental unit, built for only $4,500 for John DeKeyser, the manager of a Hollywood Boulevard music store.[18] The other was an apartment inserted on the ground floor of the little cabin owned by DeKeyser's brother, Peter, a furniture salesman, which had been the first house on the hillside (see fig. 2-2). Bella Lewitzky, prima ballerina of Lester Horton's dance company in the 1930s, and her husband, dancer turned architect Newell Reynolds, lived in the Peter DeKeyser house apartment for fifteen years after

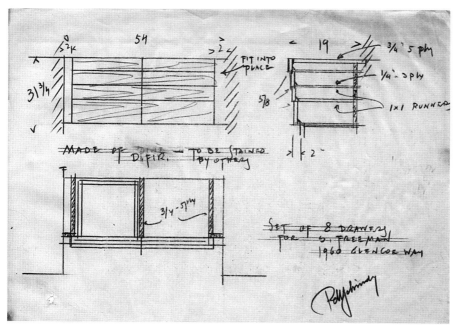

6-23. Schindler dresser design, 1930s. These dressers were set between the pilasters along the west wall of the loggia. Mirrors and shelves were installed above them.

6-24. Exterior of the laundry apartment bedroom showing a portion of the wall and roof structure Schindler designed to transform the loggia into the apartment bedroom.

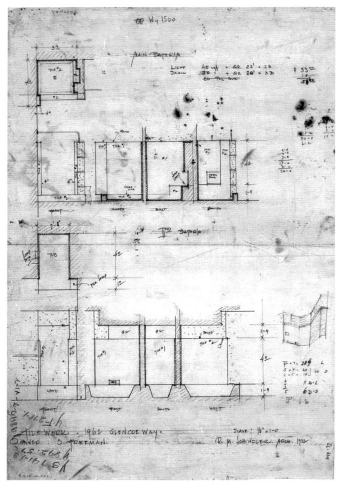

6-25. Schindler drawing of tilework for the shower in the main bathroom and the tub enclosure in the new apartment bathroom, 1932. At the same time the new apartment bathroom was being built, the original bathroom shower enclosure was retiled.

their wedding reception at the Freeman House in 1940. "Schindler cared about the fact that architecture should serve humanity," Reynolds reflected. "Everyone should be able to afford it. These rental units were part of making the homes affordable."[19] Reynolds became a second set of hands, assisting Sam on a multitude of projects around the house during the 1940s and 1950s. Lewitzky, who went on to found a highly regarded dance company in 1946, held the press conference announcing its disbanding at the Freeman House in 1996.

In the mid-1930s, Sam did live at least some of the time in his apartment, because his nephews remember him there when they were in their early teens, and he had been diagnosed with early-onset arteriosclerosis. He took up wrestling as a form of exercise. "He was constantly down on the floor with us," Gary Lovell remembered. Hap added, "He used to take me down to the wrestling matches and boxing matches at the Hollywood Legion. He was actually going to a gym and working out with some guys on the mat. It was a commercial gym. He was a very devoted fight addict."[20]

In 1937, Schindler reworked the laundry apartment. He installed large windows on two sides of the room directly under the garage and added a built-in kitchen and a projecting shed that contained a refrigerator off the north side. The following year he added the fireplace.

A new wall between the kitchen and living room in the main house was a major change because it removed one of the most progressive ideas from the original Wright design: transparency between served and server spaces. Wright's octagonal table housed in that wall no longer had a place: Schindler cut it down and made it into a coffee table. From a purely aesthetic standpoint, the new kitchen wall was successful. Its Mondrian-like composition of operable and fixed panels made a strong, clean, modern backdrop for the northeast corner of the living room. In a rather optimistic gesture, Schindler's wall even included a metal-lined container for a plant. No photograph of that wall shows anything growing out of it, but it did contain dirt into the 1990s.

Also in 1938 Schindler placed two parallel picture rails 32" apart along the north side of the entry hall, again employing the tripartite motif of the original Wright ceiling battens. The Freemans set large prints and paintings between sheets of glass and placed them between the railings; small works rested on the top rail. Two Japanese prints, both showing a small pavilion set on a hillside overlooking a picturesque landscape (evoking the siting of the Freeman House) were among these; they may have been gifts from Frank Lloyd Wright.[21]

In 1938 and 1939, four separate households were living in the house. The Freemans

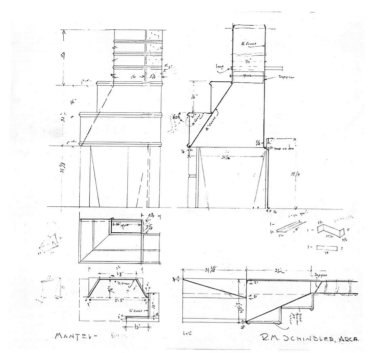

6-26. Schindler drawings for fireplace "mantel," ca. 1938.

6-27. Schindler-designed fireplace in laundry apartment living room. Schindler also installed the new large windows, drapery pockets, and window seats.

6-28. The Freeman House with two adjacent Schindler projects: the John DeKeyser cabin, to which he added an apartment, and the Peter DeKeyser House in the foreground, both from 1935.

shared Harriet's bedroom; Fritz Zwicky occupied the laundry apartment; actor Albert van Dekker[22] and his wife and child lived in Sam's apartment, and Wyn Evans slept in the living room. The Freeman House is comfortable for one or two. It is a bit crowded with seven. And yet, remarkably, each "family" had its own door to the outside, and its own outside space.

In 1940 the van Dekkers hired Schindler to build a house for them in the San Fernando Valley, a strong endorsement of the modifications he had made to the single room at the Freeman House in which they had lived for nearly a year. Nearly fifty years later, Esther Dekker reminisced about the Freeman House:

> The Freeman House as a dwelling presented problems . . . and the roof and walls made of concrete blocks, cast on the place, leaked. . . . However, awkward details had to be forgiven when one entered the truly beautiful living room; half the wall space was open, floor to ceiling, to sun and sky and the roofs of Los Angeles. . . . The house has one living room, one bath, one kitchen and two bedrooms, one of which had been designed partly as a private study for Sam [another take on the Schindler remodeling of 1928]. . . . There was also a pleasant patio outside with a gnarled tea tree.
>
> One might wonder how such a house, designed for a single couple, could accommodate an additional couple with a child. A great part of the answer was the compassionate nature of the Freemans. Sam moved out of his own bedroom and pleasant patio so that we would have our own space.
>
> The Freemans liked people, especially young people. Harriet tried to avoid age, in herself as well as in others. . . . [She] held a weekly dance exercise class in her living room—women should keep their bodies young. She taught the class in her living room, not in a practice hall, because she wanted the students to enjoy the beauty of the room. She was generous in inviting anyone interested to visit the house. She was proud of it. She enjoyed watching others enjoy it. "This is the most beautiful room in the country!"
>
> Once a week there was a cleaning woman and about her work Harriet was punctilious. Particularly about the living room, I never saw her go over the shelves with a white glove but that was the idea. And the floors of thirsty concrete block—they were fed and polished every week responding with a dull, beautiful glow. [The "thirsty" nature of the block floor was likely why it needed to be painted from the beginning, and was continually repainted and waxed.]
>
> During our eight months' joint residence, we four adults became good friends with very little contact inside the house. I managed with the "Pullman" kitchen, never using theirs. Harriet and I might go shopping in the mornings, leaving my husband and

6-29. Original Wright bookcases and store-bought couch, ca. 1950. This image from an unidentified newspaper article shows the two Wright-designed bookcases seen in fig. 4-30 still present in the house even after the original kitchen wall was rebuilt. They were no longer in place in Julius Shulman's photograph (fig. 6-31).

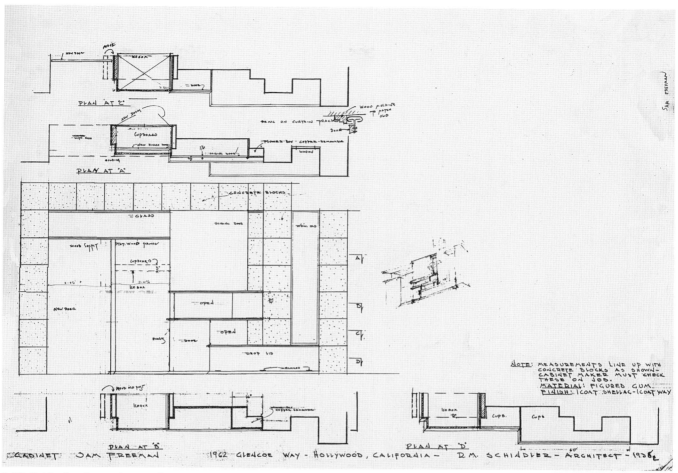

6-30. Schindler design for a wall between living room and kitchen, 1938. This replaced the wall assumed to have been built in 1925 (and depicted in fig. 4-29).

6-31. Schindler's kitchen wall, ca. 1950. All of Schindler's pieces in the living room were finished in a highly figured gum veneer with a warm stain meant to go with the orange shellac used by Wright on the original woodwork in the room. The painting of the horse is by artist and director—and one-time tenant—Jean Negulesco.

6-32. Harriet and Oso sitting in front of the Schindler kitchen wall. The lower part of the wall contained a large storage unit, the lid of which formed a seat.

child in each other's care—or Sam would guard the crib while he watered plants on the terrace. We didn't get entangled indoors. There was an atmosphere built into the very design and materials of the house which allowed, perhaps fostered, an individual aloofness.

From the bedroom along a dark stone corridor to the bathroom or up a dark stairway to the door to the left along a dark hallway to the living room, one felt a personal isolation. [The result of the Schindler additions.] There were windows in the bedrooms but they never seemed flooded with sunshine—but hemmed in by thick stone walls. For us in our room at the far side of the house we were private rather than isolated. No one had to pass our door to get outside or elsewhere in the house. Our life centered on the patio where the infant's crib was and from which a narrow flight of stairs led to the street. I suspect when Sam was occupying his own room his pattern might have been similar to ours. He and Harriet lived somewhat independently.

There was no door at the head of our stairway to the street. Nor, to my recollection, was the front door to the house ever locked. It seemed the solid wall of stone blocks was sufficient to discourage any intruder. The place had a magic, an ancient feeling, like a stone fortress that has withstood and sheltered and abides. How much of this was from Wright's inspiration and use of materials matched to the shape of the house and how much of that feeling came from the solid warmth and tact, their grace in living, that characterized the Freemans—I have never sorted out. Certainly, that building and those people belonged to each other and provided a special haven to a young family at a crucial time. The experience gave ideas for us to shape our lives by.[23]

Rosalind Schaeffer DeMille, a dancer and dance teacher who grew up next door to the Freemans, was also struck by the cultural environment of the Freeman House: "Harriet had all kinds of the most interesting guests. Harriet was a 20th-century Proustian salon lady, who loved to adopt and sponsor people, primarily dancers, but other artists as well, who she was fond of, or who she thought she could learn from. They were also the kind of people who stayed at the house. I have a great deal to thank Harriet for. I cultivated a passionate interest in the arts and modern dance because of her. Meanwhile, my brother was close to Sam. They used to sit and discuss politics."[24]

A series of further alterations in 1939 focused on a long-time problem: the cold. Schindler priced at least half a dozen different heating units and systems, and the Freemans investigated the possibility of central forced air. A gas heater was installed in the living room, in an elegant container of gum wood with brass trim; other units subsequently were placed in the two bedrooms and the laundry apartment. The gas heater in Harriet's bedroom was later replaced by an electric unit, but the others remained unvented gas heaters through the Freemans' tenure at the house.

The electrical wiring, inadequate to the demands of modern life, was an ongoing problem at the house. The nonflammable walls, fortuitous in the case of the frequent short circuits, nevertheless made the house susceptible to another problem: the subterranean termites that built mud tubes in the damp space between the block wythes all the way to the roof. Repairing the damage (the contractor was Clyde Chace, the engineer with whom Schindler had built his double house[25]) was another in the long list of items addressed during this period.

The source of funding for the work in 1937–39 probably came from the increased value of Sam's portfolio, as well as from rental income. Sam could now retire. He spent most of his time working around the house, gardening and laying brick. "Always got to do something around here,"[26] he would say with a mixture of annoyance and pride to visitors. Harriet may have had the lead role in the choice of architects and in initiating major modifications, but Sam shouldered the practical responsibility of keeping the house functioning and livable.

Much of the work at the Freeman House during the next decade focused on the grounds. Lloyd Wright had addressed the landscape during the construction of the house, mostly by ordering plants for planters and ivy to cover the walls. However, any broader vision had not been fully implemented, and what was planted was likely overrun by native vegetation in the intervening years, because few of the original plantings still remain. Richard Neutra's design for the landscape also remained unfulfilled. In 1943, Schindler designed the concrete stair that connected Glencoe Way on the north side of the house to the laundry apartment terrace, continued down the hill to another staircase that led to the DeKeyser houses, and then descended to Highland Avenue. This apparently replaced an earlier path that had served the same little community. Gary and Hap Lovell recalled that as children, "One of the most exciting things about living at the Freeman House was taking the long stairs down the hill to Highland Avenue."[27]

Around 1947, Sam and Newell Reynolds built two small terraces on the west side of the house and paved the slumber terrace, which until then had been grass, although Wright intended it to have block pavers. Sam bricked one of the little terraces and surfaced the slumber terrace and the terrace outside his apartment with square concrete pavers to match the block of the house. Schindler enhanced Sam's terrace projects with two elegant wood lattice structures, one to shade the entry to Sam's apartment from the west terrace, the other to provide a (rather minimal) visual barrier between sunbathers on the slumber terrace and the Schaeffer house next door.

Sam built additional terraces, dirt-floored, around the south and east sides of the house,

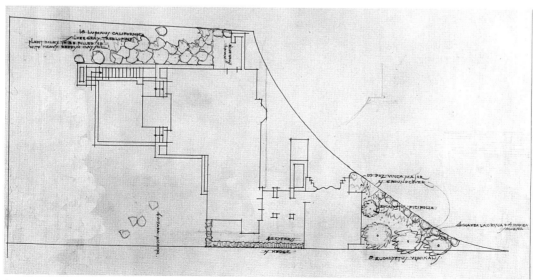

6-33. Landscape plan by Richard Neutra, ca. 1927, not executed. Schindler asked both the Freemans and the Lovells to hire Neutra to design their gardens at a time when he was otherwise unemployed, and before Philip Lovell fired Schindler and hired Neutra to design his new house in Hollywood.

using rubblestone for retaining walls. He and Reynolds connected these terraces with concrete paths and steps. Most of the terraces still exist in some form, although in places they are buried under soil excavated during subsequent repair projects at the house. On these terraces, Sam planted lantana, jade plants, cacti, euphorbia, and other succulents and tropical plants.

Harriet liked having plants indoors; she grew some in containers set on the projecting ceiling in front of the clerestory windows in the middle section of the living room, just above the doors to the balcony. These produced a waterfall of leaves that was much commented upon by visitors, not always favorably.

Lloyd Wright's purchases for the landscaping of the house had included ivy, and by the late 1920s, vines were clearly visible on the building. Trumpet vine also grew thick on the exterior walls, often sending shoots into windows and cracks between the blocks. The appearance of the house was substantially altered by these plants, and opinions may differ on whether they undercut Frank Lloyd Wright's vision for the house or simply expressed the owners' tastes. Only three planters were built as part of the architecture: one outside the kitchen window and two flanking the bedroom doors to the slumber terrace. Otherwise, Wright's renderings depict the house as an angular, concrete counterpoint to the topography and the surrounding eucalyptus.

During the 1940s, the Freemans also addressed the leaks, which were so bad they were staining and damaging floors and walls throughout the building. Sam's pragmatic approach to his job eventually brought him into direct conflict with Frank Lloyd Wright. His friend Murray Niedich, who lived down the street, recalled the incident, providing one version of a story with multiple variations:

6-34. Exterior of the house, ca. 1955. The image can be dated from the new sheet-metal cap on the parapets.

The last encounter between Sam Freeman and Frank Lloyd Wright took place, unfortunately, in the rainy season of about either '48 or '49. Because of the inherent problem in the structure, there would be a water leakage through the parapet section of the roof and that would show up on the walls as residue and on the floor as puddles. Sam very cleverly solved this by taking five-gallon tins, cutting out the short ends and one long end, creating a long, elongated section, a U-channel, which he would then place all along the parapet. These, of course, shed water and kept the place comfortably dry. Wright announced that he was going to be [in Los Angeles] and would like to come by and visit with Sam. Sam invited him up for lunch and completely forgot that he had the tin covering the parapet. Sam, anticipating Wright's arrival, was waiting at the front door and as the cab pulled up Wright got out of his cab, paid the cabbie, and started to walk toward the entrance. His eye was drawn to the tin, which was lining the top of the walls, whereupon he looked in horror, flung the cape over his shoulder, and turned around and left. He walked away, and never spoke to Sam after that, and that was the end of their relationship.[28]

Another version held that Wright saw a metal roof while driving up Highland Avenue toward the house—it was indeed clearly visible even from many blocks away—and never came any closer. Harriet herself is reported to have said: "One day, Wright made a brief surprise inspection. He was angry and started shouting, 'What have you done to my house? What have you done to my house?' We hadn't done anything, except to fix the leaking roof, and he had seen the narrow band of new metal flashing at the roofline. He considered this house a treasure that he had created, and we were the guinea pigs for his ideas."[29] If Harriet is correct, the visit would have had to have happened some five years later than the winter recalled by Murray Niedich, after a sheet-metal cap replaced Sam's oil cans. Whichever version of the story is true, they concur on two points: Wright did not see the interior of the house on that occasion, and he never returned. However, numerous Taliesin apprentices visited the house from the late 1930s on.

Rudolph Schindler's last project at the Freeman House, designed in 1952 and constructed the following year, replaced the assemblage of furniture that had sat to the east of the hearth, the two Wright-designed bookcases and the store-bought couch described earlier. Schindler created another complex piece similar in nature, if not in design, to the couch/bed/table/shelving installed in 1929 on the west side of the hearth. It included a couch with shelving above, behind, and to the north, and a countertop that connected to one constructed earlier at the end of the entry hall. Although the scale, complexity, and materials (gum wood and tufted fabric) of the 1929 and 1953 units were similar, formally they were quite distinct, reflecting Schindler's evolution as a designer. The new couch, cantilevered from the shelving unit, floated in the air. A broad V in plan, it echoed the angles of the octagonal hearth and the coffee table (Wright's octagonal dining table). The two suites of furniture and the rebuilt kitchen wall joined other pieces Schindler designed over the years for the living room, including lamps and ceiling fixtures, a dining table and chairs, a rolling tea cart (that transformed into a serving table), and two armchairs (with rotating drink trays), to create one of his most significant interiors. And yet at the same time, he still allowed the room to achieve the same importance for Frank Lloyd Wright by celebrating the architecture and making it a place people could spend time in with comfort and grace.

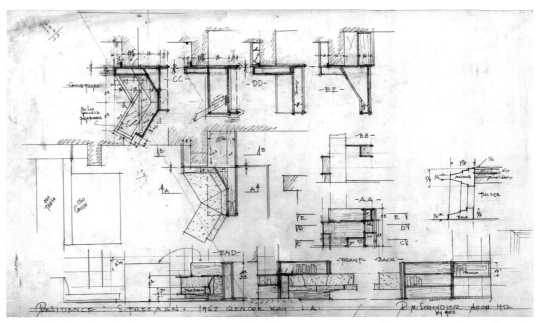

6-35. Schindler plans for furniture group, east side of living room, 1953. In addition to a cantilevered couch, there was shelving behind the couch and wrapping the pilaster.

6-36. Schindler-designed dining chairs, ca. 1950. These elegant cantilevered chairs were upholstered in black leather. Note the water damage on the wood floor.

6-37. Schindler-designed dining table. The original black top was replaced around 1970 with white Formica.

Schindler died in 1953. He had been largely responsible for keeping the house alive, albeit in a state of perpetual change, for over a quarter of a century; he had made Wright's problematic experiment into a home for Harriet and Sam, and for others. But Schindler was more: friend, lover, colleague both political and artistic. Even twenty years later, when the Freemans talked about Schindler, their affection and sense of loss were palpable.

6-38. Living room, looking northwest, 1953. A Schindler-designed upholstered stool can be seen at the end of the table. The cantilevered couch is not yet installed; a slatted arm-chair, also by Schindler, is at the lower right.

6-40. Rolling tea cart, Schindler, 1938. Pushing the top shelf to the right lowered it and raised the bottom shelf up, forming a serving surface on the level of the middle shelf.

6-39. Schindler's cantilevered couch group, 1986, with Wright's original moveable octagonal dining table coverted into a coffee table.

6-41. Harriet in the living room, ca. 1940.

6-42. Living room, looking south down Highland Avenue, 1953. The iconic view from the Freeman House, showing Wright's propulsive design, with beams, battens, mullions, and flooring all shooting toward the view, as well as Schindler's dining table and seating. This photograph captures the Freeman House at its peak.

ASSESSING SCHINDLER'S WORK

Henry-Russell Hitchcock, in *In the Nature of Materials*, wrote that Schindler's furnishings "produce a more homogeneous effect than the antiques" in the Millard House.[30] Interestingly, Schindler followed what today would be considered good preservation practice, by clearly distinguishing his work from Wright's. Except for the area of the lower hallway where he matched the existing doors, Schindler's furniture employs either a lighter wood—gum—or painted finishes.

However, there are undoubtedly conflicts between the Schindler additions and Wright's house. Schindler's approach to the relationship between container and object was different from Wright's. Wright seemed to want the furniture to be separated from the block in the same way that movement was separated from the orthogonal grid. He intended elements such as the carpet of oak in the living room or the inglenook to create their own realms within the larger composition of free-flowing space and continuous block grid. Schindler, in contrast, set furniture into corners, blurring the cubist geometry. Through their own visual intricacies, the pieces establish more complex spaces both vertically and horizontally. Tendrils of wood molding extend outward from furniture, often in two different directions, while cantilevers and floating sources of light further blur the nature of the larger volume. Furniture is often deliberately offset from the grid, providing another sense of movement. Schindler tends to reinforce the horizontal, while Wright meant to reinforce the vertical.

Schindler's beautiful, clever, and useful pieces could sometimes seem to chip away at Wright's architecture, which is most powerful when it is stripped of almost everything except glass and concrete. That is the great conundrum. The original design never provided more than a few uncomfortable pieces of furniture, and even those seem to be reluctant concessions to occupancy. Schindler essentially built a second house within the first, jazz variations on a classical theme. As Wyn Evans put it, "The furniture was done over the years . . . the way it should be, rather than having it all done and moving in and finding out it doesn't work."[31]

Even more damaging than the furniture to Wright's vision was the way Schindler reconfigured the plan. The

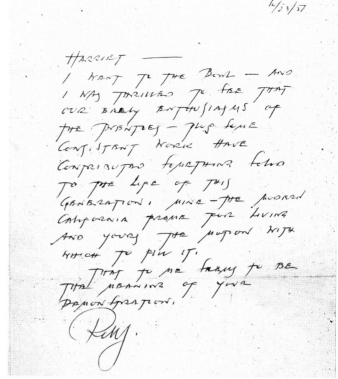

6-43. Letter from Schindler to Harriet, 1951. Sent after Harriet's class performed at the Hollywood Bowl, it reads: "I went to the Bowl—and I was thrilled to set that our early enthusiasms of the Twenties—plus some consistent work have contributed something solid to the life of this generation: mine—the modern California frame for living and yours the motion with which to fill it. That to me seems to be the meaning of your demonstration. RMS."

6-44. Harriet leading a dance class, ca. 1945.

6-45. Original kitchen as designed by Wright, ca. 1954, views showing some of the original casement windows replaced by jalousie windows, apparently by Gregory Ain.

incorporation of the west end of the lower hallway into an apartment and the east end into a bathroom made the area dark and dank. Wright's design principle that every axis of movement in the house should terminate outdoors vanished from the lower floor. And the loggia, once a pleasant breezeway between house and laundry, and the source of both light and air for the lower hall, was replaced by a narrow, low-ceilinged interior space. Yet, according to Robert Clark, who worked on the house later, if any one person could be said to have loved the Freeman House, even more than the clients who kept directing its transformation, it was Schindler.[32] Ultimately, the tension between Schindler and Wright at the Freeman House became a significant part of the experience for inhabitant and visitor alike.

AFTER SCHINDLER

Over the years Sam developed a coterie of young friends willing to help him fix worsening roofs and other failing parts of the house. Following Schindler's death, he turned to another close friend and ex-Schindler employee, architect Gregory Ain. In 1955, Ain apparently ordered the sheet-metal cap on the roof parapets and the chimney that replaced Sam's low-cost but inelegant cans; the cap remained on the roof until 2000. Throughout the house, the windows with the greatest horizontal proportions failed more rapidly than those that were relatively tall and narrow. The thin wooden sash and simple framing, weakened by the damaging effects of sun and rain, did not stand up to the repetitive movement of a heavy window. Ain replaced six casement windows—in the two bathrooms, the laundry apartment, and the kitchen—with one of the most recognizable elements of fifties' modernity: jalousie windows, with their horizontal strips of rotating glass set in aluminum frames.

Although the wall between kitchen and living room had been redesigned by Schindler in 1939, the kitchen itself evidently had not changed substantially since its completion in 1925. It still contained the original cast-iron sink and cabinetry. Ain boxed in the hall coat closet by the front door and opened a hole in the block wall behind it so that it became a receptacle for a wall stove. He added a small table by projecting a piece of plywood from

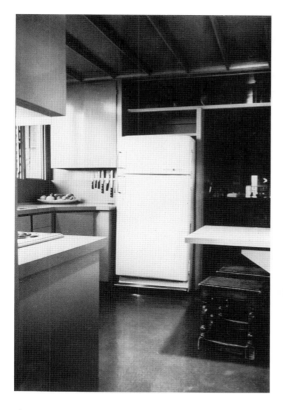

6-46. Kitchen after remodeling by Robert Clark, 1956.

the counter that ran along the north wall, and he may have begun some demolition work on the cabinets themselves. His involvement then ceased for unknown reasons. Sam's regard for Ain was well known by his friends, and he himself praised the young architect.

About three years after Ain's brief involvement, Sam hired Robert Clark to finish remodeling the kitchen. A young architect who had been a Taliesin apprentice in 1951–52, Clark came to the Freemans through Chris Thompson, a Danish cabinetmaker who was already on the job and who executed the work. According to Clark, Sam complained that "nothing in the kitchen was working properly, everything was falling apart, he wanted everything redone. He just felt that everything in here was very inefficient." Clark's goals were "to stay with compatible colors, do a simple job; and keep on budget."[33] Thompson applied taupe-colored sheet vinyl to new cabinets and shelves and placed a built-in sink with drawers and cabinets below it into a continuous counter along the south wall. (The same vinyl was used on the bathroom in the laundry apartment, which apparently was remodeled by Thompson alone about the same time, giving it a new counter, sink, and fluorescent light fixture.)

Of the Freemans Clark said: "I don't know how much understanding they had of Mr. Wright. They tried to stay in tune. I know Sam did. I know [Harriet and Sam] did not see eye to eye, or even get along. . . . Sam was a very sincere person, very honest. And he enjoyed people. He was outgoing. He had good values. He didn't talk people down. He didn't complain about others. We didn't have many deep, philosophical conversations. But he was just an enjoyable person to be with."[34]

For his ongoing struggles with the outdated and inadequate electrical system, Sam turned to Murray Niedich, who recalled:

There was a lot of dangling wire because they ran wires from one place to another just the way people do when there's not a lot of wall plugs. So there were always extensions with clusters of plugs in them. And so like I do whenever I see a situation like that, I'd straighten them out, or recommend that they get another one, or say this one is wearing . . . people don't see that. So that was how I started to do that. It wasn't a hellish mess, there weren't that many appliances in those days. So people didn't have that many things hooked in. But lamps, or a radio. . . . Or [Sam would] call me over to give him some advice about whether I thought this was a good way to fix it. Just little details, so I'd do various jobs around here, fix switches. . . . There was always something going on, not particularly because this was a Frank Lloyd Wright house, but every house has things that don't suit people right. I said he had a sense of humor and it was caustic. . . . And he said some things [about] how this place never will be finished.[35]

Roof leaks continued to plague the house despite the sheet-metal cap. Black fungus and white efflorescence stained the walls, not just in the lower hallway where it had become visible early on, but eventually almost everywhere. Wood ceiling panels and furnishings were water stained and cracked. The living room oak floor buckled; in 1955, new flooring was set on top of the original oak square, with the boards turned 90 degrees.[36] When leaks resumed, a wool carpet was laid over the new floor. (The 1929 furniture was recovered at the same time.) The roof continued to thwart repair attempts. Over the living room, a series of scuppers that brought water from one roof level to the next and then to two corner drains leaked into the parapets through which they passed. The corner drains, no longer securely attached to the surrounding roofing, leaked. Water entered the roof where holes had been cut into roof beams at the southeast corner of the living room to prevent the buildup of water over the kitchen, another unforeseen consequence of lowering the kitchen roof from its original design height.

The Freemans called their home a "17-bucket" house—meaning, in the language of Frank Lloyd Wright houses, that it took seventeen buckets to stanch leaks during a rainstorm. It certainly took ten. During a heavy rain, two pools of water would form on the floor of the living room, each about five feet in from the corners and directly under a principal roof drain. More water blew in through the two-story windows themselves, which were separating at the corners more and more with each passing year.

Another decade passed without any major changes. The couple, now in their seventies, no longer had as broad a circle of friends or activities or as much energy as before. Sam organized lunch debates among his friends at various nearby restaurants, tinkered with his stock portfolio, and did minor repairs around the house. Although Harriet continued to host the occasional dance and exercise class, she spent most of her time traveling: in a fifteen-year period, she visited forty-three countries, several more than once.[37] On those trips she shopped, mostly for her friends, but also for the house: a Russian samovar, stools from Hong Kong, a reproduction pre-Columbian head from Mexico. The house, filled with a jumble of objects from around the world, assumed the character that people in later years associated with it.

Meanwhile, the perennial onslaught of water and winter from multiple leaking roofs, porous parapets, and the two-story corner windows continued. By 1974, the windows gaped so much that one "could put a hand through the opening. . . . The wind was always blow-

6-47. Living room, ca. 1972. The Jawlensky painting Harriet obtained from Galka Scheyer is in a Schindler-designed frame, and one of a pair of Schindler folding chairs is visible to the left of the balcony doors. A Schindler-designed stool sits next to dining table. The oak floor has been carpeted because of water damage. (See jacket for the image in color.)

ing the water right into the living room, especially from the corners."[38] Gary Lovell now approached John Lautner about fixing the windows.

Lautner had come to Los Angeles to supervise the construction of the Sturges House for Frank Lloyd Wright in 1939. He stayed and developed an important practice[39] just four blocks from the Freeman House, on Hollywood Boulevard and Sycamore. He visited the house with his long-time, highly regarded, meticulous contractor, Wally Newiadamsky, who had also worked for Frank Lloyd Wright in the late 1940s as a builder on three of Wright's block houses in central Michigan.[40]

Lautner and Newiadamsky chose an off-the-shelf aluminum window mullion that resembled the original Wright wood design. Cutting each down to make it more closely match the original, Newiadamsky then rebuilt the window frames in aluminum (with small wood muntins). At the same time, he performed minor repairs of several doors and other windows, adding metal brackets to the outside of the french doors and windows in the living room and bedrooms, and splicing new wood into the door to the roof and the doors to the living room balcony. He replaced Schindler's original wood and glass door to the north terrace from the laundry apartment with a solid wood slab. Finally, Newiadamsky chased bats from the roof. All the exterior woodwork was then repainted in ochre, with the exception of the soffits outside the living room windows, which were painted in mauve to recall the original redwood stain. This was the fourth, and final, paint job for the exterior (first was Wright's application of shellac on most of the woodwork, with green and gold on the fascias, followed by two applications of green paint directed by Schindler).

In 1979, both Harriet and Sam were in wheelchairs, and they asked Gary and Hap Lovell to figure out a way to get them from one floor to the other. As their nephews later recalled, "One company was going to put a wheelchair lift on the stairs, but they couldn't figure out how to do the sharp turn at the bottom. So eventually, we engaged another company to put in the elevator."[41] Another local architect, James Reneau, who had done some work on the Lovell Beach House, was hired to design an enclosure for the elevator and make some other small repairs around the house. Reneau remembered the couple as not suffering quietly from the infirmities of old age. Sam was losing mental focus; the formerly active and independent Harriet had become partially paralyzed. "They were," Reneau said, "rather crabby."[42]

6-48. Elevator installed by James Reneau in 1980. The horizontal wood members are part of an earlier Schindler trellis structure.

Reneau's goal was to make the elevator enclosure easily reversible. He succeeded to an extent, although to provide access to the elevator he had to heighten the northernmost window on the west side of the living room into a doorway 6'8" tall by removing the row of blocks at the top and shorten the decorative Schindler molding, which had run along the block joint at 5'4". Downstairs, he removed the two blocks that were set under the window in the west wall, converting the window into another doorway. In each opening he set a wooden door, divided horizontally by trim every 16", with wood panels mimicking the glass in doors and windows elsewhere. Part of the roof of the outside tool shed had to be demolished to accommodate the elevator shaft. The elevator itself was a package unit, with an inexpensive imitation wood-grain interior, a luminous plastic ceiling with fluorescent lighting, and an accordion gate. The motor sat in a large box adjacent to the elevator on the west side of the house. On the exterior, the elevator shaft was surfaced in gray stucco. Finally, Reneau placed a sheet of plywood on the living room floor so the Freemans' wheelchairs could move from the carpeted section to the perimeter block pavers in front of the elevator door.

Harriet's and Sam's final years were difficult ones. The family was dying—the house and its owners. A few friends remained close; Gary and Hap Lovell looked after the couple's affairs. In 1980, Harriet Freeman called Eric Lloyd Wright and asked him to come and see if he could fix the doors leading out to the living room balcony, which had been repaired previously in 1974 by Wally Newiadamsky. Eric had visited the Freeman house in the 1970s, when he and his father were working on a restoration project at the Storer House (Eric remained involved through the early 1990s with both the Storer and Ennis Houses), but he had not been inside on that occasion. Wright (born Lloyd Wright, Jr., in 1929) had studied with his grandfather at Taliesin in 1948 and then worked with him on a number of important projects, including the Walker House in Carmel, California, and the Guggenheim Museum in New York City. In 1956, Eric returned to California to join his father's practice, working with him until Lloyd's death in 1978. Evidently, Harriet's rather exaggerated concerns about the cost of the various projects undertaken by James Reneau and her nephews impelled her to approach Eric in some desperation. When he arrived, he found some of the glass panes from the balcony doors replaced with plywood, other parts rotten, and the doors themselves hanging askew. The living room was cold and drafty; the wind blew directly onto Sam Freeman, who lay ill on the living room couch.

Wright designed new doors to match the originals, but Harriet said she could not afford the $300 estimate for the job.[43] She told Eric what a wonderful man Rudolph Schindler had been, bringing lumber and tools in his car when he came to the house and fixing whatever was needed at no charge. Praising Schindler and criticizing Lloyd Wright, she clearly expected

6-49. Living room shortly after Harriet's death in 1986.

Eric to take on the cost as well as the responsibility for fixing the doors. Eric demurred, but designed a repair for half the price, to which Harriet reluctantly agreed.

Sam died in the living room of the house in November 1981. For the next four years, Harriet and Noel Osheroff, daughter of the Freemans' friends Bill and Stephanie Oliver, lived at the house. (I was the last of the various tenants in the laundry apartment.) In 1985, Harriet suffered a stroke, which prevented her from speaking and left her paralyzed. A bed was set up in the living room, where she spent her final months. At the end of February 1986, almost sixty-one years after she moved in, Harriet Freeman, age ninety-six, died in the home she loved.

7

STEWARDSHIP

In their last years, the Freemans were anxious to find an owner for their house who would value it as much as they did. They discussed their concern at length with family and friends, none of whom wanted the house even as a gift. By the late 1970s, they had narrowed their choice down to the University of Southern California and California Polytechnic State University (Cal Poly), San Luis Obispo. But in a preliminary conversation with USC, the school's representative immediately discussed selling the house for cash and the Freemans turned to a third alternative, the nonprofit Trust for the Preservation of Our Cultural Heritage, established by August Brown when he purchased the Ennis House in 1968. The deal was concluded, but after Sam's death Harriet had second thoughts. She feared that the Freeman House would play second fiddle to the Ennis House, and her relationship with Gus Brown was rocky. Eventually, as I describe in the Preface, Harriet came to an agreement with Dean Robert Harris of USC in 1984 and gave the house to USC, retaining the right to live in it until her death. Harris also persuaded her to leave $200,000 for repairs. The occasion was important enough to warrant numerous local newspaper articles and an approving editorial in the *Los Angeles Times*.[1]

Harriet and Harris negotiated one more provision. To ensure that USC did not see the house as a potential source of ready cash, USC accepted the responsibility to maintain the house and its furnishings in good condition; failing to do so would require the school to sell the house, with proceeds from such a sale to fund a scholarship in Harriet's name. This provision became a consideration a decade later, when USC was trying to devise ways to pay for repairing the house after the Northridge earthquake and its financial investment in the Freeman House became significant.

Still, Harriet was anxious. USC co-owned another large, glamorous home, the Gamble House in Pasadena, designed in 1908 by Charles and Henry Greene. Though USC was having an easier time funding and managing the Gamble House than Gus Brown with the Ennis House, Harriet still found the prospect of comparisons odious. She wrote the following note by hand (the spelling and grammar are hers):

1. No connection or similarity to Gambell H,
2. Not to be thot of in the same breath

3. <u>Compare silver & platinum</u>.
4. Not a complement to Gambell House,
5. Don't even think of the 2 together.
6. Think of our house as a single gift.
7. A practical house for work—students—teachers, etc
8. All the house needs is what is necessary to be made efficient not a rebuilt house.
9. Not large house like Gambell or gigantic Ennis House just a private house of 4 rooms which Mr. Wright said would cost us between 8 & $10,000. If it would cost us more he would be responsible.[2]

That difference between "a practical house for work" and a "large house like Gambell" in part motivated Dean Harris's interest in the Freeman House. Because of Wright's intentions regarding affordability and the modernist experimentation with construction, Harris viewed the Freeman House as a heuristic contemporary model for design students. He also envisioned it as a short-term residence for distinguished visiting faculty at the School of Architecture.

When USC first took over the Freeman House in March 1986, it was still a home. Even the way the house was suffering from neglect and the casually placed and mismatched furnishings were obscuring the architecture proclaimed that it was a home, not an architectural showplace. In the ensuing months and years, the house transitioned; though it remained a residence, it was now a part of a larger cultural institution. Soon it was hosting classes, cultural programs, fundraising events, and community meetings. It opened to the public for tours, at first by appointment, later on a regular schedule. And it was being studied and evaluated in detail. It was undergoing a change of use, a significant event in any historic site. As often happens, not all the changes were conscious, deliberate, or tied to an overarching vision of the building's future. For many of the people involved, it was a learning experience, and we wrote the rules as we went along.

In the preservation field, cultural resource stewardship (sometimes also referred to as cultural resource management) means ownership of a historic site that is undertaken with conscious consideration for the site's ongoing viability and utility. It covers a range of short- and long-term activities, such as maintenance, more substantial capital preservation projects, interpretation and programming, community engagement, legal and physical protections, financial security, and long-term planning. All of these activities are aimed at delivering the site in good condition to future generations. There is no question that Harriet Freeman saw herself as the steward of an architectural treasure, and she was passing that responsibility to USC.

I had been Harriet's tenant, and now I was a caretaker for the school, the appointed "resident administrator." (Over the next few years, that title changed several times, eventually becoming director.) I spent the initial months familiarizing myself with the house and its contents in ways not previously available to me as a tenant, organizing papers, photographs, and other documents, and identifying friends and family who could be sources for research. It was, as is normal in such situations, a confusing period in terms of responding to the building's physical needs. A lot of damage was visible, but its significance was not. Operating with limited funds, we worried about spending money on repairs that would not really address underlying problems and neglecting problems that would only get worse and more expensive to fix in the future.

However, the early discoveries in some ways were the headiest. I found Harriet's scrapbook, which contained dozens of wonderful pictures of her days as a dancer and then a teacher, and Edward Weston's brilliant photographs of Schindler, the Lovells, and Harriet's father, Mose—the first portraits of the photographer's career. Schindler drawings, construction photographs, and the original legal documents concerning the construction of the house were all at the house. Family and friends shared their remarkable recollections, some memories going back more than half a century. And in a box in a locked cabinet in the garage I found a complete block mold, including two face plates (for a plain and a left-hand patterned block), a coffered back piece, a tin liner, and the hinged flask that held all the pieces in place. This would turn out to be the only intact set from the textile-block houses still extant.

PROTECTION AND STABILIZATION

Preservation projects usually start with a "step 0" that tackles immediate problems even before planning for major work begins. These early efforts are aimed at protection and stabilization of the site, buying the time necessary to research and develop an overall scope of work. At the Freeman House, our first interventions were intended to achieve those goals, and also to present the building as being "under new management"; to improve its appearance and signal that its new owners cared about it and were monitoring it. This was important both for gaining neighborhood support and for safety.

To deal with the termites, Rose Pest Control encased the house in a large blue bag and fumigated; they also drilled holes around the perimeter and injected poison into the soil. This seemingly straightforward project revealed how tricky it would be to work on a house that stepped down a steep hillside and around a bend in the street. The building's complex shapes and geometries made analysis, access, and implementation difficult even for a mundane termite eradication.

Fumigation killed some of the ivy and vines that had covered much of the house for most of its life. The plants on the building had been important to Harriet, so they were not removed casually. In 1986, the purple trumpet vine on the stair tower was beautiful when it blossomed, as was the night-blooming cereus with its enormous fragrant white flowers that grew on the slumber terrace. Ivy softened the outlines of the walls (it also disguised the real condition of the blocks). The plants had another important role that was not evident until they were removed: the layer of green provided climate control, shading the south-facing walls and keeping a cooler layer of air next to the building in the summertime, when the concrete would otherwise bake in the California sunshine.

Nevertheless, the plants had to be removed in order for us to assess the condition of the blocks, and to fix them. Plants can be destructive even under the best of conditions: they trap moisture against the building, provide nesting places for vermin, and often send roots into joints and cracks in the building walls. At the Freeman House, the plants had exploited every opportunity to penetrate joints. Virtually every window at the lower level had vines growing both outside and in. (One tenant in the 1930s even complained about it.[3])

We had the hillside surrounding the house cleaned up to afford easy access to all parts of the house for repair and restoration, deprive vagrants of loitering and sleeping places, and remove the significant fire hazard of accumulated dry brush, pine needles, and other debris. Trees and shrubs to be saved were identified and pruned.

In response to the realities of modern city life, small surface-mounted deadbolts were installed on four exterior french doors that lacked locks, and an alarm system was installed. The house was also equipped with a fire extinguisher.

Lavey Roofing Services donated time and materials to try to stop the roof leaks. (Over the next several years, USC's own in-house buildings and maintenance staff also spent considerable time patching the roof.) The Freeman House has eighteen different roof areas and terraces that sit over inhabited spaces. All were in bad shape, despite the years of struggle to remediate the problems detailed earlier. We hoped that another round of patches would give us time to design a new roofing system. As already noted, though Wright had specified flashing and counterflashing at the roofs and parapets, none had been drawn or detailed and none was installed. Since the house was built, roofing had been applied four more times, each time over the previous layer. We needed to figure out what to do.

In addition to taking these immediate measures and beginning to research the history of the house and the Freemans, I worked on gaining a deeper understanding of the building. How did the textile-block system work? What structure transmitted loads through the building to the ground? What was the condition of the materials, the assemblies, the overall building? What caused the damage I saw as I moved around the house, now as a representative of its owner?

Some of the research into the building's condition had actually begun in 1984, shortly after the agreement between Harriet and USC was signed, under the direction of a committee that included Dean Harris, architect Stefanos Polyzoides, Gamble House director Randell Mackinson, and landscape architect Emmet Wemple. Walk-throughs had identified areas of the house that needed major work, including the roof and the double-height windows in the living room. The group had also compiled a short list of cosmetic repairs and some system upgrades and obtained an estimate for the proposed repairs of $200,000, the amount requested of Harriet to supplement her gift. Immediately following the school's takeover, that figure still seemed reasonable, and the description of work accurate. However, after several months of examining the entire house, the true condition of the property began to emerge.

By January 1987, the school had identified three areas for immediate work: shoring the foundations, replacing the doors and windows, and upgrading the electrical and mechanical systems. A geotechnical consultant found the house to be inherently stable but settling, because of the inadequacy of the fill under the floors in the southeastern quadrant of the building. The lower floor rested on bedrock in the northwest corner of the site but was supported on up to eight feet of fill under the stair tower at the bend in the house. The lower parts of the south and east walls of the house were supposed to contain the dirt fill but had begun to bulge, and the fill had compacted and possibly even drifted out from beneath the walls.

The electrician who reviewed the building's electrical and mechanical systems warned that the electrical system was on its last legs. Fire, not just lack of power, was the concern: outlets all over the house produced sparks and flames before expiring. Some Schindler light fixtures were powered by two thin individual strands of fraying, cloth-wrapped wire, and the portable electric heaters used to keep the house warm added to the already overloaded system once we disconnected the unvented gas heaters the Freemans had installed to replace the original wall heaters.

Of the three issues we had identified, the electrical service got the immediate response; the others were subsumed within the widening scope of the project. Now a new concern arose: the condition of individual blocks. Both porous and friable, they were so soft in some areas that material could be scooped out with our bare fingers. The deterioration was obviously linked to their porosity—they absorbed a tremendous amount of water during a rain—although we did not yet understand the full decay mechanism. But we had to find some method of waterproofing (or, more accurately, create a system for minimizing water penetration and its effects).

At the end of 1987, a new estimate based on the work identified to date came to $461,300 for construction costs alone (not including design fees, permits, and so on). Although we did not have a complete grasp of what it would take to restore the Freeman House, it was increasingly clear that it was a major project, of broad enough scope to raise significant questions about how to approach preservation. Repairs to a relatively intact residence had elicited mainly technical questions; now the school had to consider what the building should look like when the project was finished. Was there a "period of significance" to which the house should be restored? Was a restoration going to result in a Wright-designed house, a Schindler-designed house, the house as it appeared upon the client's death, or something else altogether?

And how was the project to be funded? The need to pay for minor repairs, utilities, and consultant studies was depleting the $200,000, while the scope of the work was growing.

THE WHITTIER EARTHQUAKE

On Thursday, October 1, 1987, at 7:42 A.M, the Los Angeles region was rocked by the Whittier earthquake. Centered ten miles east of downtown Los Angeles—twenty miles east of the Freeman House—with a magnitude of 5.9, it caused eight deaths and extensive damage, especially to older buildings in the northeast part of the county. Small aftershocks continued over the next two days, followed by a 5.3-magnitude aftershock on Sunday. Altogether, the four days of quakes caused some $215 million in damage to 10,500 residential and business structures.[4]

These were the first damaging earthquakes to occur in the Los Angeles area since the great San Fernando earthquake of 1971, a destructive event that had been widely studied in architecture schools because of its catastrophic impact on the Olive View Hospital, a brand-new, supposedly resistant structure. The Freeman House had survived that earthquake (and the even more severe Long Beach earthquake of 1933) apparently unscathed, although unnoticed damage could have been a contributing factor to leaks and other perennial problems.

The earthquakes underscored the vulnerability of unreinforced masonry construction. Most earthquake deaths in California have come from the collapse of all or part of masonry buildings, especially their street façades. The Whittier earthquake brought home the urgency of figuring out whether Frank Lloyd Wright's textile-block construction system behaved more like a reinforced or an unreinforced masonry system, and whether Wright's seismic engineering could be trusted.

Wright's ability to understand and design for seismic forces is still a matter of debate, even after the survival of his Imperial Hotel in the Tokyo earthquake of 1923. Eric Wright maintained that the inherent flexibility of the textile-block system would help protect the houses from the usual fate of traditional unreinforced masonry structures: the collapse of the façades after they separate from the building's structural system or the collapse of the entire building if the masonry walls are the supporting structure (as in an adobe house). He had complained about a previous owner of the Storer House who filled the major columns, making them solid and thus stiffer and more likely to concentrate seismic forces and possibly snap—though of all the block houses, the Storer House suffered least from seismic damage over the years, perhaps because it is built on bedrock, has no significant retaining walls, and has the most protective roofs. The textile blocks, Eric Wright said, should be free to rotate slightly around the grout tubes, with the steel reinforcing providing a flexible mesh to hold the system in place. This behavior is theoretically possible if, first, the blocks are so wet when the grout is poured that only a weak connection is made between the grout and the block. Second, if the grout is weaker than the block so that it can absorb seismic forces by crushing or bending without the edges of the perimeter channels snapping off—much as the crumple zone of an automobile absorbs the impact of a crash. Finally, if the various planes of block are anchored adequately to the major structural components of the house, and those, in turn, are strong and resilient enough to transfer any shaking to the ground without collapsing.

The ability of the block houses to perform well in a major earthquake was still unproven in 1987, and the system had not been analyzed or modeled in a way that could demonstrate its reliability to the degree of certainty necessary to reassure a public institution that anyone in the house during an earthquake would be safe. Did the system really have the flexibility Frank Lloyd Wright intended, as well as the strength required to stand up to both horizontal and vertical shaking? We needed confirmation not just for a theoretical house, built as designed and well maintained, but for an actual house that at sixty-two years of age had rusting rebar, crumbling block, termite- and water-damaged wood framing, inadequate fill, and possibly other problems not yet identified.

Analysis of a textile-block wall, for example, would need to consider both the strength of the block based on its composition, size, and shape, and the capacity of the grout tube and reinforcing steel to transfer forces through the system. Did the condition of cracked or crumbling block, rusted or missing rebar, and cracked or missing grout mean a percentage reduction in overall capacity or introduce discontinuities that radically changed their performance altogether?

In the weeks that followed the Whittier quake, careful inspection of the house revealed damage in a number of areas, most noticeably sagging of the lower floor pavers at the base of the main stairs and cracks between the cross walls and the exterior wall at the bathroom. These signs validated concern that fill under the southeast corner of the house was inadequate to the task of supporting the house. Now structure became the principal focus of our attention. Could we develop a useful model of the structural system and all of its various elements (piers, columns, single-wythe walls, double-wythe walls, concrete beams, wood beams, nailed connections, no connections)? Such a model would allow us to evaluate how the house was likely to perform in another earthquake. Moreover, we could assign values to the existing members and connections that reflected their resistance to seismic forces and then calculate what was needed to bring the building's performance up to current code requirements. Finally, we could evaluate different ways of achieving the desired capacity in terms of their impact on the historic character of the building, their cost, their ease of implementation, and the level of maintenance required.

7-1. Settlement at entry, ca. 1990. This was exacerbated by water movement and the Whittier earthquake. The area to the right of the large vertical crack is supported by the loggia.

7-2. Differential settlement in the bathroom, ca. 1990. The wall on the left rested on fill that compressed over time, while the wall with perforated blocks had a more substantial footing.

However, assembling all the data such a model required was impossible with any reasonable accuracy and, in fact, unnecessary for action because it made the structural analysis too complex to conduct, evaluate, or act upon. We had been seduced by Frank Lloyd Wright's vision of a mono-material building into thinking of the house as a continuous fabric. Though the pieces (sometimes) connect, the building was far from Wright's ideal construction. The most effective strategy, we came to realize, was not to fit the components into a single conceptual model, but rather to separate the house into discrete systems and projects: the block walls, the major structural columns and beams, the floor and roof planes, and the foundations. First we needed to ensure that they were all up to their tasks and then physically tie them together. Along the way we gained many smaller but valuable insights. Engineer Melvyn Green deduced that the grid of grout tubes and reinforcing steel was as important as the blocks, if not more so, in evaluating the capacity and performance of the textile-block system. We also realized that even if the footings were upgraded to the specifications that had been drawn (but not built), they would be undersized for the house and its hillside location. What, then, constituted a reasonable scope of repairs? And, given the complex nature of the building—its configuration, its position set partway into the hillside, and the interconnected nature of the construction, how much historic fabric were we willing to demolish in order to save the house? How much could the house be changed before it was no longer the building we started with?

The expanding scope and complexity of the project meant that USC had to consider additional measures for stabilization and repairs to prevent further harm. We met with craftsmen and engineers to carry out a program of further roof patching, a system of new (temporary) roof drains, repairs to several of the french doors, a cap for the planter outside the kitchen window to keep it from filling with water, the design and construction of new iron security gates and fencing, and other cosmetic and safety measures.

At this point, the house was neither undergoing preservation (beyond the early protection and stabilization measures) nor being used for the purpose for which the school had accepted it: housing distinguished visitors and guest faculty. (In fact, it was not a comfortable place to live.) What, then, was its purpose? This became a critical question if we were to justify continued ownership, especially as the financial responsibilities were growing. The answer was to make it a more active part of the school and direct energies to education, restoration research, and fundraising to support the ongoing operations, the interim projects, and whatever the final preservation project turned out to be. While still owned and controlled by USC, the Freeman House became a quasi-autonomous organization with me as its full-time director, a part-time caretaker, volunteer docents, student researchers and interns, and a Friends group with its own board of directors.

EDUCATION AND RESTORATION RESEARCH

Once the Freeman House was owned by an educational institution, requests for information about the building and its potential restoration poured in from students, scholars, and Wright aficionados, and there was a growing demand for public access. The first of a series of six newsletters summarizing the work being done at the house and the challenging issues the school faced was published in September 1987.

Weekly public tours brought over a thousand people a year to the house; special events could bring three hundred in a weekend. Adult education programs, such as "master classes" taught by photographer Julius Shulman and lectures by Wright scholars such as Aaron Green and Kathryn Smith, were presented. The Freeman House organized architectural tours of Palm Springs, Chicago, and Phoenix and assembled or contributed to exhibitions on the house, Frank Lloyd Wright, and Rudolph Schindler at the Municipal Art Gallery, the Schindler-Chace House, Gensler and Associates, the University of California at Santa Barbara, the Feldman Gallery at the Pacific Design Center, the San Diego Museum of Art, and USC.

Above all, the Freeman House became a case study in design for students at the School of Architecture and at other institutions in Southern California. It offered a research course to USC students, primarily undergraduates enrolled in the Bachelor of Architecture five-year professional program, who were invited to work in four areas:

- Research on the cultural, social, and political worlds of the avant-garde in Los Angeles in the 1920s–1950s through oral history interviews and visits to the Archives of American Art and other special collections
- The history of the built structure through study of the original drawings, correspondence, and job records of Wright and Schindler, and through physical investigations

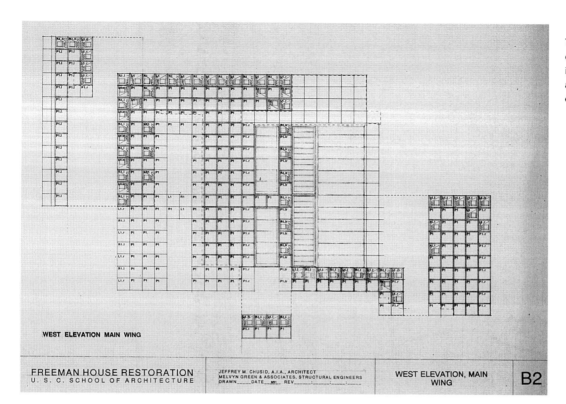

WEST ELEVATION MAIN WING

FREEMAN HOUSE RESTORATION
U. S. C. SCHOOL OF ARCHITECTURE

JEFFREY M. CHUSID, A.I.A., ARCHITECT
MELVYN GREEN & ASSOCIATES, STRUCTURAL ENGINEERS
DRAWN_____ DATE____ REV____

WEST ELEVATION, MAIN
WING

B2

7-3. Block survey, west elevation, 1991. Each visible block was identified as to which of the seventy-four variants it was.

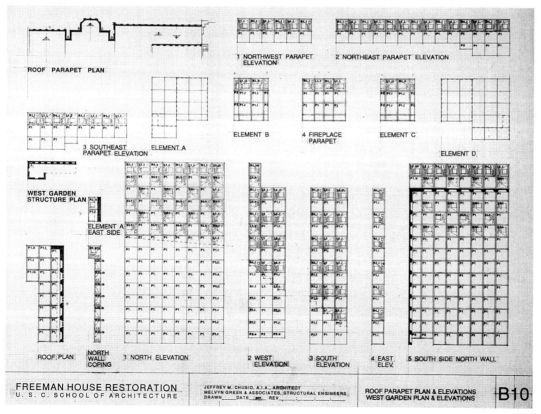

ROOF PARAPET PLAN

1 NORTHWEST PARAPET ELEVATION

2 NORTHEAST PARAPET ELEVATION

3 SOUTHEAST PARAPET ELEVATION

ELEMENT A

ELEMENT B

4 FIREPLACE PARAPET

ELEMENT C

ELEMENT D

WEST GARDEN STRUCTURE PLAN

ELEMENT A EAST SIDE

ROOF PLAN

NORTH WALL COPING

1 NORTH ELEVATION

2 WEST ELEVATION

3 SOUTH ELEVATION

4 EAST ELEV.

5 SOUTH SIDE NORTH WALL

FREEMAN HOUSE RESTORATION
U. S. C. SCHOOL OF ARCHITECTURE

JEFFREY M. CHUSID, A.I.A., ARCHITECT
MELVYN GREEN & ASSOCIATES, STRUCTURAL ENGINEERS
DRAWN_____ DATE____ REV____

ROOF PARAPET PLAN & ELEVATIONS
WEST GARDEN PLAN & ELEVATIONS

B10

7-4. Block survey, north elevation and chimney, 1991.

- Preparation of measured drawings to discover what was actually built, to locate what was added or altered, and to provide a base for the reconstruction work
- Participation in actual reconstruction efforts as they arose

Between 1987 and 1997, over thirty students took on projects, and they started producing useful information immediately. Along with the consultants, especially preservation architect Martin Eli Weil, we studied paints and finishes, counted block types, analyzed the design geometries of Wright's block houses, and built paper and wood models of the house. We also made several sets of drawings:

1. Plans, sections, and elevations of the house in AutoCADD, showing the house as built in 1925 and as found in 1986 (see page 2).
2. Thirty sheets of measured drawings (the base for figs. 7-18, 7-19, and 7-5).

The measured drawings in turn were used as the basis for two additional sets of drawings:

3. The type, orientation, and location of each block in the house (see figs. 7-3 and 7-4).
4. A record of building damage (see fig. 7-5).

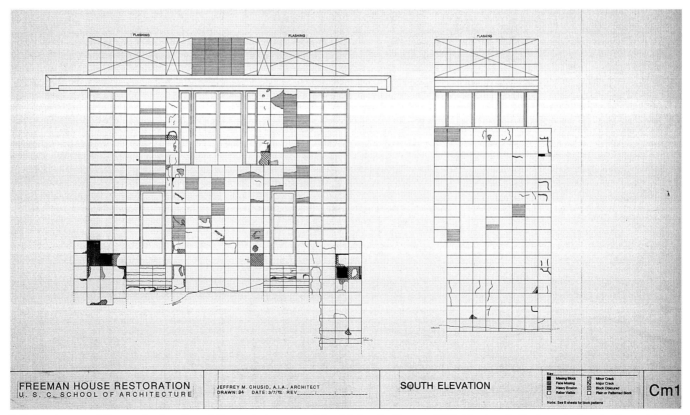

| FREEMAN HOUSE RESTORATION | JEFFREY M. CHUSID, A.I.A., ARCHITECT | SOUTH ELEVATION | Cm1 |
| U. S. C. SCHOOL OF ARCHITECTURE | DRAWN: B+ DATE: 3/7/92 REV | | |

7-5. Crack map of the south elevation of the main house and the kitchen/bathroom, 1992. The key indicates missing, broken, deteriorated, and hidden blocks.

Buildings being measured become remarkably variable. Walls that were sixteen blocks long by six blocks tall on Tuesday somehow become fifteen blocks long on Wednesday. A wall that is a row of sixteen 16" blocks should theoretically be 21'4" long. However, we typically found it an inch or more longer or shorter, a discrepancy that we later discovered was, in part, a function of the uneven thickness of the walls. The measurements posed an interesting problem not uncommon in modern architecture. The buildings are usually designed on a module, with the intention that they will be built on one as well; however, the realities of construction and settlement or modifications over time often alter the module when measured years later. In some buildings, planes turn out to be not truly vertical or horizontal. When we began to draw the Freeman House, we needed to decide whether the most important information was

7-6. Measured drawing details of roof conditions, 1993.

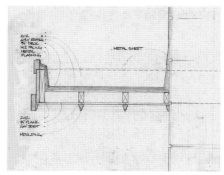

Section through east cantilever, looking south.

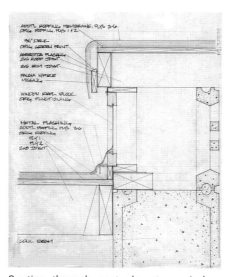

Section through east clerestory window, looking south.

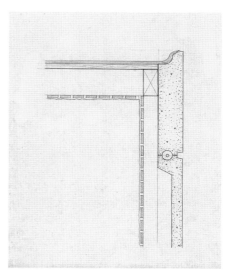

Typical section through penthouse roof.

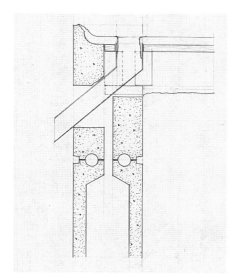

Section through garage roof at roof drain.

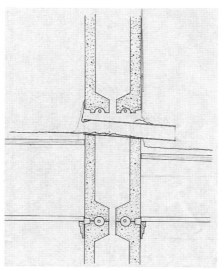

Section through scupper at roof landing outside penthouse.

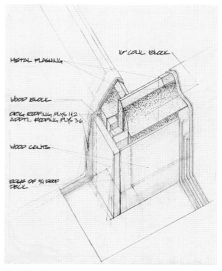

Detail of corner parapet above east clerestory roof.

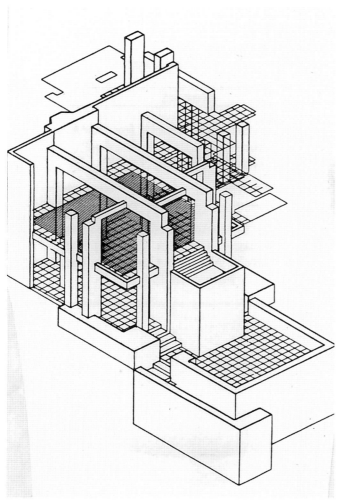

7-7. Sketch model of the structure of the house showing major columns, beams, and bearing walls.

the number of blocks and the home's intended geometries or the distortions to the grid and the actual dimensions. We remembered that the initial construction was plagued by this discrepancy (especially when it came to fitting windows and doors into openings), and we did not want to create unclear or deceptive drawings.

In the end, we used different strategies for the different kinds of drawings needed. The four sets of drawings listed above were drafted according to the intended design grid (all block joints were 8" or 16" apart) and focused on locating all the features and elements of the house. We assumed that any future design team or contractors using these drawings would not scale off them but rather measure the existing building when undertaking work. But additional drawings were made to record other information:

5. Details that examined particular areas or phenomena in depth, focusing on local conditions and uncovering information missing from the original drawings. These were dimensioned, and drawn as measured.
6. Analytical drawings, often more abstract than literal and sometimes without any scale, covering information such as the reinforced-concrete structural system, the geometries of the architecture, or the form, pattern, and size of the different types of blocks used in the house.
7. Historical recreations of the living room and the front of the house as originally built, giving us views not seen in the early photographs of important features now missing.

THE HISTORIC STRUCTURE REPORT

A Historic Structure Report (HSR) is the core document for any substantive preservation project. The HSR establishes the significance of a historic property through a retelling of its history and an evaluation of its architectural and historical meaning to a community. It describes the property, paying special attention to character-defining features; details the construction and any physical changes over time; and assesses its condition and integrity. It usually discusses potential future uses for the site, recommends a treatment (some form of preservation, rehabilitation, restoration, or reconstruction), and provides guidelines for the design of the interventions.

The National Park Service, in its Standards for the Treatment of Historic Properties,[5] outlines four potential treatments for historic sites. They are *preservation*, which essentially maintains the property as found while addressing code requirements and other conditions that might endanger its future; *rehabilitation*, which keeps the character and important features intact while introducing sympathetic changes that accommodate contemporary functional requirements or new uses; *restoration*, which takes the site back to its appearance during its period of significance; and *reconstruction*, which, as the name implies, reconstructs a significant property that was somehow lost. The profession is generally biased toward the less invasive treatments, such as preservation, and also toward treatments that best reflect historical reality. Which treatment was appropriate at the Freeman House was much debated from 1987 on, and continues to be argued today.

Professional consultants who contributed to the HSR were Marc Goldschmidt of Emmet Wemple and Associates, who studied the landscape; Martin Weil, assisted by Linda Lefever, who developed a chronology of the various colors and finishes at the house as well as recommendations for cleaning and treatment; and Melvyn Green, who wrestled with the structure. The effort was funded in part by a Getty Grants Program Project Preparation Grant. It was completed in 1989.

Initially, student research was incorporated into the broader investigation required for the HSR. Much of the historical background for the report came from recorded interviews and less formal but extensive conversations with surviving friends and family members, architects, and builders who had worked on the house, scholars of Wright and California architecture, architects who had worked on other Wright sites, owners or curators of other Wright sites, and conservation and preservation experts. Interviews were either video- or audiotaped and then transcribed. (As with all other aspects of research, information that seems unforgettable at the time soon is forgotten unless recorded, dated, and attributed.) Oral histories and interviews have to be treated with the same degree of skepticism as any other source. For example, some parts of the story that original crew member Byron Vandegrift told about the construction of the house were not borne out by the job records in the Lloyd Wright materials kept in Eric Wright's possession. However, Vandegrift's memories were extremely helpful, and the discrepancies highlighted the need for further research rather than invalidating either source. Job records can be altered or mistaken almost as easily as memories fade or are rewritten.

Other sources of information for the HSR were the original drawings, viewed at the Frank Lloyd Wright archives at Taliesin West and then studied in photographic reproductions; working drawings sets and job records from the Lloyd Wright Archives (also kept by Eric Wright); contract documents, photographs, and other material kept by the Freemans; drawings, letters and photographs in the Schindler Archive at the University of California at Santa Barbara; the Security Pacific Bank Photographic Archives (housed at USC) and the *Los Angeles Times* Photographic Archives (at the Los Angeles Public Library); visits to other Frank Lloyd Wright–designed buildings, especially those undergoing preservation themselves; and visits to other sites designed by those who worked on the house in later years, especially Schindler, Ain, Lloyd Wright, and Lautner.

Developing a clear understanding of Wright's design involved reading his sometimes helpful, often impenetrable texts, as well as the work of others about Wright, and visiting other Wright sites. Above all, it involved spending time at the house, learning to see. Drawing and photographing were a part of that seeing, but living in the house was key. Sam once commented

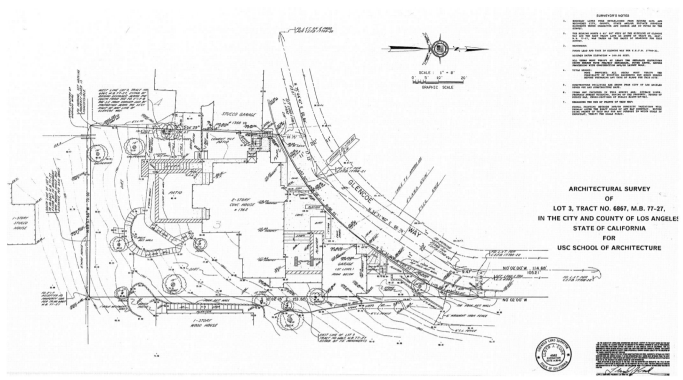

7-8. Architectural Survey of the Freeman House Property, 1989, Lloyd J. Cook, Surveyor. Drawing depicts paths, terraces, major trees, surrounding buildings, Glencoe Way, and the house.

that he had been coming into the living room of his house every morning for fifty years, and every day he saw something new.[6] I had the same experience: discoveries never ceased, and each helped in assessing the significance of the building, in formulating treatment decisions, and most critically, in informing the debates about original intent versus original materials, the relative importance of Wright versus Schindler, and 1925 versus 1925–53 or 1986.

The HSR summarized everything known about the house, its occupants, and its preservation issues in 1989. It is still referred to by scholars and others interested in Wright's work in Los Angeles. Even after it was completed, however, students produced considerable material of use to the project over the course of the next several years. Ideally, HSRs are viewed as living documents, and such work is appended, but in this case information collection was more casual, and additional material arrived and was evaluated in bits and pieces.

FURTHER RESEARCH

In addition to documentary research and recordation drawings, another source for investigation and testing of potential solutions to conservation problems was the fabric of the building itself. The Getty Conservation Institute volunteered to help with the challenge of saving the block. Conservators removed pieces to their laboratories (then in Marina Del Rey, Los Angeles), cored them, and sliced the cores into thin discs for testing. First, they measured the stress needed to break the discs. Then they applied various chemical treatments in the hope of consolidating and strengthening the fragile material and making the discs less vulnerable to water penetration; ultimately, they suggested epoxy consolidants for both purposes. That was useful information. However, the research did not extend to an application strategy or outdoor testing. Moreover, the experimental solutions could only be applied to blocks that held their shape when cut; the blocks in the worst condition were too friable for slicing and therefore could not be included in the testing protocol.

Mason Peter Purens (who worked with Eric Wright at the Storer House) developed a technique for replacing the face of blocks suffering from the ring fractures described in Chapter 5. He removed the face if it was still present but only loosely attached, cleaned what remained of the rusted steel with a tiny sandblaster and then primed it, cleaned and smoothed the surface of the portion of the block left in the wall, cast a new face, and reattached it with concrete cement. These repairs could only be made to plain blocks or those that used the reproduction we made from the left-hand pattern face plate we had; the cost of producing a new right-hand mold was beyond our budget. (A new right-hand mold created from scratch would have required making a wood model from measured drawings of existing blocks—the left- and right-hand variants are not quite mirror images of each other—and using that to cast an aluminum mold; because aluminum shrinks as it cools, all of the dimensions would have had to be slightly enlarged in order to create a final product exactly 16" on a side.) Casting blocks to match the pieces that were removed or missing (and to fit what was left of the grout tubes) in turn meant experimenting with the composition of the mix. Purens also tested waterproofing compounds for their efficacy and impact on the appearance of the block. Some caused temporary yellowing; water resistance seemed to last about three years.

As the work progressed, we learned more about the mixes and techniques required to make attractive, sound, and durable blocks. All aspects of the manufacturing process, from mold making to mixing to casting to curing to cleaning the surface of the finished block, required precision, skill, and consistency. Peter Purens conducted a program of block reproduction, which had the dual benefits of developing expertise in the process and fundraising: patterned blocks sold for $200, perforated ones—made as they were originally, by cutting out parts of the pattern from an uncured left-hand block—for $250.

Norman Weiss and Stephen Gottlieb, then with Wank Adams Slavin Associates (WASA), a New York preservation firm with experience at Fallingwater and the Guggenheim Museum, conducted tests at the house to find where water entered the walls, how long it took, and where low spots on the roofs were. Weiss trained a hose on specific sections of wall and created ponds on the roof to track the path of water through walls and roof surfaces. He also examined the grout and steel reinforcing assembly, experimenting with various superplasticizers in an attempt to develop a replacement grout that could be injected through joints or cracks into the many cavities in the system where steel lacked protection and was corroding. At the time, the effort was unsuccessful.

Finally, WASA architects examined the roof design and construction and the connection of roofing to block parapets. Even conceding that Wright had a somewhat cavalier attitude toward leaks, the condition of the Freeman House was astonishing. It was supposed to be an affordable, simple construction system, yet there were more square feet of roof than of

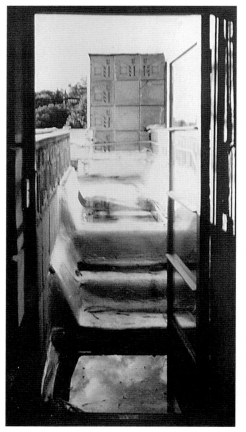

7-9. Passage from penthouse to roof, ca. 1986. Water has ponded at the base of the steps and extensive metal flashing.

7-10. Water saturating a portion of the north façade. The source of the water is visible in the photo at the left.

habitable space inside the two-story building. The roofs joined in such complex ways, intersected the vertical planes in so many different situations, and the blocks themselves formed so many different kinds of exposed horizontal surfaces that WASA identified seventy-five different potential details for controlling water on the roof. As has been noted, there were no original drawings detailing how to seal the joints between wall and roof, between roof and downspout, or between fascia and roofing. Wright was ambivalent about the watertightness of the block assembly; he counted on the grout tubes to seal the block joints, and the blocks themselves to be dense and sufficiently well formed to prevent seepage. He also seemed to anticipate water entering the wall cavities, although only a handful of drainage weepholes were ever found. But he also specified the application of Barlith, a waterproofing compound introduced in California in 1922,[7] on the back of blocks on the exterior of the building. But because the grout tubes rarely sealed the joints, the blocks were porous, no flashing was installed, and the builders had not grouted the joints, rainwater could pour into the house. Because no bills for Barlith were found in the job records, it is assumed that none was actually used at the Freeman House.

PHYSICAL PROJECTS

Tests were interesting and useful, but each led to yet more steps or a realization that fixing the house was a much larger project than previously assumed, and each investigation required funding. The largest project undertaken during the early years was the stabilization of the slumber terrace, funded by the Andy Warhol Foundation. (Both of the projects described here, the terrace and the door, were executed by California Waterproofing and Restoration under the direction of David Charlebois. Except for roofing, plumbing, and electrical upgrade, this firm did most of the work on the house from about 1989 through the first response to the Northridge earthquake in 1994.)

The terrace retaining walls, some of which were as high as 13 feet, had cracked during construction in 1925 and were on the brink of collapse by 1990. Foam-lined wood shoring was installed around the terrace perimeter to keep the walls standing. The pavers installed by Sam Freeman and Newell Reynolds in the 1940s were removed and the top several feet of the fill excavated. The fill adjacent to the three retaining walls was removed all the way down to the original grade to relieve pressure on the walls and then cut back at its angle of repose (the angle at which it would be stable and no longer slide against the walls). A new redwood deck was installed on new footings that threaded between the deadmen from the original construction. This solution saved the historic fabric of the walls, provided a pleasant place for visitors and residents to spend time outdoors, and for fundraising events, but added a new material (the deck), used in an ahistorical way.

7-11: Slumber terrace, 1988. Compare to fig. 4-13, the retaining wall during construction. The cracks continued to grow over the ensuing decades.

The terrace project revealed how much actual construction at the Freeman House differed from what was on the working drawings or from what one might reasonably expect. During excavation of the fill adjacent to the terrace walls, the concrete placed against the interior of the corners of the terrace, which first appeared to be reinforcement for the walls and parapets, fell out as the fill was removed: it not only provided no support, but actually seemed intended to deceive anyone inspecting the project. Similarly, the pilasters cast against the inside of the retaining walls at the south face did not go all the way up to the parapet; they stopped two inches short, so the 16"-thick parapet wall that should have rested on two modest 8"-thick pilasters instead sat only on the 3½"-thick block wall, which was now buckling from the weight. We quickly inserted 2 x 4s into the gaps, planning to add more structure later. In addition, the deadmen, which were supposed to help the south wall resist the pressure of the fill, lacked steel reinforcing and lay in pieces in the fill.

7-12. Shoring the terrace. Prior to excavating the terrace, the walls were shored with wood members. Those touching the wall were lined with Styrofoam.

7-13. The new cedar deck installed, 1989.

Making the project much more labor intensive than originally planned (and providing a good lesson for the future), the fill dirt turned out to be densely packed with original construction debris. It had to be excavated by hand, piece of broken block by piece of broken block. In the debris, however, we made several useful discoveries, including full bags of the original Riverside Cement used in making the blocks. This confirmed at least some information on the job invoices.

Another project, useful as a test of replacement in kind versus repair, with broader implications for the overall restoration, focused on the french door leading to the slumber terrace from Sam's apartment. The original, poorly designed and constructed, had been badly damaged during a break-in and appeared beyond salvage. We decided to construct a new door, of Douglas fir, using the original glazing, which had survived. Unlike the original, the new door was made to fit the actual opening (the wood of the original door, it may be recalled, had been "shaved" to fit). This resulted in a proportionally smaller door with smaller openings for the glazing, which was trimmed to fit. A new element was the insertion of steel rods in the stiles as post-tensioners to keep the door from sagging—a problem that developed in many of the doors and windows over time, especially those that had been altered to fit on site. The replacement door looked good and worked well, although it was visually heavier than the original door or Harriet's bedroom door (which had also been shaved down to fit its opening in 1925). Unquestionably, the minimal framing of Wright's original achieved a level of transparency that we lost in reproduction. On the other hand, the new, slightly beefier door has operated well for twenty years, and is still secure and tight. The ideal solution in terms of a combination of strength and delicacy would turn out to be the steel windows Wright used from the 1930s on, but those were not available in 1924, and thus not a preservation option at the Freeman House even if we weren't just replacing a single door.

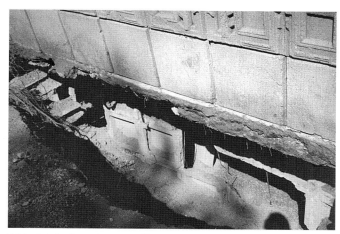

7-14. Original retaining wall construction. The 16"-wide parapet rested on a 3½"-wide single-wythe wall with only two vertical pilasters (and broken deadmen) as bracing. These were set in line with the main columns of the house.

7-15. The beam, triangular in section, that ran under the parapet wall actually sat almost 4 inches above the pilaster meant to support it. The wood blocks were added after excavation to prevent the parapet from toppling inward.

7-16. Excavation of deadman by USC student Gregory Downs. These members were meant to use friction to resist the pressure against the south wall of the terrace. However, they failed.

7-17. The living room at night, with the newly reupholstered Schindler armchair, and a polished wood floor catching the light.

7-18. Living room, ca. 1994. Removing the carpeting revealed a second wood floor laid over the original. Only the lamp, the andirons, and the cut-down dining table, remain of Wright's original furnishings.

Our new door needed a clear finish that resembled the original orange shellac but was more durable. We delayed applying any finish for a year so the sun could darken the wood through oxidation; otherwise a treatment could affect the parts of the wood grain differently, and seal in unwanted graining. By the time we applied a marine varnish, the door had acquired a beautiful, even, orange color on its own, and against the surrounding concrete it had the effect Wright had desired—two materials meeting in a relatively natural condition.

At the end of 1993 the Schindler furniture in the living room—both couches and both armchairs—were reupholstered. The upholstery that was removed was, as best we could tell, installed by Harriet in the 1950s, and was not Schindler's original choice (if he was even involved in fabric selection). Still, the change was controversial. Carried out at the insistence of dedicated volunteers who had been raising funds for the Freeman House for four years, the refurbishment enhanced the room's appearance, but it changed historic furnishings before a decision had been made about their final disposition or whether the home's period of significance included changes made by Harriet.

At the same time, the gold shag carpeting was taken up with the intention of replacing it with a new low-pile wool carpet. However, when the wood floor beneath it was revealed, its impact on the room was spectacular, despite the water damage. For the first time in forty

7-19. Laundry apartment living room, 1953. The table in the foreground was attached to the windowsill at one end. The block has been painted.

years, the floor mirrored the sky and the lights of the city, demonstrating the importance of this square of shimmering reflection within the matte-textured block walls. The two Wright-designed standing lamps, long neglected, were now refinished by Buffalo Studios and lent elegance and drama to the room.

While most of the house was considered historic and subject to debate over appropriate treatment, the apartment under the garage that Schindler designed in 1932 was considered space that could be altered with impunity, in part because of its remove from the rest of the house, in part because the importance of Schindler and his work to the preservation mission was uncertain. An enhanced apartment could house a permanent occupant, either a USC faculty member, a student caretaker, or a resident administrator, leaving the main house for a short-term architect-faculty member-in-residence and educational programs. The apartment needed to be made more comfortable and the bathroom relocated to bring light back to the east end of the lower hall. USC contacted John Lautner, who had overseen the reconstruction of the two-story corner windows in the living room twenty years earlier, and offered the commission as a contemporary intervention, with the aim of engaging and recapitulating the tradition of new work by former Wrightians. Unfortunately, Lautner died in 1994, and the apartment remains the least altered area of the house.

SIGNIFICANCE, FUTURE USE, AND RESTORATION GUIDELINES

At the end of the 1980s, we began to believe that a single large-scale restoration was unlikely; rather, work on the house would take place in a series of projects over several years, each addressing a separate set of concerns. This called for the articulation of a restoration philosophy, independent of any specific projects. I wrote a preliminary version of *A Program for Future Use and Restoration Philosophy* following the HSR in 1989; it was revised and expanded in 1992 to reflect what had taken place in the interim.

The *Program for Future Use and Preservation Philosophy* began with a short restatement of the building's proposed use as a home for a short-term visiting faculty member, formally referred to as an Architect in Residence.[8] The mission statement, a critical item for any historic site (in fact, for any nonprofit arts institution), laid out the premise: "The Samuel and Harriet Freeman House is a facility of the School of Architecture at the University of Southern California. Its restoration and future use should reflect the highest standards of care commensurate with its inherent qualities, as well as its ownership by an academic institution. It will be primarily maintained in its original use and occupancy: as a single-family residence with a small 'in-law' apartment. Other uses include classes and seminars, research, and periodic public tours. Its restoration will be that required to make the house livable, minimize future deterioration, and demonstrate clearly those qualities of its architecture and history which make the building significant."

The *Program* discussed issues associated with its proposed use, such as how the transient nature of the visitors necessitated keeping the apartment under the garage as the home of a more permanent resident, possibly a student. It examined building-code issues, access, and utilities and raised a host of questions with the expectation that they would inform and be answered as much by the course of the project as by decisions made in advance: Should visitors use the original Schindler furniture or should it be removed and replaced by reproductions? If used, certain historic furnishings, such as the cantilevered couch in the living room, would need to be reinforced, and more durable coverings installed, which would entail a loss of integrity. Should the kitchen be upgraded for visitors? For catering social events? Should there be limits on crowd size? Where should visitors park, and how would they be transported to the house (a consequential question for the neighbors)? When the architect-in-residence was present, should the house be open for tours? If so, was the resident required to keep his or her spaces immaculate? (At the Gamble House, the rare visitors who stay there are required to return their rooms each day into "unlived-in condition" by 8 A.M.) Did transient visitors require a fully furnished house, with linens, dishes, etc.? Was laundry service needed? Should keeping the house clean and the grounds maintained, jobs each taking about eight hours a week, be the responsibility of the permanent apartment resident or an outside contractor? Should there be an administrator in addition to the apartment dweller to oversee programs, conditions, repairs, and neighborhood and public relations?

The document addressed these issues and considered the future of the house in light of the much more profound understanding of the site developed in the years since Harriet had given the house to USC. And the more we learned, the more complicated the preservation choices became.

The Freeman House presents a particularly interesting example of contested significance.

What is its importance and its value on a local, state, or national level? The National Register of Historic Places—which was founded by Congress as the official "list of historic properties worthy of preservation" and which, as of early 2011, has more than 80,000 listings representing some 1.4 million individual resources—has established four criteria to be used in nominating properties.[9] Criterion A addresses historical events; Criterion B, the role of significant people; and Criterion C, design, technology, or craftsmanship. (Criterion D is for properties that provide historical or prehistorical information and is generally reserved for archaeological sites.) Using those criteria, the Freeman House can be considered significant:

A. As a prime example of the development of an avant-garde artists community in Southern California, and the home of people intimately connected to important political and social movements that marked Hollywood and the United States in the first half of the twentieth century. As a salon of the arts. As the physical and historical center of a set of houses both architecturally interesting and inhabited by important people in the arts in Hollywood. As an exemplar of a new architecture for the automobile and the automobile-accessed hill communities emblematic of Los Angeles's extraordinary growth in the 1920s.

B. As the home of Harriet Freeman, architectural patron, supporter and friend of the arts, dancer, and educator, who with her husband hosted a wide cast of dancers, actors, architects, and political activists during a period of artistic ferment.

C. As an important work in the life and career of Frank Lloyd Wright, a pivotal design in his transition from Arts and Crafts to Modernism. As the first known example of a (residential) two-story glass curtain wall with mullionless corner windows. As the first work designed and constructed in the textile-block system. As the setting for a quarter century of Rudolph Schindler's designs for both furniture and architecture. As a unique example of collaboration by three generations of architects practicing in Los Angeles: three Wrights, Schindler, Lautner, Ain, Clark, and Reneau.

The Freeman House might also be considered significant under Criterion C as an example of interventions required to keep Wright's experimental work standing and functional.

(Notably, the theme of the 2010 Annual Meeting of the Frank Lloyd Wright Building Conservancy was Modifying Wright's Buildings and Their Sites: Additions, Subtractions, Adjacencies.) Wright's work often pushed the limits of what materials and structures could do. Hence, interpreting interventions is not merely an exercise in self-congratulation but an important aspect of understanding the buildings and the architect's intentions, successes, and limitations. In the Los Angeles textile-block buildings the system was inherently flawed, with consequences that ranged from relatively modest (if expensive and frustrating) in the case of the Storer House to near catastrophic in the case of the Freeman and Ennis houses. Thus, the interventions are not only part of the history but also part of the ongoing reality of the textile-block system. Because much of the interest in the Freeman House lies in its construction system, the repair and upgrading of that system belongs to the story. It is therefore a reasonable conclusion that everyone involved with the house from 1986 to the present is relevant.

Designation may be based on multiple criteria, but at the Freeman House the physical features associated with the three criteria described above coexisted uneasily. The modifications that the Freemans requested of Schindler and their other architects after 1925 diminished Wright's intentions and the force of his design, yet Wright's experiment could not be lived in without them. Although the Freeman House is an extreme example, most historic sites present a similar set of conflicts between a kind of ideal state, either historical or architectural, and the changes that occurred or may be required to make the site function.

Our method of addressing the question of significance was to share our research with as many interested parties as we could, to expand the opportunity for input. We brought up the flawed block system and the history of constant change to varied audiences and kept a kind of informal poll of visitors' opinions. These ranged from support for restoring the house to its original state in1925 to keeping Schindler's work at the house, or even all those elements that interpreted Harriet Freeman's life. Discussing the period of significance was a teaching tool for students and the public, and it became central to understanding both the history of the house and where preservation practice potentially falls short.

In 1993, the State of California designated all four concrete-block houses—Millard, Ennis, Storer, and Freeman—as Landmark No. 1011 on the California Register. This multiple-property listing recognized them as a single historical phenomenon with four distinct elements. The effect was largely symbolic at the time, although it did recognize the houses' importance to the cultural and social history of the state and helped validate fundraising efforts and other programs. It would become more germane, however, the very next year.

THE NORTHRIDGE EARTHQUAKE

On Monday, January 17, 1994, at 4:31 A.M., an earthquake with a magnitude of 6.7 struck the San Fernando Valley, some fifteen miles north of the Freeman House, centered under the community of Northridge. Less than thirty seconds of shaking left 57 people dead and more than 1,500 seriously injured. About 12,500 buildings were moderately or severely damaged, and 20,000 inhabitants were left temporarily homeless.

7-20. Interior damage from the Northridge earthquake, 1994. Left, the main stairs were littered with pieces of the perforated block windows and the plaster ceiling of the penthouse. Right, inside the chimney.

7-21. Stair tower braced on the interior.

7-22. Bracing the east balcony and stair tower on the exterior following the earthquake.

Architecture student Gregory Downs was housesitting the Freeman House during the Martin Luther King, Jr., holiday weekend. In the predawn darkness, he was jolted awake by the violent motion of the quake and the sound of the contents of the kitchen cabinets smashing onto the concrete floor. Rolling off the 1929 Schindler couch, where he had been sleeping, and out from underneath the massive concrete beam supporting half the roof, he lay on the floor and heard thousands of textile blocks groaning as they moved. The noise masked the sound of blocks popping out of the stairway walls and the partial collapse of the chimney structure on the roof. When the shaking stopped, Downs ran outside and climbed in his car to wait for daybreak. The morning light revealed his car untouched but surrounded by chunks of the chimney and north wall of the house.

A hastily assembled team surveyed the house that evening. The damage seemed fairly limited at first, but over the next several days we began to realize that it was extensive. A bit of floor was bouncier. Cracks were wider and more numerous. The stair tower was bowing out and leaning to the east. The floor in Harriet's bedroom had separated from the walls. The floor in the lower hallway had dropped.

The Northridge earthquake nearly destroyed the Freeman House. Instead of years of slow deterioration, it suffered a major attack. Engineer Melvyn Green and restoration contractor David Charlebois were soon on the job and a skeleton of wood and metal began to grow inside and around the house. Within a month, we submitted a damage report to USC and contacted the Federal Emergency Management Agency (FEMA). As a (just designated) state historic landmark and a property owned by a nonprofit educational organization, the Freeman House was entitled to federal funding to repair the earthquake damage. It also appeared that it was eligible for funding to mitigate future damage by bringing the structural system up to code.

And so began a six-year process of design, negotiation, redesign, and renegotiation leading to a seismic rehabilitation project in the fall of 2000.

8-1. Harriet's bedroom, looking south down Highland Avenue, 2007.

IMPLEMENTATION

In 1994 the School of Architecture had been in control of the Freeman House for almost eight years. Despite a full calendar of classes, research projects, public programs, tours, and fundraising events, to most observers the house seemed no closer to its critically needed restoration than it had been in 1986. The technical problems still eluded solution and the money required to undertake the work was lacking. Local newspapers highlighted the house's ongoing deterioration; volunteers were discouraged and felt that the school was not fully committed to the project; USC feared it was saddled with a money pit at a time when its own finances were pushed to the limit.

The Northridge earthquake changed the context; it greatly accelerated the building's decay and demonstrated the consequences of waiting for every question to be answered before taking action. Realizing how close we had come to losing the house was both terrifying and energizing. Although another five years would pass before work actually commenced, much of that time was taken up by the challenge of developing a seismic repair and mitigation scheme that would not be prohibitively expensive and would bring the building into compliance with current codes for life safety, yet would not result in a significant loss of historic building fabric. Two substantially different schemes were developed, evaluated, and then discarded before a third scheme was adopted and implemented. Debates with and among federal and state agencies centered on what work was repair of earthquake damage, what was mitigation to prevent future damage, and what was neither and therefore not fundable with public monies. FEMA considered whether it could impose a funding maximum on the project based either on use or square footage. Frequent changes in agency staff in both state and federal agencies and the multiple layers of approvals required complicated the discussion. Temporary FEMA staff based in California often disagreed with permanent staff in Washington, D.C., about both the nature of the damage and the interpretation of rules and regulations. The various agencies—local, state, and national—debated what constituted compliance with the Secretary of the Interior's Standards for the Treatment of Historic Properties, the document that the National Park Service uses to "promote responsible preservation practice" and that serves as a template for preservation regulations across the United States.[1] And both the School of Architecture and USC questioned what I, as the preservation architect, and the various project consultants and local FEMA staff proposed. Finally, in 1998, Robert Timme,[2] the dean of the school at the time, adopted the project as his mission, directed the school's efforts and the work of the many consultants and others involved in the project, and found the substantial additional funds required to do the work. That the house stands today is a tribute to his determination and perseverance. (Dean Timme died in 2005, but the Freeman House has many more decades of life thanks to him.)

THE DAMAGE

The Historic Structure Report had predicted what to expect at the Freeman House in the event of a major seismic event, based to a large extent on how the house had reacted to the Whittier quake: cracking throughout and sagging of parts of the lower floor. Hence, the damage from the more severe Northridge earthquake presented few surprises.

The earthquake traveled north to south through the house in the form of a hard lateral acceleration and waves that shook it up and down and side to side. The movement dislodged blocks at the top of the house and induced a permanent deformation of a half-inch or more in several areas. The two concrete "frames" in the living room were bent to the south and spread apart. The upper floor also moved south, deforming the south wall and causing separations between walls running north–south and the floors and ceilings. Similar separations ran between roofs and parapets or walls. The block membrane of the walls stretched and bent, opening numerous cracks between individual blocks as well as separations between major building components.

The southeast corner of the building sank and tilted eastward as the supporting fill compacted and pressed out against the retaining walls, and the house settled in response. Treads in the stair tower separated from the walls on either side because of the outward bowing of the tower, and the east end of the lower-floor hallway began to collapse. The east wall of the garage bowed away from the rest of the structure, and a regular pattern of cracking (ring fractures) could be seen in each block.

The concrete beams in the corner cantilevers of the living room floor broke. Some floor and ceiling joists slipped off their supports. Other damage included broken windows, cracked wood ceiling panels, cracked and fallen plaster, and bowing and cracking of the retaining walls inside the house and the laundry apartment. Over the next months and years, the cracks and gaps introduced throughout the building by the earthquake led to even more than the usual amount of water infiltration, which caused further deterioration of building components, as well as more settlement and more cracks.

The Northridge earthquake exploited every weakness in the materials and assemblies, as well as previous damage from rain and prior earthquakes. The structural system, essentially adequate for vertical gravity loads, was ill prepared for the lateral forces of the earthquake. The minimal connections between elements could not channel the earthquake-induced movements through the building to the ground. Long-term exposure to water due to the failures in the design of the multiple roofs and roof penetrations, internal roof drains, planters without drains, windows sitting in puddles, and other "courageous details,"[3] created ideal conditions for damage throughout the house, especially rusted reinforcing and crumbling block, which further compromised its ability to resist earthquakes. The missing foundations, columns lacking reinforcing steel, inadequately cured blocks, retaining walls without functioning deadmen, and parapet joints missing grout and steel—all of these deviations from the original drawings also contributed to building failure.

SEISMIC REPAIR AND MITIGATION

The first engineering firm hired to develop a structural repair scheme following the earthquake was Nabih Youssef and Associates. Over the next two years, their scheme was designed, reviewed, modified, and debated, while, I, as lead architect, and Martin Weil, as a consultant, developed a detailed scope of work for review by the university's construction and accounting offices and by government agencies. FEMA and the California State Office of Emergency Services then developed their own scope of work based on our proposal and their understanding of what the government would fund. It was submitted to FEMA in Washington, D.C., for review, and came back substantially cut. We argued, mustered our political forces, and resubmitted, and the process was repeated several times. Typically, the teams with whom we were negotiating were swapped out every few months, and it would take a while to bring the new agency staff up to speed on the project.

Time and again the question of how to repair the textile-block system came to the fore. The teams agreed that the blocks were character-defining features, and that they had to survive any treatment. But it remained unclear how to achieve that.

After my departure in August 1997 for a new position in Texas, Dean Timme undertook an in-depth reexamination of the project. He gave primary responsibility to Frank Dimster, an associate professor in the school who had been the architect for the early 1990s rehabilitation of Villa Aurora, writer Lion Feuchtwanger's house in Pacific Palisades, California. USC needed to figure out what to do next. Public pressure was building to do something, but the structural rehabilitation alone was now estimated at nearly $1 million, and a more comprehensive restoration would likely double that figure. The school could not proceed without a guaranteed contribution from FEMA that covered most of the cost, and it could not sell the house because FEMA funds critical to any project were only available to an educational nonprofit owner. Still, USC spent several months looking for a way to transfer the house to another person or entity and break Harriet's gift of deed, until Dean Timme bowed to the inevitable and began raising money for the project. At the same time, more protection measures were undertaken, including placing a tarp over the house to minimize water damage.

Timme and Dimster, along with a new engineer, Jeff Guh of EQE International, settled on three actions needed to ensure the survival of the Freeman House. First was achieving continuity, meaning that all parts of the house had to be tied together so that it did not collapse in a future earthquake and so that lateral forces at the top of the house could be brought down and transferred to the ground. Second, individual elements in the structural system had to be upgraded so that they could resist lateral forces without cracking or failure. Guh described this as "technical surgery, replacing the bones within the skin."[4] Finally, the house had to be securely anchored to the ground to prevent additional damage through slipping or settling on the site during a future earthquake and to ensure that the lateral forces transferred

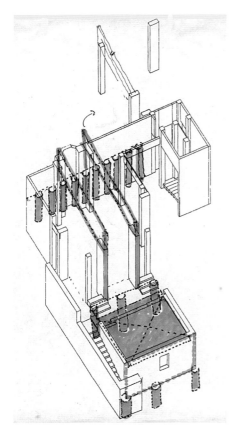

8-2. Sketch of the schematic design for the structural repair by USC professor Frank Dimster illustrating the two sets of caissons connected by the two large trusses in the living room ceiling.

8-3. Working session at the Freeman House planning the seismic repair. At the head of the table is Eric Lloyd Wright. To his left, Dean Robert Timme, Arne Mikkelson (site superintendent), Stan Westfall (standing, USC), Frank Dimster.

to bedrock. Later, the City of Los Angeles added another requirement that significantly enlarged the scope of work: the stone retaining wall that was part of the original construction of Glencoe Way had to be reinforced and supported independently from the structural system of the house.

To achieve these goals, the team chose an approach that was based on one used on the Villa Aurora: a series of caissons connected with grade beams to anchor the building to bedrock. They proposed using shotcrete, or gunnite (a lightweight concrete sprayed onto a reinforcing mesh, requiring minimal formwork), to create shear panels around the building, replacing numerous structural components and reinforcing connections. The shear panels would transfer horizontal movement in the building from columns to the foundations. This solution was favored because much of the historic fabric was brittle and had to remain in situ, and the bulk of the work could be done from the exterior, where most of the existing deterioration was found. It would, as Guh put it, shift from the "haphazard construction of the original building to a better model: a box, with edges, and planes, not necessarily continuous, but sufficiently connected to transfer loads appropriately."[5] He proposed the strategy to FEMA in October 1998, suggesting it would be less intrusive, less costly, and more effective than the two previous schemes. FEMA in turn explained its requirements for protection of historic fabric, and everyone left with a sense of renewed purpose and direction.

Joining the new project team at this point were Stan Westfall, a USC alumnus, who was the project manager for USC Construction Management, and Steve Lohr, from the same department, who did much of the negotiation with FEMA and the California State Preservation Office (SHPO). Jeff Guh was assisted at EQE by Bill Yang. Eric Lloyd Wright came as a consultant and advisor (as he has been for all the textile-block houses). In December the team presented a new formal proposal to FEMA. Construction documents were completed by the end of February 1999 and submitted to the city on March 8; they approved the design, but added the requirement for an independent structural system to hold up Glencoe Way.

THE DESIGN OF THE PROJECT

The final design for the seismic repair and mitigation consisted of interventions intended to accomplish the three objectives of continuity, upgraded structure, and secure anchorage. The first step in the process of achieving continuity was to tie the roof structure together from east to west and north to south. The discontinuity formed by the two living room clerestories was especially problematic. The solution was to insert a steel Vierendeel truss in each clerestory and align the top and bottom chords (principal structural elements) and web members (the connections between the chords) of the trusses with the structure and design grid of the house. (The advantage of a Vierendeel over other truss types is its lack of diagonal members; hence the new trusses became essentially invisible from inside the house despite their considerable heft and location in the clerestory windows.) The original 1" x 12" roof sheathing was replaced with plywood. Loads from the joists, side-walls, and parapets would be transmitted by the plywood to the new trusses, which would carry the loads to the columns at the north and south ends. These columns, starting in the foundations and laterally braced at the floors, previously had essentially acted as two-story-tall cantilevers; now they would be anchored at three points. On the underside of the living room floor, drag struts (linear elements intended to transfer forces) were inserted to take loads to the columns on the east and west sides of the room.

The initial concept for upgrading structural elements inside the house was to remove some blocks from the major columns at the north and south sides of the main volume of the house, and put new steel and concrete in the portions of the columns that were shown as empty on the plans, to bolster the existing columns' ability to absorb lateral forces. Additional new concrete beams were to be poured into the living room floor between the columns, at the roof, and at the cantilevered corners. In addition, 3" x 3" tube-section steel columns were to be inserted into the two smaller columns in the south elevation outboard of the major frame

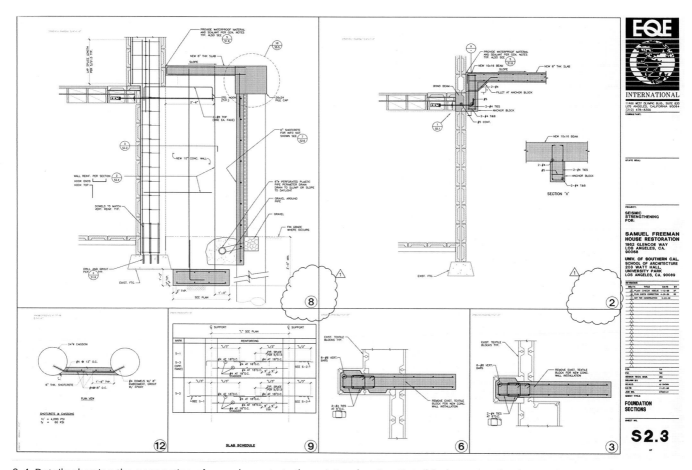

8-4. Details showing the connection of new elements to the existing framing. Detail 8 shows new footings, caissons, and entry terrace, along with drag struts and french drain. Details 2, 3, and 6 show the insertion of new concrete elements into existing fabric.

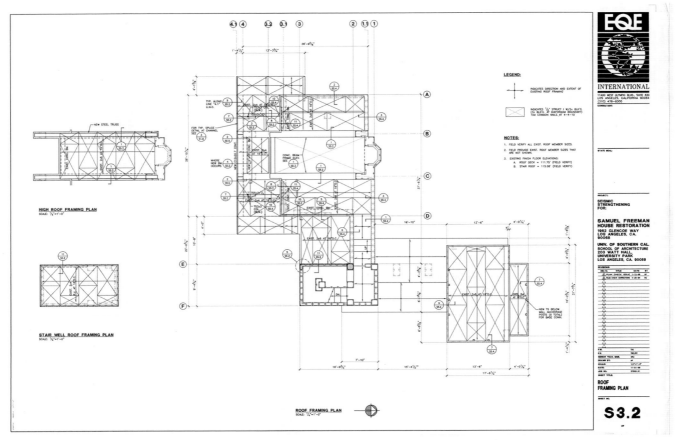

8-5. Seismic repair project roof plan, showing location of new steel roof trusses and plywood sheathing.

elements. All the structural steel was at odds with the materials and language of the original house, but the most visible of these interventions was the insertion of a 34-foot-long steel C12x20.7 beam to support the living room roof at the south façade and make a rigid connection between the two Vierendeel trusses at their south ends.

The foundation was to be reinforced by pouring large concrete blocks underneath the principal columns and tying those blocks to the new caissons anchoring the building to bedrock. A row of fourteen 24"-diameter caissons would be placed along Glencoe Way, and a separate series of six 12"-square concrete columns would support a new concrete terrace poured between the street and the house. Below grade, the north wall of the house was to be sprayed with four inches of gunnite. At the south side of the house, a new set of poured-in-place concrete walls for the slumber terrace would rest on a series of twelve 24"-diameter caissons set deep into the earth. These caissons would also support the south wall of the main cube of the house via massive concrete grade beams running diagonally up the slope until they engaged the blocks beneath the columns of the south façade. The caissons were set five feet apart (2½ times the diameter of the caissons), which allowed the soils upslope of the caissons to develop an arching effect (in other words, enabling the dirt to support itself instead of pushing against the retaining walls as it had before). The two sets of caissons and girders at the north and south sides of the house, to use a familiar Wrightian image, formed hands with fingers that reached out to anchor the house on each side. The team thought of them as "bookends."

Other interventions planned in support of the three goals included increasing the size and number of joists in floors and ceilings; inserting substantial steel connections between wood members and both new and existing concrete elements; adding new footings; and pouring new concrete beams set into the block walls, especially at the roof and floor level. The "box" formed by the bedroom closets and living room balcony was to be rebuilt in poured-in-place concrete as an additional brace and transfer element for forces transmitted through the south columns. Similarly, the projection that contained the east end of the lower hallway and the small balcony by the front door would be rebuilt in poured-in-place concrete. The exterior wall outside the main bath and kitchen was replaced with a gunnite shear panel; and a gunnite shear panel replaced the plaster wall on the west side of the stair tower.

Finally, the stairs in the stair tower were to be set into a new concrete bond beam (a beam set into a wall to cinch it together) that ran diagonally around the tower and not only secured the steps but helped to stabilize the tower. The bond beam also tied into the new concrete

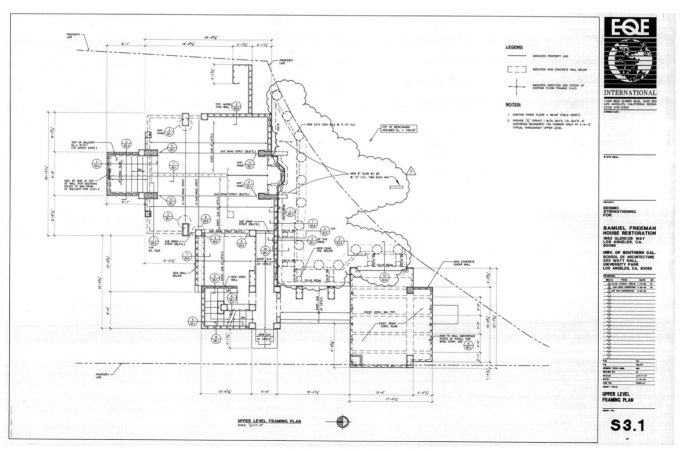

8-6. Upper-level plan for the structural repair project, showing the addition of caissons to support Glencoe Way. Other work shown includes four reconstructed columns in the main house, new concrete living room balcony, drag struts in the floor to connect all structural elements, and a new concrete wall in the stairwell.

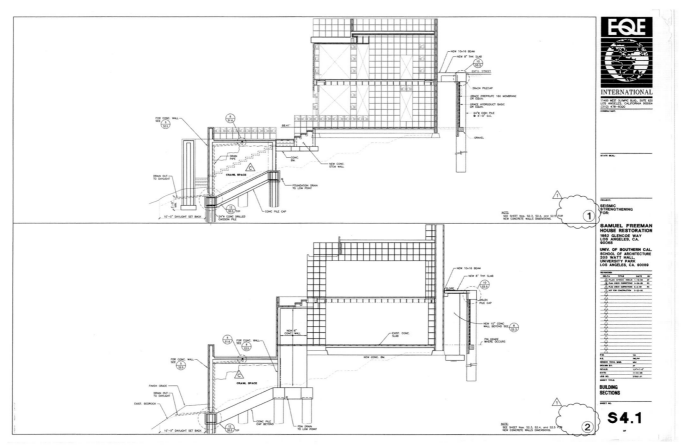

8-7. Cross-sections through the living room, bedrooms, and slumber terrace, cut at the doorway to Sam's apartment and through the balcony/bedroom closets, showing new caissons at the street and under the slumber terrace, connected by a bond beam going up the hillside, and new shear walls and beam under the house. The slumber terrace is completely reconstructed. New columns and the steel truss in the roof (not seen in this view) complete the new structural "frame."

structure at the east end of the hallways. The solution was designed to be largely invisible, while fixing the tower securely in place.

Everywhere that block walls were replaced with gunnite or poured concrete, the work was dimensioned so that the original blocks, new blocks, or at least face blocks (half the thickness of the originals) could be set in front of the intervention, hiding the new work and retaining the original size and shape of the feature. The only area where it was acknowledged that no block would go back after the work was finished was the interior of the bedroom closets. Because the walls there had only been single-wythe in the first place, it was impossible to pour new walls that allowed block to be visible on both the inside and outside of the structure.

In late March 1999, the USC project team met with FEMA to discuss the blocks. Citing Section 106 (a part of the National Historic Preservation Act that requires federally funded or approved projects to attempt compliance with the Secretary of the Interior's Standards), FEMA asked what was going to happen to the blocks. Which ones were to be removed? Where would blocks be replaced? What were the criteria for deciding which blocks to reuse and which to replace? Who was to be the conservator? And what was the conservation approach to wood panels, doors, and windows?

The team's responses were somewhat contradictory. Preservation architect Peyton Hall and materials conservator Duane Chartier were brought onboard to ensure maximum conservation of the blocks. But at the same time, Dean Timme and Eric Wright argued that the entire house was the artifact at risk, not just the blocks, which were mass-produced elements meant to be replicable, inexpensive, and not viewed as individual artisanal productions. This position would allow work that damaged or caused the removal of blocks from the house to proceed while waiting for solutions to the failures of the textile-block system and the blocks themselves. Even though there was as yet no plan to repair or reproduce the blocks, the proposed interventions would render moot most of the structural role played by the textile-block system.

At first FEMA did not accept the proposal; Hall and Chartier also were skeptical. FEMA demanded that the house be returned to its "pre-work condition" at the end of the project. However, the uncertainties associated with the block and the potential cost concerned USC. FEMA was willing to commit approximately $700,000 to the project, but the more requirements added to the scope of the project, the higher the price tag rose beyond that amount. Dean Timme and Eric Wright continued to argue that if the School of Architecture could not carry out the project, the house would likely collapse, taking the blocks with it. If the house could be made structurally sound, then the problem of the textile blocks could be addressed in the future by other architects, preservationists, and scholars, and the Freeman House could survive.

USC and FEMA finally agreed that at the conclusion of the project, the house would be left as a "restoration in process." USC committed to make the repair and manufacture of blocks an ongoing focus for restoration after the seismic rehabilitation project was completed, and the Getty Grants Program agreed to help fund that research. Despite the agreement, the preservation community in Los Angeles remained divided about the threat to the original historic fabric of the Freeman House.

In September 1999, FEMA and the California State Historic Preservation Office (SHPO) circulated a memorandum of agreement allowing the project to proceed. EQE issued a Scope of Work to bidders, a two-and-a-half-page list of items to be included in the project. Two or three firms were involved in the first stages of bidding, but by the end of the year only one, Matt Construction, demonstrated the capacity and willingness to do the project and would commit to a guaranteed maximum price contract. It helped that one of Matt's principals, Trent Anderson, a USC alumnus, encouraged it to participate. In early 2000 the company started work on a cost estimate, helped to refine the scope of work, and began preconstruction planning.

Matt Construction had no comparable precedent on which to base their estimates (the Ennis House Seismic Rehabilitation was being developed at the same time by a different team but had not advanced as far as the Freeman House project). According to Jeff Jarrett, who helped manage the project for Matt Construction, it was particularly hard to estimate the length of time it would take to remove individual blocks from the building and to account for the difficult site logistics. The first estimate came in at $1,515,698 in March 2000. This was not good news for USC.

A month later Matt Construction revised the estimate to $1.1 million by refining the process, reducing the scope, mostly by eliminating work on the garage and the laundry apartment, and assuming some risk on the costs. (Eventually, Matt Construction did the project at cost, and a few years later did the seismic rehabilitation at the Ennis House.) Meanwhile, FEMA and the SHPO developed a set of formal requirements for "recordation and assessment of existing conditions, and inventory and salvage documentation," which were incorporated into the Section 106 memorandum approving the project. The documentation was to include eighteen views of the house recorded with large-format, black-and-white photography, with copies for the State of California archives, FEMA, SHPO, USC, the Los Angeles Central Library, and the Los Angeles Conservancy. A "qualified preservation professional" was required to conduct the photographic documentation and to prepare the reports.

Peyton Hall was designated to oversee the conservation and reproduction of the blocks. However, while considerable time and effort was spent on block making, the results were not significant for the project. Few new blocks were made and even fewer of those removed were reinstalled. Eric Wright assumed responsibility for overseeing documentation, inventory, and storage of the blocks removed during the repairs. He also took on the task of putting a functional roof on the building—perhaps as challenging a job from a technical and design standpoint as any other aspect of the project.

Eric Wright's role was critical in two other ways. His authority relative to his grandfather's intentions was accepted by FEMA and (almost) everyone else. His experience working for both his father and grandfather and on the other block houses gave him, in the words of the USC project team, "a balanced view about what was achievable. He understood cost, and pragmatic reality."[6]

The summer of 2000 was spent negotiating a contract and outlining the procedures USC would use to manage the contract. Although USC and FEMA had finally agreed on project scope and budget after almost six years of give and take, FEMA did not immediately write a check to start the work. The entire project had to be completed, reviewed, and approved before FEMA would hand over any funds. This placed the School of Architecture at risk, and USC had to agree to let the school proceed under those conditions.

The first construction meeting was held on September 22, followed by regular Friday project team meetings, typically attended by Dean Timme, Frank Dimster, Jeff Jarrett, and Arne Mikkelson, the project superintendent from Matt Construction. They were joined on occasion by Stan Westfall and Steve Lohr from USC, and Eric Wright. [Ill. 8-2] One or another of the changing cast from FEMA and the somewhat more stable representatives from the SHPO participated as needed. The neighbors were always invited, and several attended the first few meetings; as they became more comfortable with the process, they stopped coming. In October, the project budget was finalized at $1,206,045, which included the extraordinarily low contingency of $50,755, or 4.21 percent. This worked out to approximately $400 per square foot. FEMA had agreed to contribute $767,300, leaving $438,745 to be raised by the USC School of Architecture, in the person of Bob Timme.

In November the required photo documentation of the house was completed. USC removed the Schindler built-in furnishings and stored them at the Power Station, a facility owned by the School of Architecture near its downtown campus. Eric Wright developed directives for Matt Construction to protect the historic fabric that remained in the house. Because FEMA and the SHPO insisted that as many blocks as possible be saved and treated

8-8. Before the damaged chimney mass was dismantled, each block was labeled. The blocks were then removed, and the code written on the back of each.

as potential future conservation projects, the blocks had to be identified and recorded as they were removed. Matt Construction developed a procedure, using the thirty sheets of block identification drawings that had been prepared by USC students in the early 1990s as a key (see ills. 7-18 and 7-19), tagging each block with a code indicating its location on the building before it was wrapped in bubble wrap. Outside each package another tag repeated the location, and the wrapped blocks were placed on palettes in sequence and shipped to the Power Station. An inventory log, consisting of reduced copies of the drawings with the relevant blocks marked in red, documented which blocks were removed, their type, location, and condition, and noted the palette on which the block was stored.

CONSTRUCTION

Glencoe Way is a 22-foot-wide cul-de-sac. Houses located beyond the Freeman House had no egress when construction blocked the street, and the city's requirement that the street be re-supported meant that part of Glencoe would be temporarily unusable. Because the Freeman House pushed up to (and maybe a few inches past) the property line on the east and within a few feet of the property line on the west, there was no ready access to the portion of the site below the house where much of the work was to occur. The neighbors on both sides of the house and across the street were apprehensive about how the project would affect them and their tenants (most houses in the area include rental units). Fortunately, the owners of a small vacant lot 25 yards down the street rented it for construction crew parking; additional parking was arranged at the Hollywood Bowl parking lot several blocks away. To protect the neighbors to the east who used the historic paths down to Glencoe Way, Matt Construction built scaffolding over the path.

Trees and plants around the site were tagged to identify those to be trimmed, cut, or removed, largely based on their health and proximity to the work site rather than on whether they were historically significant. Almost all the vegetation at risk from the project had already been documented previously, and most would be easy to replace. A pair of enormous pine trees and the spectacular two-story-tall euphorbia outside the southeast corner of the living room needed protection in place. By early November, the landscape was prepped and ready.

On November 1, 2000, Matt Construction hosted a neighborhood reception and kick-off party. The company was keenly aware of the necessity of keeping the wary and very active community informed about progress and mollified in the face of any inconvenience. Jeff Jarrett and Arne Mikkelson gave out their cell-phone numbers and announced their willingness to hold meetings with neighbors at any hour of the day or day of the week. The construction office was set up in the laundry apartment. Excavation began next to the street, to access its retaining wall, and removal of the blocks from work areas around the house commenced.

It soon became clear that only 10 percent of the blocks were surviving the removal process intact. As noted earlier, some of them had but 1 percent of the strength of the concrete blocks used in construction today; FEMA directed the team to collect the pieces. How many pieces could a block be in and still be called a block or be worth saving? FEMA representatives came by the house to watch the removal process and discuss the possibility of modifying it. Six months later it was agreed that USC could dispose of patterned blocks in five or more pieces and plain blocks in three or more pieces. Ultimately, 1,233 blocks, or about 14 percent of the total, were removed; of those, 23 were reinstalled on the building as part of the work.

The block problem inflamed passions on all sides. Conservator Duane Chartier deplored the losses and what he felt was a lack of concern for the hand-crafted historic fabric and for making matching new block. Matt Construction tried to be careful and economical. It took about thirty minutes to remove each block. But could more have been saved if the process had been slowed down? Arne Mikkelson remains skeptical: "It would have been 15 hours versus a half hour. For thousands of blocks, that would have been totally impractical."[7] Could chemically consolidating the block before removal, or using another cutting technique, or binding the block faces, have saved more of the block? Possibly. But feeling the pressure of time and money, in the end Timme and Dimster opted to proceed with saving the building, even at the expense of blocks.

By mid-November Matt Construction was ready to drill the caissons along Glencoe Way, which would be 24 to 30 feet deep. The metal cages of reinforcing steel that would go into each caisson arrived along with a drilling rig. Each caisson had to be drilled, the hole cleaned, and the concrete poured in a single day, or else the hole might close up again.

While the work on the north side of the house proceeded relatively smoothly, the principal questions about how to proceed on the south side were still unresolved: how to get a drilling rig to the south side and how to get the dirt from that excavation back up to the street. One proposal was to dismantle the "tool shed," construct a ramp from the street down to the terrace level, and another from there to the level at which the caissons were to be drilled. Matt investigated using a conveyor belt in lieu of the ramp, and digging by hand instead of using a rig. The company also looked at burying the excavated dirt, or spoils, in the open space under the reconstructed slumber terrace. Meanwhile, the north caissons supporting Glencoe Way were finished, allowing excavation of the dirt between the street and the house. The sequence essentially reversed the original construction process. Those areas, such as the entry, that were last to be finished in 1925 were the first attacked in 2000. (The same happened inside the house, of course, because finishes had to be removed to allow access to the structure.[8])

8-9. Caisson installation at the street. The sequence runs from upper left, showing caissons supporting street, inspection of exterior of north wall at the lower level, foundation work under lower level of house and addition of concrete to lower-level north wall, formwork for new entry deck, and waterproofing at the pool.

Once the fill was removed from between the street and the north side of the house, attention turned to the wall of the house at the lower level. Over the years, it had bowed several inches into the lower hallway from hydrostatic pressure and dirt pressing horizontally against the block system. Diagonal cracks had spread across many of the blocks, and water and soiling had followed. The project team decided to attempt a risky straightening of the wall. Usually preservationists seek to stabilize features to prevent further damage but avoid trying to move things back into place because sudden changes that reverse years of slow movement can cause elements to fail. However, this wall was already failing and unsightly, and with the fill now permanently removed from behind it, which lessened the load, the wall would no longer have to perform as it had. The work required to effectuate this one repair is a good example of how laborious and painstaking the entire project was. First, the crew placed jacks between the floor and the ceiling, to take vertical loads off the wall. They then set 1 x 12 planks of wood (all dimensions here are in inches) across the entire wall at a point about four feet above the floor, secured 4 x 6s to the 1 x 12s, and anchored a series of large, threaded nuts, spaced equally along the length of the wall, to the 4 x 6s. From these nuts, all-thread rods were stretched through small holes in the wall all the way to the new caissons holding up the street. Over the course of two hours, four men "walked" the wall into place, each in turn tensioning their all-thread rod by only a half turn. Nothing snapped (although a crack did appear in the floor). When the wall was within ½" of vertical, the men stopped. Then a 4" layer of gunnite was sprayed on the opposite side. Seven days later, the cables were cut. The wall stayed in place.

By the middle of December, 472 blocks on 29 pallets had been shipped to the Power Station. Matt weatherproofed the house in anticipation of winter. Site drainage was addressed with french drains (buried perforated pipe that takes water away from building foundations susceptible to saturated soils) in gravel at the base of the wall on the north side and area drains at the lower entry terrace. The rest of the month was spent removing the block at the slumber terrace, and finishing the concrete subterranean structures on the north side.

Matt Construction and the caisson subcontractor arrived at a solution to the problem of accessing the south hillside: they would use a crane with a 90-degree boom to deliver a hydraulic drilling rig to the locations where they needed to drill the other set of caissons, and the same crane, equipped with a bucket, would then remove the debris. Two dump trucks' worth of debris was taken from the slumber terrace (in addition to the debris already removed in the earlier terrace stabilization project). By the end of the year, the slumber terrace and its footings were gone, and work began on a pad for the crane. Drilling on the south caissons commenced in early February. Almost immediately, there was trouble: the rig hit bedrock three feet down. It took over a month, marked by unhelpful cold and rainy weather, to drill the twelve holes needed, even with a second rig delivered to the site.

At the end of January, work began inside the house with the dismantling of the living room ceiling. Among the interesting discoveries was the technique used to slope the roof for drainage: nailing 1 x 1s to the roof joists, under the sheathing. At the stairwell, lath and plaster were removed from the west wall in preparation for an application of gunnite. The kitchen was also dismantled and the outside wall of the kitchen and the bathroom below prepped for gunnite. Scaffolding was erected at the east and south sides of the house. The process of dismantling the east balcony began.

8-10. Foundation work at the south side of the house. Digging the caissons for the slumber terrace (a, b). Checkerboard excavation to provide footing for new gunnite walls at the kitchen and to support new work at bedroom planters and the east balcony (c, d, e, f).

8-11. Reconstruction of the main columns from roof to lower-level foundations. Investigation of the four principal columns in the living room revealed that they had no vertical steel reinforcing except that connecting the block and lacked the cavity spaces shown on the drawings that the seismic repair scheme anticipated using to strengthen the columns (a). In addition, the columns rested on wood framing and were not continuous from ground to roof (b). As a result, they were completely removed (c, d), and reconstructed from new footings through the lower floor (e) and upper floor (f) to the roof.

At the beginning of March, Matt Construction reported that they had failed to find any footings under the two north columns flanking the hearths, and each supported one end of the massive concrete beams in the living room; a few weeks later they discovered that the columns on the south side, which were supposed to be partially hollow, thus allowing for the insertion of new steel reinforcing and new concrete, were actually solid concrete without any reinforcing steel at all. And the concrete was very soft. This meant that the four columns lacked the structural capacity that they had been assigned in the design of the seismic repair. Replacing the columns completely would mean the loss of more blocks, including highly visible blocks inside the house. The design team explored the alternatives open to them. Trying to shift the loads to other columns was not practical because it would impair the structural performance, and changing the basic design would mean having to go back through the approval process on the city, state, and federal levels. After six weeks of discussion and redesign, the design team decided to demolish the four two-story columns and rebuild them, from new footings to the living room beams and the new Vierendeel trusses.

By the end of March, construction of formwork for the new walls of the slumber terrace had begun, while dismantling continued indoors. The design team decided not to touch the two-story glass windows.

In early April, Matt started to insert foundations below the southern and eastern half of the house. The (minimal) foundations of the western part of the house, which sat on the portion of the property that had been cut and leveled with the Fresno Grader back in 1924, were not touched. The 2001 foundation was largely handwork. Dirt was removed beneath the walls in a checkerboard pattern, new footings were poured, and when those had set, the dirt in between was removed and the process repeated. At the same time, parts of the wall and the planters outside the bedrooms, which had framed the slumber terrace, were propped in the air while work on the terrace was ongoing, and repaired while suspended.

The two columns on either side of the main structural columns at the south façade contained their own unpleasant surprises. Shown as hollow on the working drawings, they were supposed to have steel tubes inserted that would connect to the new steel framing in the cantilevered roof. But they were found to be solid. The design team decided to attach a steel plate to the top of the columns to anchor horizontal tube sections inserted in the living room ceiling.

Work also began on the stair tower. Blocks had to be removed from the outside in order to cast the bond beam that ran along the steps; fortunately, most were plain, not patterned.

The original termite- and water-damaged roof framing was removed, leaving nothing overhead in the kitchen or living room. The crew had a surreal view of open sky between the massive concrete beams spanning the living room, which were supported on a row of thin little metal poles while the four columns were being rebuilt. During this time, Arne Mikkelson was awakened one night by a minor earthquake, and lay awake until dawn fearful that disaster had struck the house. Not until he got to the site the next morning and saw that everything was still securely in place did he realize that the quake was probably only a dream.

Work proceeded intensely during May. The gunnite on the kitchen wall and most of the new concrete beams, footings, and columns were completed; the roof joists were replaced. The two Vierendeel trusses to support the center roof were delivered. Eric Wright approved the reinstallation of blocks brought out of storage at the Power Station for the outside wall of the stair tower.

8-12. Demolition and reconstruction of bedroom closets. Compare these to the construction photographs in Chapter 4. The bedroom closets and living room balcony were constructed from single-wythe walls lined with wallboard on wood framing at the exterior (a). Original construction debris under the bedroom floor is typical of that found virtually everywhere under the house (b). After removal, it is clear that the closet/balcony structure was built essentially as an independent structure attached to the main house at the columns (c). After installation of caissons (d) and a new footing (e), the closet and balcony is reconstructed in poured-in-place concrete (f).

8-13. Construction of bond beam at grade, slumber terrace, and bedroom planters. The grade beam (a, b) connected caissons being dug in fig. 8-10, and served as the footing for the new walls of the slumber terrace (c, d). The terrace floor has been poured (e). The completed terrace, along with a new bedroom planter (f). The vertical stripes are grooves intended to assist the future application of textile-block pavers, half the width of a full block, to the poured-in-place elements, in order to achieve the original appearance.

8-14. Revealing the original roof framing. After removal of the sheet-metal cladding seen in (a), and multiple layers of roofing, the original roof construction was revealed. Planks of Douglas fir were used to construct steps, crickets, and roof sheathing (b–f). The parapet wall along the north side of the main roof terminated in patterned block on both sides, with a coping block covering the air space between the wythes (c), whereas the remaining parapets were single-wythe, terminating in a mitered block. (See figures 7-6 for detailed drawings of how roofing met mitered edges and other conditions visible here.) The vent stacks for the kitchen and bathroom fixtures, along with the electrical conduits added to the house over the years, can be seen (c). The cantilevered roofs required beams deeper than the rest of the roof framing, essentially creating bathtubs on top of the cantilevers (a, e). The windows for the living room clerestory were rotted out by water (f).

8-15. Demolition of floor and roof framing. The original floor framing consisted of Douglas fir planks on joists 16" on center, with diagonal struts (a). The joists rested on walls or hung from black metal joist hangers as seen here. Original electrical conduit can also be seen in (a), along with the base of the concrete column from the living room just to the left of the wood framing sitting on top of the block column in the lower hallway (see arrow). Roof sheathing removed, new joists are installed in the living room (b) and kitchen (c), along with more substantial metal connectors. After removal of roofing and columns, the cantilevered roof framing along the south side of the living room forms a delicate tracery against the sky (d, e, f).

8-16. Adding structural steel to the roof. Horizontal steel tubular member being installed, after analysis revealed that the two small concrete columns outboard of the block screens and main columns in the living room lacked the capacity to anchor the new steel channel spanning the south façade (a, b, d). Bracket connecting wide flange to new columns on either side of balcony doors (e). One of the two new Vierendeel trusses installed in the clerestories (c).The south end of one truss is visible to the left, the new steel channel runs along the edge of the cantilevered roof, and one of the new steel tubes intersects the channel (f). New plywood sheathing is visible as well (c, f).

8-17. New roofing and framing. After installation of the truss, it is painted to match the block color, and then new framing and sheathing are installed (a). New framing at the west side of the cantilevered roof (b). Roof framing at the underside of the upper roof and cantilevered roof (lower right); one of the trusses is installed behind the perforated-block clerestory at the middle left (c). In order to drain the roof, the penetration through the upper portion of the wood girder is retained (d). The roof project after installation of new roofing and flashing (e). The lower-floor ceiling at the same location as in 8-13 a, showing the new poured column, wood blocking, and metal drag strut and joist hangers (f).

8-18. Completed roof, kitchen, and east balcony. The finished roof has metal flashing covering all the exposed tops to single and double-wythe parapets, as well as the backs of the parapet walls (a, d). The new flashing has a minimal profile when seen from street or garden (a, f). The exterior wythe of blocks removed from the south façade of the kitchen and bathroom in preparation for application of gunnite (b). Formwork and reinforcing installed for gunnite (arrow points to reinforcing outside of kitchen planter) (c). Completed gunnite installation (f). Like the living room balcony, the east balcony is reconstructed in poured-in-place concrete, to anchor the house in the east–west direction (e).

The crane was removed, marking the completion of work on all of the structural elements on the south side of the house. During its three months of operation, it had lifted thousand-pound buckets of dirt regularly up and over the house to waiting dump trucks on the street. According to the crew, every load swinging overhead triggered apprehension about potential disaster until the process was finished.

With the installation of the new trusses atop the beams, roof framing accelerated. Roofing went on in early June. Plumbing connections to the roof scuppers were installed. Doors and windows that had been removed were reinstalled, and in place of the original perforated blocks, plexiglass panels were set into the new walls of gunnite or poured concrete, in the same locations as the original windows.

Work on the Freeman House was finished in the middle of the month. Despite the surprises and the logistical difficulties, Matt Construction had completed it within the budget. The company did some of the work with their own crews, instead of hiring subcontractors, which allowed them to reduce some fees. They constantly sought ways to accomplish their tasks more efficiently and dropped some items from the project, such as the manufacture and installation of new blocks, and the reinstallation of the wooden ceiling at the upper floor. FEMA approved the funding in February 2002, a little less than a year after the work was finished and eight years after the Freeman House asked the agency for help.

THE PROJECT CONTINUES

The seismic rehabilitation was always seen as an incremental project—"Doing what one can as one can," in the words of Bob Timme.[9] It was a response to the Northridge earthquake and to the structural vulnerabilities that had resulted in damage, not a complete and final restoration. In the years since, more work has been done at the house. A new wood floor and radiant heating system was installed in the living room, and new tiles made by students at USC have been set in the floor of the living room and kitchen. The kitchen has been furnished with simple stainless-steel appliances and fixtures, allowing the school to use the house for meetings and events. In 2004 the living room balcony was reconstructed and lined with sheet copper, and other new details to prevent leaks were incorporated. It also now had block steps and pavers, as Wright once envisioned, instead of the as-built poured-in-place concrete steps. A new set of doors for the opening between the balcony and the living room replaced the pair that Eric Wright so unhappily repaired while Sam lay dying. Reconstruction of the pool by the entry was finished in 2005, complete with koi. A local weather station, with thirty-eight monitors that measure relative humidity around the house, has been installed and sends the information to a computer that can both record and transmit the information to the school.

Large projects remain. The most critical is reinforcing the garage and the laundry apartment, which was dropped from the scope early in the project. The other is reconstruction of the two-story corner windows, a technical problem that is likely to challenge the preservation of Wright's aesthetic vision for the building, even as it engages elements that remain an undervalued part of the house's design. And finally, of course, there is an ongoing need for new blocks, both half thickness for covering the gunnite panels and poured-in-place elements and replications of the original block for reconstruction of areas that are still missing such as

8-19. The project is complete, but not the house. At the conclusion of the seismic rehabilitation, the house sits securely on its site, has some elements of Wright's original vision restored, but much more work is needed. The lower hall ends in a large window, awaiting reproductions of the original french windows; the area from the frosted glass panel back was the bathroom for the apartment from 1932 to 1999 (a). New doors lead to a living room balcony awaiting block parapets (b). Harriet's bedroom (c). The living room has a new floor reproducing the original, and the former door to the elevator is now open, but needs to be one block shorter to match the original Wright window, and awaits casement sash (d). Then entry has a restored, watertight, and functioning pool for the first time since the 1930s, although it still needs block facing (e).

the chimney mass at the top of the house. A small block-making plant now sits outside the School of Architecture at USC, with new molds and a press, anticipating the next step in the restoration of the Freeman House. No one knows when that will happen, or when all the finishes and furnishings will return from storage. But the Freeman House itself still stands, at least physically more secure today than at any time in its long and eventful life.

9-1. The Freeman House in 2007, seen from Highland Avenue.

WRIGHT AND
HISTORIC PRESERVATION

In Chapter 1 I discussed briefly the two dilemmas of preservation at the Freeman House: one concerning integrity; the other, significance. Does the site still retain its authenticity as an experiment in modernist construction if the textile-block system that is central to its story has been significantly supplemented or even replaced? And how much significance should be given to the clients and their other architects in designing a future for the Freeman House? In one form or another, these dilemmas of integrity and significance underlie all of preservation.

Questions about why, how, and for whom we preserve have accompanied the actual work of preservation for hundreds of years. At times these debates have been linked to issues of national identity, culture, and material progress, and have taken place in the popular realm as well as within architecture or art circles. Indeed, the rise of Modernism, in all its political, social, and artistic manifestations, has been accompanied by a rise in preservation as a discipline and a cultural phenomenon. As antithetical as they may appear, Modernism and Historic Preservation need each other as a kind of counter-model; they share a sense of time as a linear, propulsive thing. There has probably never been a time in which preservation, of both natural and cultural resources, has played a greater role in public policy and in design than it does today. Widely used in urban design, public policy, and economic and community development, preservation has also been addressed in international and national charters, laws, and regulations, and the practice has codified around certain principles, which aim to minimize bias in the selection and treatment of sites, create normative models for preservation practice, and maximize the longevity of those aspects of a site that best characterize its meaning to the community. Applying these principles to the Freeman House project has always been a challenge.

It is almost never the case that history or science tells us exactly what to do in a preservation project. Nor does the program for a property's future use or even an interpretive plan. Furthermore, relying only on those sources to try to come up with the most "authentic" restoration or rehabilitation can rob a site of its vitality. To paraphrase philosopher Jean Baudrillard's commentary on our contemporary engagement with the real, the simulacrum, and the hyperreal,[1] the more a site strives for authenticity, the more it risks becoming unreal and the more the reconstruction eliminates the original.

But the opposite tack can also be problematic. Dismissing a site's real history and material reality, and relying instead on intuition, taste (contemporary or otherwise), or speculation about what might have been intended or might have happened if, for example, Wright had finished the building or been around to do the preservation project himself, can lead to a site that has either finally achieved its original intentions or one that has lost its historic character and become something new and compromised. (For example, the removal of the Freeman House's original poured-concrete steps at the living room balcony, and their replacement with block pavers, brings the house into compliance with the drawings but not as it was actually built.)

Design—informed, thoughtful, and creative—is central to a good preservation project. And it relies on a willingness to surrender to the object while maintaining a coherence of vision and purpose. This is hard to do, however, so traditional preservation practice seeks to minimize the amount of intervention at a site and utilizes a process of public review that makes innovation difficult.

These restrictions certainly were fought at times in the case of the Freeman House. Robert Timme proposed designs (unfulfilled) for interior lighting that were meant to celebrate the architecture in self-conscious ways never intended by Wright—or at least not available to him historically. And during the seismic rehabilitation project following the Northridge earthquake, as noted earlier, Eric Wright is reported to have said that certain decisions being imposed by government agencies were "not what my grandfather would do," and winning the argument.[2]

By the same token, since 1926, when Rudolph Schindler started his own quarter-century of reworking the Freeman House, close to a dozen architects have done things to the building. They generally operated with sympathy for Wright's ideas, with varying degrees of success. Change and intervention were the norm at the Freeman House. That is part of the challenge for all historic sites that don't seek to capture a moment in time long gone: change is the norm in life. And as various writers have pointed out, a building is a functional object that must continue to adapt and evolve by its very definition. It is not an archival document, but a living one.[3] And as with the United States Constitution and other living documents, much debate accompanies change and interpretation at a historic site.

A building is a particularly rich historical document. It records how we build, as individuals and as a culture, and through its program and symbology, why. Embedded in every site are essays in aesthetics, economics, politics, physics, engineering, anthropology, and so on, and each site's stories represent a unique nexus in the web of human history. We save sites because losing them deprives us of a physical manifestation of these stories, as well as of the space that constructed and was constructed by them. We need to be cautious in preservation because with our work it is so easy to erase a part of the record and its related stories—both those we know, and, even more dangerously, those we don't yet know.

As mentioned at the beginning of the chapter, preservation centers on the concepts of significance and integrity. The first tells us *why* we should preserve a site, while the second tells us, basically, *how*: by preserving its physical fabric. Put another way, significance deals with the meaning of a site, while integrity deals with its materials. Because significance relates directly to why we preserve, it depends as much on the beliefs of the stakeholders as it does on the stories associated with the site. Significance varies not only from person to person and community to community, but over time. And it is attributed both when a place is created initially, and retroactively when we seek to save it. People continue to invest significance in a site as they view or experience it.

Significance is communicated through interpretation, educational programs, tour spiels, signage, brochures, and other messages that tell about a historic site. Interpretation is also political—people rarely tell stories they don't buy into—and typically directed to a self-selected audience. Good interpretation can reach across different experiences, perceptions, values, and ages. Sophisticated site interpretation programs are also continually updated and checked, so that they remain fresh and accurate.

In the United States, we generally equate authenticity with integrity. We believe that a site really is historic if most of the physical fabric of the property, whether buildings, landscape, or furnishings, date from the period of significance. In places that are much older (such as China), or where resources are continuously repaired or reconstructed (such as the pueblos of the American Southwest), authenticity can be situated in the cultural practice of traditional building, either with or without attention to the materials. Increasingly, preservation is also paying attention to intangible cultural heritage. This includes language, music, social practices, and craft traditions that are essential to understanding a culture but may have no intrinsic built manifestation. As a result of this expansion of the idea of integrity, we are increasingly challenged to redefine what exactly it is that constitutes the thing we need to save at a site. In the preservation of modern architecture, for example, many advocate for the intention of the architect, as if it were an intangible characteristic of the site that can even outweigh the value of the historic fabric, pointing out that the materials themselves were often expedient choices or prototypes awaiting better solutions that are now available. Yet by privileging the intentions over the fabric, we can end up erasing the story of that struggle, of the innovation in the face of difficulty.

Architecture conveys experiences and meanings to a visitor beyond those that arise from the physical materials. And we recognize that those aspects of a site can be compromised over time. But it is not clear that those intangible qualities can be or should be manipulated or somehow preserved independently of the physical fabric.

Authenticity is a tricky term, and an even trickier concept, especially when Wright-designed buildings are at issue. Some believe that Wright's involvement is, by virtue of his importance, more significant than other potentially significant historical events, and thus the historic fabric specifically associated with Wright is more important than other historic fabric. They further believe that integrity at a Wright-designed site is as much about the ideas and vision of Wright as it is about what was actually built. Thus, a site such as Auldbrass Plantation in Yamasee, South Carolina, includes not only recently constructed structures that were designed by Wright but never built but also remade details in copper that originally were crafted in wood because copper was unavailable during World War II when Auldbrass was built.

In 1997, the restoration committee of the Frank Lloyd Wright Building Conservancy proposed Conservation Guidelines for the Designs of Frank Lloyd Wright. The guidelines were modeled on the Secretary of the Interior's Standards, but started with a clear bias about significance. Guideline Seven read, in part, "Later changes or additions, if limited in scope and fully complementary to Mr. Wright's original design, may be retained." The language shifted the onus for keeping historical material onto the material itself—a very dangerous proposition, as it put the integrity of the site at risk from the always limited information available to those associated with the project. But the guidelines' presumption that most people who save Wright sites care more about the architect and his work than about the history of the clients or subsequent interventions is probably accurate. In fact, the guidelines, which were ultimately not adopted, were redundant.

In trying to determine appropriate treatments at Taliesin, in Wisconsin, the restoration staff have had to address the long period of Wright's residency, which was, of course, from when he built the house and studio complex in 1911 until his death in 1959, as well as the regular campaigns of redesigning and rebuilding that he conducted over that time. In addition, Wright's third wife, Ogilvanna, lived at Taliesin until 1985, making many of her own changes to the site, and the Wright Fellowship continues to occupy and transform parts of the site even today. Taliesin Preservation, Inc., has adopted a fairly sophisticated and nuanced response to the complexity of the preservation challenge.[4] While the exteriors of the buildings are all highly protected, they have zoned the interiors into primary spaces, warranting a full restoration treatment; secondary spaces, which can be rehabilitated, restored, or preserved; and utility and storage spaces, which are expected to be modified as needed functionally. In general, the site adopts a "period of restoration" that is the last decade of Wright's life (with priority given to the later 1950s),[5] even though the period of significance would likely cover Wright's entire life at the house. However, individual structures, and even individual spaces, are evaluated independently. The result may be that some rooms get restored to an earlier period than other adjacent spaces, such as is currently planned for the bedrooms that were traditionally occupied by the apprentices in the teens and twenties, because the documentation is there, the work is reversible, and there is a lesson to be learned from seeing the rooms as they were at that time. The same approach can be used for some of the accessory buildings on the site. In this flexibility, Taliesin has chosen not to become a site that interprets or represents a step back to a static moment in time, but rather a self-conscious, designed aggregation of various aspects of the site's past, forming a new, living document that interprets itself even as it becomes its own future.

At the Freeman House, as at every historic site, the ideal solution will always be elusive, because it depends on perpetually evolving knowledge about the site's story, and on changing conditions, audiences, and uses. It has now been the most altered of all Wright's block houses; although with many of its finishes gone, the house somehow feels even more modernist and radical than when it was built. And very little of the history of the house after 1925 is left. The Schindler furniture is in storage, along with the ceiling panels, artwork, and all traces of the Freemans' daily life. The textile-block system remains a focus of study even as it no longer has to support the building.

There is no doubt that the Freeman House has been more of an educational experience for me and for a quarter century of students and visitors than if it had "worked" and never required the level of study and intervention that it did. And it continues to be a valuable pedagogical tool for the School of Architecture, a rich subject for seminars and theses. But for the sake of the house, and because the building remains an extraordinary architectural achievement, we have to look forward to the day when the house lives again as it did before, with the furnishings and finishes in place, inhabited by creative people doing interesting things, and at the forefront of the cultural conversation in Southern California.

CONTRACT DOCUMENTS

The Contract Documents for the Freeman House consist of the various legal agreements that enabled its construction, including agreements, working drawings and specifications. In late January 1924, copies were prepared for the signatures of the clients, architect, and contractors (Wolff and Hackenschmidt). One bound set of several of the documents was labeled "Owner's Copy" and given to the Freemans. It included an Agreement between Owner and Contractor, an Architect's Contract, and a Receipt. The clients and contractors also signed each page of the working drawings at that time. All documents are transcriptions by the author of the originals.

AGREEMENT. . .

THIS AGREEMENT, made this Twenty-ninth day of January, 1 9 2 4, by and between . . .H. J. D. Wolff, of the City of Los Angeles, County of Los Angeles, State of California, party of the first part and hereinafter designated the Contractor; and Sam Freeman, of the City of Los Angeles, County of Los Angeles, State of California, and herein after designated the Owner.

WITNESSETH, that the Contractor, in consideration for the sum of NINE THOUSAND ONE HUNDRED. . . . . . . DOLLARS, to be paid by the Owner in installments as herein after described, hereby agrees and contracts to furnish all the material and tools to perform all the labor required to complete the Excavation, Grading, Masonry, Carpentry, Mill Work, Plumbing, Heating, Electric Wiring, and Fixtures, Hardware, Painting, Glass, Roofing, Sheet Metal, and Iron Work, Plastering, or whatever may be shown on plans and specifications, including permits and insurance, as necessary to complete the building owned by Sam Freeman to be erected where shown on plans and on Lot #3 Glencoe Way, Highland View Estates, Hollywood, Los Angeles, California, as shown by plans and specifications prepared by Frank Lloyd Wright, Architect. This work to be done under the superintendance of the said Architect and to his entire satisfaction, the plans and specifications being part and parcel of this Contract and identified herewith by initials of the contracting parties.

THE CONTRACTOR further agrees to proceed with said work immediately and at all times without delay also to complete same by August First, 1924. He will also deliver to the Architect a surety Bond for a sum equal to Fifty per cent (50%) of the contract price. This will be returned upon Completion of the Contract to the satisfaction of the Architect.

IN Consideration of the above the Owner hereby agrees to pay to the said Contractor, NINE THOU-SAND ONE HUNDRED . . . . DOLLARS, in five installments of Eighty-five per cent (85%), of actual work done or material delivered for same at the time of payment, as the work progresses, and as estimated and certified to by said Architect, and the retained Fifteen per cent (15%) of the last installment, thirty-five days, (35 days) after acceptance and when said work shall have been completed to the satisfaction of said Architect, and so accepted and certified to by him. Waivers of Lien for materials furnished or work done shall be furnished whenever and as required by the Architect or Owner.

When the building is finished the Architect will give a written acceptance of same and issue a final certificate to the Contractor.

IN WITNESS WHEREOF, the parties to these presents have hereunto set their hands and seals, the day and year first above written.

H.J.D. WOLFF
EMIL HACKENSCHMIDT
CONTRACTOR

SAMUEL FREEMAN
HARRIET PRESS FREEMAN
OWNER

WITNESS
WILLIAM A. KOCH
WILLIAM B. S. SMITH

ARCHITECT
CONTRACT

IN RE. . FREEMAN HOUSE

LOS ANGELES. . .JANUARY 26th. 1924. . .

SAMUEL FREEMAN agrees to employ FRANK LLOYD WRIGHT, ARCHITECT, to furnish designs and superintendence for the erection complete of a house to be built at HIGHLAND VIEW ESTATES LOT 3, Hollywood, California, and agrees to pay the aforesaid Architect ten per cent of the total cost of building, in installments as follows,-

When plans are ready for letting contracts 7 1/2% of estimated cost of $9,100,000. When building is completed additional 2 1/2% of completed cost and adjustment of total commission to equal 10% of cost of complete operation. Plans and specifications are the property of the Architect and are to be returned to him on completion of the contract. . . .

Samuel Freeman
Owner
Frank Lloyd Wright
Architect
Witnesses
Emil Hackenschmidt

RECEIPT

(Printed on FLW stationery)

Los Angeles
Jan 29th 1924

Received of Samuel Freeman ($682.^{50}) Six Hundred Eighty Two and $50/00$ Dollars - being first payment of 7½% of Contract for Residence-
Bal 2½% - and adjustment - to equal total of 10% of the total cost of building - to be made at completion of structure.

Frank Lloyd Wright

Using the 1907 version of the "Uniform Contract" for Architects and Builders issued by the American Institute of Architects, the contractors from January (Wolff and Hackenschmidt), joined by C. S. Holman, submitted the following agreement in February 1924. However, there are no signatures, and changed just a week later.

AGREEMENT

This Agreement, made the Nineteenth day of February in the year one thousand nine hundred and twenty-four by and between

> D. S. Holman, H. F. D. Wolff, Emil Hackenschmidt...all of the City of Los Angeles, County of Los Angeles, State of California...
>> party of the first part (hereinafter designated the Contractors), and
>
> Mr. and Mrs. Samuel Freeman, of the City of Los Angeles, County of Los Angeles, State of California...
>> party of the second part (hereinafter designated the Owners),

Witnesseth that the Contractors, in consideration of the agreements herein made by the Owners, agree with the said Owners as follows:

> Article I. The Contractors shall and will provide all the materials and perform all the work for the erection and entire completion of a Pre-cast Concrete Slab Residence located on Glencoe Way Lot #3 Highland View Estates in the City of Los Angeles, County of Los Angeles, State of California...

It is hereby understood and agreed that no methods or machinery whatever will be used in this work except that expressly ap[p[roved by the Architect. The dies, moulds and block-making apparatus proper are the property of the Architect and are all to be returned to him at the completion of the building or disposed of as may be directed by him. Dies for special pattern blocks such as may be peculiar to the building are to be paid for by this Contractor but to be the property of the Architect and returned to him at completion of work or upon demand. Other necessary dies, flasks, saddles, etc., are to be furnished by the Architect to the Contractor who will be held responsible for safe return of same in good order at completion of the job or when demanded by the Architect. This Contractor shall pay to the Architect a rental for the use of same to be agreed upon and a royalty of three cents per block for every block made and set in this work as compensation for the use of the System hereinafter specified in connection with patent sheet diagram.

The Concrete mixer, shovels, wheel barrows, and whatever labor or materials are necessary to the proper setting up and working of the System are to be furnished and paid for by the Contractor. The Contractor shall also pay for the transport of all the above mentioned apparatus to and from the job, as directed.

as shown on the drawings and described in the specifications prepared by FRANK LLOYD WRIGHT Architect, which drawings and specifications are identified by the signatures of the parties hereto, and become hereby a part of this contract.

Art. II. It is understood and agreed by and between the parties hereto that the work included in this contract is to be done under the direction of the said Architect, and that his decision as to the true construction and meaning of the drawings and specifications shall be final. It is also understood and agreed by and between the parties hereto that such additional drawings and explanations as may be necessary to detail and illustrate the work to be done are to be furnished by said Architect, and they agree to conform to and abide by the same so far as they may be consistent with the purpose and intent of the original drawings and specifications referred to in Art. I.

It is further understood and agreed by the parties hereto that any and all drawings and specifications prepared for the purposes of this contract by the said Architect are and remain his property and that all charges for the use of the same, and for the services of said Architect, are to be paid by the said Owners.

Art. III. No alterations shall be made in the work except upon written order of the Architect; the amount to be paid by the Owners or allowed by the Contractors by virtue of such alterations to be stated in said order. Should the Owners and Contractors not agree as to the amount to be paid or allowed, the work shall go on under the order required above, and in case of failure to agree, the determination of said amount shall be referred to arbitration, as provided for in Art. XII of this contract.

Art. IV. The Contractors shall provide sufficient, safe and proper facilities at all times for the inspection of the work by the Architect or his authorized representatives; shall, within twenty-four hours after receiving written notice from the Architect to that effect, proceed to remove from the grounds or buildings all materials condemned by him, whether worked or unworked, and to take down all portions of the work which the Architect shall by like written notice condemn as unsound or improper, or as in any way failing to conform to the drawings and specifications, and shall make good all work damaged or destroyed thereby.

Art. V. Should the Contractors at any time refuse or neglect to supply a sufficiency of properly skilled workmen, or of materials of the proper quality, or fail in any respect to prosecute the work with promptness and diligence, or fail in the performance of any of the agreements herein contained, such refusal, neglect or failure being certified by the Architect, the Owners shall be at liberty, after three days written notice to the Contractors, to provide any such labor or materials, and to deduct the cost thereof from any money then due or thereafter to become due to the Contractors under this contract; and if the Architect shall certify that such refusal, neglect or failure is sufficient ground for such action, the Owner shall also be at liberty to terminate the employment of the Contractors for the said work and to enter upon the premises and take possession, for the purpose of completing the work included under this contract, of all materials, tools and appliances thereon, and to employ any other person or person to finish the work, and to provide the materials therefor; and in case of such discontinuance of the employment of the Contracts they shall not be entitled to receive any further payment under this contract until the said work shall be wholly finished, at which time, if the unpaid balance of the amount to be paid under this contract shall exceed the expense incurred by the Owners in finishing the work, such excess shall be paid by the Owners to the Contractors; but if such expense shall exceed such unpaid balance, the Contractors shall pay the difference to the Owners. The expense incurred by the Owners as herein provided, either for furnishing materials or for finishing the work, and any damage incurred through such default, shall be audited and certified by the Architect, whose certificate there shall be conclusive upon the parties.

Art. VI. The Contractors shall complete the several portions, and the whole of the work comprehended in this Agreement by and at the time or times hereinafter stated, to wit:

August First 1924...

Art. VII. Should the Contractors be delayed in the prosecution or completion of the work by the act, neglect or default of the Owners, of the Architect, or of any other contractors employed by the Owners upon the work, or by any damage caused by fire or other casualty for which the Contractor are not responsible, or by a combined action of workmen in no wise caused by or resulting from default or collusion on the part of the Contractors, then the time here fixed for the completion of the work shall be extended for a period equivalent to the time lost by reason of any or all the causes aforesaid, which extended period shall be determined and fixed by the Architect; but no such allowance shall be made unless a claim therefor is presented in writing to the Architect within forty-eight hours of the occurrence of such delay.

Art. IX. It is hereby mutually agreed between the parties hereto that the sum to be paid by the Owners to the Contractors for said work and materials shall be

NINE THOUSAND ONE HUNDRED DOLLARS ($9,100.00)

subject to additions and deductions as hereinbefore provided, and that such sum shall be paid by the Owners to the Contractors, in current funds, and only upon certificates of the Architect, as follows:

In five installments of Eighty-five per cent (85%), of actual work done or material delivered for same at the time of payment, as the work progresses and as estimated and certified to by said Architect, and the retained Fifteen per cent (15%) of the last installment, thirty-five days (35 days) after acceptance and when said work shall have been completed to the satisfaction of said Architect and so accepted and certified to by him...

The final payment shall be made within thirty-five days after the completion of the work included in this contract, and all payments shall be due when certificates for the same are issued.

If at any time there shall be evidence of any lien or claim for which, if established, the Owners of the said premises might become liable, and which is chargeable to the Contractors, the Owners shall have the right to retain out of any payment then due or thereafter to become due an amount sufficient to completely indemnify them against such lien or claim. Should there prove to be any such claim after all payments are made, the Contractors shall refund to the Owners all moneys that the latter may be compelled to pay in discharging any lien on said premises made obligatory in consequence of the Contractors default.

Art. X. It is further mutually agreed between the parties hereto that no certificate given or payment made under this contract, except the final certificate or final payment, shall be conclusive evidence of the performance of this contract, either wholly or in part, and that no payment shall be construed to be an acceptance of defective work or improper materials.

Art. XI. The Owners shall during the progress of the work maintain insurance on the same against loss or damage by fire, (Contractors will pay Workmens Compensation Policy) the policies to cover all work incorporated in the building, and all materials for the same in or about the premises, and to be made payable to the parties hereto, as their interest may appear.

Art. XII. In case the Owners and Contractors fail to agree in relation to matters of payment, allowance or loss referred to in Arts. III or VIII of this contract, or should either of them dissent from the decision of the Architect referred to in Art. VII of this contract, which dissent shall have been filed in writing with the architect within ten days of the announcement of such decision, then the matter shall be referred to a Board of Arbitration to consist of one person selected by the Owners, and one person selected by the Contractors, these two to select a third. The decision of any two of this Board shall be final and binding on both parties hereto. Each party hereto shall pay one-half of the expense of such reference.

The said parities for themselves, their heirs, successors, executors, administrators and assigns, do hereby agree to the full performance of the covenants herein contained.

In Witness Whereof, the parties to these presents have hereunto set their hands and seals, the day and year first above written.

In Presence of

At the end of February 1924, a new set of documents was prepared. This consisted of a Memorandum of Agreement between owners and architect that supplemented the previous month's Contract, a new rather brief Agreement between owners and builder (since Lloyd Wright had replaced Holman, Wolff and Hackenschmidt as contractor), and a Specification, which is undated, and may in fact have been prepared the previous month.

MEMORANDUM OF AGREEMENT

THIS AGREEMENT made this Twenty-sixth day of February, 1 9 2 4 by and between MR. & MRS. SAMUEL FREEMAN AND FRANK LLOYD WRIGHT. . .

It is hereby agreed between MR. & MRS. SAMUEL FREEMAN and FRANK LLOYD WRIGHT that the cost of the building covered by percentage contract with LLOYD WRIGHT - said contract identified herewith - shall not exceed the sum of TEN THOUSAND DOLLARS ($10,000.00) without Architect's fees.

Should the cost of the building exceed that sum, then FRANK LLOYD WRIGHT hereby agrees to furnish whatever sum may be necessary to complete the work according to Plans and Specifications and to become a partner with MR. & MRS. SAMUEL FREEMAN to the extent of such payments as he - FRANK LLOYD WRIGHT - may be called upon to make and be reimbursed when, within such time as may be agreed upon between them, the property may be sold as an investment. The share of profit to FRANK LLOYD WRIGHT shall be pro rata to the amount of the sum invested.

It is understood that the superintendence fee of 2 1/2% is to be allowed by the architect to go to make up the Builder's fee of ten per cent. The total compensation to remain reckoned upon a contract price of $9,100.00 unless the building is sold as an investment in which case the full commission of ten per cent upon complete cost is to be paid the Architect and the fee of ten per cent in addition paid to the Builder.

Samuel Freeman
Harriet Press Freeman
Frank Lloyd Wright

AGREEMENT

THIS AGREEMENT made this Twenty-sixth day of February, 1 9 2 4 by and between LLOYD WRIGHT, party of the first part, hereinafter designated as the Builder and MR. & MRS. SAMUEL FREEMAN, hereinafter designated as the Owners.

WITNESSETH that the Builder in consideration of the conditions herein made by the Owners, agrees with the said Owners as follows ;

It is hereby understood and agreed that the work to be done is to consist of the building of a Residence, Garage and Garden Work for same, all located on Site designated on Plot Plan as Lot #3, Tract #6867, Highland View Estates, City of Los Angeles, County of Los Angeles, California, and as shown on the drawings and described in the specifications prepared by FRANK LLOYD WRIGHT, Architect, which drawings and specifications are herewith identified by signatures of contracting parties. And the whole of the said work shall be executed according to said Architect's instructions and as ordered by him. Should any matter arise as to the interpretation of, and the nature of the work to be done and the method of it's [sic] execution, the Architect shall be the sole arbiter and the Builder will co-operate with said Architect solely and in accordance with Plans, Details or such instructions of the Architect as may be given from time to time. It is understood as a part of this agreement that no purchases of materials are to be made by the Owners nor employment of labor nor instructions be given to workmen direct by them. The Owners shall pay for all labor and material when and as necessary to properly conduct and execute the work to be done as herein described and shall maintain all liability and other insurance necessary for the protection of said work and workmen thereon employed.

The Builder is to act as the Owner's agent only, in the direction and employment of all labor and the purchase of all materials for the work herein mentioned. Vouchers and itemized bills for both materials and labor will be presented by the Builder to the Owners for payment upon the Fifteenth day of each month during the progress of the work.The Builder shall efficiently superintend and devote sufficient of his own time to the work to insure the "carry on" of the work as rapidly, accurately and economically as possible to the satisfaction of the Architect and shall see that competent men shall at all times be kept upon the work. The Builder is hereby empowered to use his own discretion in the employment and discharge of such labor during the progress of this work or to reject any materials deemed unsuitable. The Builder will at all times keep the Architect fully informed as to progress of the work and report to him any discrepancies in details and not proceed when in doubt without due reference to the Architect's advice.

For and in consideration of which service the Owners shall pay to the Builder, Ten per cent (10%) of the cost of the above mentioned work as executed and upon presentation of all vouchers and bills and as a part thereof, the Fifteenth day of each month.

A cash account such as may be agreed upon between Owners and Builder to cover weekly payroll is to be deposited to the Builder's credit by Owners or weekly payroll to be cared for by Owners - at his option. This payroll with amount paid to each workman reciepted [sic] by the signature of each workman, so paid, shall also be deposited with the Owners as voucher in accounting for same the Fifteenth of each month. The Owners shall have the privilege [sic] at all times of an accounting in detail from the Builder as to any or all moneys certified by him to the Owners as due or payable - satisfactory vouchers for same to be forthcoming on demand.

IN WITNESS WHEREOF the parties to these presents have hereto set their hands and seals the day and year first above written.

Samuel Freeman
Lloyd Wright
Harriet Press Freeman

Specifications are meant to accompany a set of working drawings, and describe verbally the materials, dimensions, and standards of quality for key elements in the building.

SPECIFICATION. . .

RESIDENCE ON GLENCOE WAY. . .
HIGHLAND VIEW ESTATES, LOT # 3 . . .
FOR SAM. FREEMAN. . .
HOLLYWOOD. . .LOS ANGELES. . .CALIFORNIA
FRANK LLOYD WRIGHT. . .
ARCHITECT. . .LOS ANGELES. . .CALIFORNIA

FOUNDATION. . .CONCRETE in trenches beneath all walls, 12" thick and 4" wider than the width of base of all walls, laid on solid ground.

MAINWALLS. . .All of reinforced construction throughout according to plans and details herewith, materials of the standard throughout of the City requirements of Los Angeles or as herein specified by FRANK LLOYD WRIGHT, Architect. Terrace Walls, Floors, Steps, and Pool to built of cement blocks as shown. See Specifications attached hereto. FLOORS AND STEPS throughout except Stairs and Living room Floor to be of cement tile throughout and as noted on the drawings. Living Room Floor to be 1/2"x 1 3/4" Oak No. 2 Grade laid on wood floor over paper and the whole supported by 2" x 12" joists 16" o.c. These joists to be Oregon Pine or Redwood.

ROOF. . .framed with O. Pine or Redwood joists 2"x 12" and 2"x 10"as shown 16" o.c. All roof surfaces to be covered with matched and dressed 7/8" fencing nailed tight and covered with approved mastic roofing. Over this lay a cement tile floor as indicated on drawings. All ceilings of Main Floor except as otherwise noted to be Redwood boards applied to soffit of joists according to detail. Other ceiling soffits and outer overhangs to be plaster,- two coats rough and sand finish colored in box to suit and applied without laps. All roofs to be flashed clear through beneath the coping walls and counter-flashed where necessary to guarantee no leaks. Terrace floors to be formed same as roof and cement tile laid thereon.

INTERIOR TRIM, Doors and Sash, of Redwood coated with oil stain or other approved coating, inside and outside. Sash, blind mortised; Doors, Sanitary Flush Slab Type. All wood inside to have coat of hot Johnson Prepared Wax brushed on and wiped smooth. Hardwood floor to be scraped, filled, shellaced, sanded and waxed.

SCREENS on all movable windows, copper mesh as selected, all as per detail.

HARDWARE - First class in every respect, Hinges, Galvanized Iron, loose pin, on doors and windows. Locks - Yale or equivalent, thrust bolts on double hinged sash, Hangers, brass thresholds, holdfasts and lever handles on all windows of bronze, as selected or directed by the architect.

PLUMBING - MAINS to be run from fixtures and make connection with sewer at S. W. corner of lot. FIXTURES. . .1 Basin, enameled iron, full roll rim and apron, concealed hangers, N. P. Fittings, 1 Shower Bath Receptor, enameled iron, roll rim, Shower head with Niedecken mixer valve or other approved. Duck curtain, and N.P. Rail. 1 W.C. Expulso Type. Bath to be California Special, tiled in or other approved. Kitchen sink to be enameled iron with roll rim, back and apron, w drain boards, enameled iron. Pittsburgh Gas Hot Water Heater, Bungalow Size, with automatic cut-out all installed where directed. Two enameled iron Laundry Trays with N. P. fittings. All this work to be according to Los Angeles Rules and Regulations. Place 4 gas outlets where directed for emergency light and heat. Provide and install kitchen range to approval. . .

ELECTRIC WIRING. . .Provided for 31 outlets and switches as marked also provide 10 electric heaters of the Cutler Hammer Type - 3 blades in each unit, Panel face registers.

WATERPROOFING. . .After completion the structure shall be thoroughly cleaned down and all ornamental blocks in horizontal courses waterproofed with Bar-lith or other approved compound and the whole left clean and complete as a whole. Contractor to guarantee building from defects of workmanship or material and maintain same in perfect condition for one year from date of completion and acceptance of same.

MASONRY CONSTRUCTION throughout to be thoroughly and carefully done in workmanlike manner according to system indicated by patent sheet attached to the plans. Steel rods to be 1/4" dia, all materials the best of their kind or as specified - the whole to the satisfaction and written approval of Frank Lloyd Wright, Architect. . .

GLASS to be Libby-Owens rolled plate through except behind perforated blocks which may be D. T. American.

(After a page break, the Specification continues as below. The "Patent Sheet Diagram" is reproduced in this book as fig. 1-18.)

To be read with Patent Sheet Diagram. . .

Reinforced Concrete Construction as shown in Fig. 3 and 16" x 16" in size 3 1/4" thick or as otherwise detailed.

All pre-cast slabs or blocks shall be made of clean sand or other suitable aggregate and Portland Cement, in the proportions of one of cement to four of sand, thoroughly mixed in a mechanical mixer to the consistency that will stand up when squeezed by the hand.

All slabs or blocks will be formed under pressure in metal molds and not allowed to dry within a period of ten days from the time they are made. All blocks shall be perfect, free from cracks or defects of any kind. The slabs and blocks will be set into the wall as indicated in Fig. 1 and Fig. 4, with 1/4" rods between them, horizontally and vertically, the joints are then to be grouted full with Portland Cement, one of cement to three of clean, sharp sand.

The joints shall be carefully filled solid in every case, the blocks being saturated with water before pouring is done.

The outer shell and inner shell to be the same. The two shells shall be tied together across the air-spaces by 1/4" steel rods hooked to vertical rods at every intersection of every joint and the rods asphalted or covered with a thickness of Portland Cement mortar- equivalent to 2" in thickness. Where the joists or rafters rest upon the walls they shall extend through the air spaces to the inside of the outer blocks and rest upon a continuous plate. Where the rafters rest the connecting rods between the course against which they rest shall be turned over and stapled to them securely.

NOTES

1. SETTING THE SCENE

1. Correspondence from the Freeman House Archives, University of Southern California School of Architecture.

2. "Historic Frank Lloyd Wright House Deeded to USC for Study, Restoration," *Daily Breeze*, Torrance, CA, May 13, 1984, p. C8.

3. Finis Farr, *Frank Lloyd Wright: A Biography* (London: Jonathan Cape, 1962), p. 13.

4. Donald W. Hoppen, *The Seven Ages of Frank Lloyd Wright* (Santa Barbara, Calif.: Capra Press, 1993), p. 11.

5. Richard C. MacCormac, "The Anatomy of Wright's Aesthetic," in *Writings on Wright: Selected Comment on Frank Lloyd Wright,* ed. H. Allen Brooks (Cambridge, Mass.: MIT Press, 1981), pp. 163–74.

6. Most dates for built works are taken from William Allin Storrer, *The Frank Lloyd Wright Companion* (Chicago: University of Chicago Press, 1993). Those in Los Angeles come from Robert Sweeney, *Wright in Hollywood* (Cambridge, Mass.: MIT Press, 1994), and Kathryn Smith, *Frank Lloyd Wright: Hollyhock House and Olive Hill* (New York: Rizzoli, 1992).

7. Frank Lloyd Wright, *An Autobiography* (New York: Horizon Press, 1977), p. 216.

8. Shirley du Fresne McArthur, *Frank Lloyd Wright: American System-Built Homes in Milwaukee* (Milwaukee, Northpoint Historical Society, 1985).

9. Smith, *Frank Lloyd Wright*, p. 166. Smith points out that Barnsdall's commission was done in part because it "buoyed Wright against the loss of the Olive Hill jobs."

10. DeLong lays out this theory in his essay for the exhibition catalogue *Frank Lloyd Wright: Designs for an American Landscape, 1922–1932* (Harry N. Abrams, 1996), available online at http://www.loc.gov/exhibits/flw/; and also in his preface to Sweeney, *Wright in Hollywood.*

11. Wright devoted a chapter to his move to Los Angeles in his autobiography and also addressed the projects in an article for *Architectural Record* written shortly after leaving California. Wright, *An Autobiography*, pp 262–75.

12. The Freeman family story about the Little Dipper differs from that described by Smith. She mentions Helen Girvin as the teacher in charge of the Little Dipper project. Smith, *Frank Lloyd Wright*, p. 181.

13. http://www.laalmanac.com/population/po02.htm, accessed January 10, 2011.

14. Ashleigh Brilliant III, *The Great Car Craze: How Southern California Collided with the Automobile in the 1920's* (Santa Barbara: Woodbridge Press, 1989).

15. Carey McWilliams, *Southern California: An Island on the Land* (Santa Barbara: Peregrine Smith, 1973), p. 12.

16. A partial list of built work includes: Frank Lloyd Wright: Hollyhock House, Oleanders, Residence A, Storer House, Freeman House, Ennis House; Lloyd Wright: Henry Bollman House, Otto Bollman House, Weber House, Sowden House, Samuels-Navarro House, Taggart House, Hollywood Bowl Shells, Lloyd Wright Home and Studio; Irving Gill: Morgan House, Dodge House, Casas Grandes Apartments, Clark House; Rudolph Schindler: Schindler-Chace Double House, How House, Helena Rubinstein salon, Floren House, Burrell Apartment, Paine House, Korsen Apartments, Kreutzer Apartments, Fisher House (and others).

17. This history is taken from Syl MacDowell, "The Magic Story of Hollywood," *Los Angeles Times*

Sunday Illustrated magazine, September 28, 1924. Even if it is a bit romanticized and abbreviated, it is a satisfying account of the Hollywood myth contemporary with the construction of the Freeman House.

18. Kevin Starr, *Material Dreams: Southern California Through the 1920s* (New York: Oxford University Press, 1990), p. 209.

19. Ibid., p. 211.

20. Brilliant, *The Great Car Craze*, p. 17.

21. John Brinkerhoff Jackson, "Truck City," in *A Sense of Place, A Sense of Time* (New Haven: Yale University Press, 1994), pp. 171–85.

22. MacDowell, "The Magic Story of Hollywood."

23. George Goodwin, "Frank Lloyd Wright's Usonian Houses for Jewish Clients," *American Jewish Archives Journal*, vol. 51, nos. 1 and 2, 1999, pp. 67–92.

24. This information comes from the 1869 Hungarian Census, through the Jewish Genealogy Web site, www.jewishgen.org.

25. Lovell had also changed his name. His progenitors were the Sapersteins and Marmorsteins.

26. Gary Marmorstein, "Steel and Slurry: Dr. Philip M. Lovell, Architectural Patron," *Southern California Quarterly*, Fall/Winter 2002, vol. 84, no. 3/4, Historical Society of Southern California, pp. 241–70.

27. Adolf and Sally's information is based on documents in the Schindler Archives at the University of California, Santa Barbara, and on comments from an interview of Sam Freeman by Kathryn Smith (see note 32).

28. Friends and family disagree about whether the inheritance came from Friedman or from Isidore or Julius Weisenberger. Sam's sisters received identical inheritances but sold their shares before the stock became valuable.

29. This information is largely taken from interviews with Gary and Hap Lovell, and from United States Census records. However, most of the 1890 U.S. census records were destroyed in a fire, and there are some inconsistencies in dates.

30. Gary and Hap Lovell, interviewed by the author at Newport Beach, 1988.

31. The birth year used here is based on the 1910 census for New York (Enumeration District 677, Sheet No. 10A), in which she is listed as twenty years old. This corresponds best with her receiving a teaching certificate in 1911, and with the ages and birth dates of her siblings. Apparently, she claimed at least two other dates. Her death certificate lists her birth year as 1893; while the public notice filed when she and Sam were married states she was born in 1899, thus making her ten years his junior, rather than six weeks. Given her active dancing and teaching career in the late 1910s, that date seems unlikely.

32. From an interview conducted by Kathryn Smith with Sam and Harriet Freeman in 1977, while Smith was assisting Esther McCoy with her book *Vienna to Los Angeles*. McCoy was gracious enough to share the interview tape with the author.

33. Diane Kanner, "Freeman House Deeded to USC: Hollywood House Designed by Frank Lloyd Wright," *Los Angeles Times*, March 25, 1984, section VIII, pp. 25, 34.

34. Ibid.

35. According to an unverified bit of Freeman family lore, Lane was the daughter of the founder of Loehmann's stores.

36. Review in the Utica press, from Harriet Freeman's scrapbook.

37. Sources differ on the birthdates and ages of Leah and Philip. According to the 1910 census in New York, Leah was born in 1885, whereas the 1920 Los Angeles census lists her as 27, hence born in 1893. Dion Neutra identifies Lovell's birth date as 1895, while the 1920 census lists it as 1890. It seems plausible that both lied in 1920 to establish a more socially acceptable age relationship. As seen in note 31, Harriet's age also varied.

38. 1920 census for enumeration district 147 in Los Angeles, sheet 19b.

39. Kanner, "Freeman House Deeded to USC."

40. Ibid.

41. *Communist Infiltration-Motion Picture Industry (COMPIC)* (Excerpts) File Number: 100-138754, Serial: 251x1, Part: 7 of 15. Page: 126. "Samuel Freeman of 1962 Glencoe Way, Hollywood, California. Freeman was identified as a communist on February 7, 1944, through information obtained from [blacked out] who furnished information [blacked out] on the Communist Party in Hollywood." The file also notes that Sam was a signatory to the articles of incorporation for the Lincoln Community Book Center, which ran the Lincoln Book Shop, in operation from 1943 to 1947 "for the sale of Communist literature to the clubs of the Communist area [*sic*] located in the Hollywood area." The FBI pointed out that the bookstore's opening had been covered in the *Daily People's World*, August 7, 1943. The store was located on Highland Avenue, within sight of the Freeman House.

42. Dorothi Bock Pierre, in a conversation with the author in 1989. Pierre was a Los Angeles dancer and critic who interacted frequently with Harriet over the years. She was also the daughter of the sculptor Richard Bock, whom Wright employed on the Home and Studio and other projects, and attended the Montessori school run by Catherine Tobin Wright in Oak Park.

43. This biography is adapted from Alan Weintraub,

Thomas Hines, and Eric Lloyd Wright, *Lloyd Wright: The Architecture of Frank Lloyd Wright Jr.* (New York: Harry N. Abrams, 1998), and David Gebhard and Harriet Von Breton, *Lloyd Wright, Architect* (Santa Monica: Hennessey + Ingalls, 1998), originally published in conjunction with an exhibition held in 1971.

44. Schindler Archive, University of California at Santa Barbara.

45. Schindler's biographical information comes largely from Esther McCoy, *Vienna to Los Angeles: Two Journeys* (Santa Monica: Arts + Architecture Press, 1979), and Judith Sheine, *R. M. Schindler* (London and New York: Phaidon, 2001).

46. Sheine, *R. M. Schindler*, p. 29.

47. Sally Kitt Chappell and Ann Van Zanten, *Barry Byrne and John Lloyd Wright: Architecture and Design* (Chicago: University of Chicago Press, 1982). John also worked in Southern California, particularly around San Diego. Like his father, John was interested both in developing a new system of construction to advance the ideas of the System-Built houses of the teens, on which he had worked in Wright's office, and in developing an appropriate architectural vocabulary for the Southern California landscape.

48. Harriet's friend Wyn Evans, for example, talked about groups starting out at the Freeman House and piling into cars for the short drive to the Schindler House, for any of the numerous scheduled events hosted over many years by Rudolph or Pauline.

49. Several friends of both Harriet and Sam described various aspects of the relationship in interviews conducted by the author from 1986 to 1990.

50. Among the Schindler clients who were also friends of the Freemans (based on correspondence and Christmas card lists kept by Harriet, now in the Freeman House Archives) were: Burke, Dekker, J. DeKeyser, P. DeKeyser, Frankel, Friedman, Horton, Kent, McCoy, Oliver, Sachs, Sax, Schaeffer, Steiner, Stojano, Westby, and Zascek. Schindler also designed a house for Sam's parents, one for Harriet's older brother Abe, and, of course, the five projects for Harriet's sister and brother-in-law. The source for the list of Schindler's clients is Sheine, *R. M. Schindler*, pp. 286–94.

51. See Sheine, *R. M. Schindler*, pp. 35–44, for a discussion of the relationship, both professional and personal, between Schindler and Wright.

52. Sweeney, *Wright in Hollywood*, pp. 204–27.

53. Andrew N. Rebori, "Frank Lloyd Wright's Textile-Block Slab Construction," *Architectural Record*, vol. 62, no. 6, December 1927, pp. 452ff.

54. Sweeney, *Wright in Hollywood*, p. 2.

55. Specifications for the Freeman House, from the "Owner's Copy" of the contract documents, Freeman House Archive, University of Southern California School of Architecture.

56. See Chapter 5 for a discussion of Robert Sweeney's theories on the development of the system, and its possible origins as Nel-Stone.

57. *Plastering and Fireproofing*, International Library of Technology 498 (Scranton, Penn.: International Textbook Company), 1919, p. 26.

58. This process was described by Byron Vandegrift, a member of the original construction crew, in an interview with the author in 1988.

59. National Register Bulletin: How To Complete the National Register Form, National Park Service, found online October 6, 2009, at http://www.nps.gov/nr/publications/bulletins/nrb16a/nrb16a_II.htm.

2. DESIGN

1. Harriet and Sam repeated this story several times in interviews, including Kathryn Smith's interview conducted for Esther McCoy. Harriet is also quoted as calling Wright "charming" in the Diane Kanner interview, "Freeman House Deeded to USC: Hollywood House Designed by Frank Lloyd Wright," *Los Angeles Times*, March 25, 1984, section VIII, pp. 25, 34.

2. Paula Kane, interview with Sam Freeman, in "Wright in Los Angeles," an unpublished research paper, July 1974, p. 4.

3. The history of site ownership is recorded in various papers, including the deed, held in the Freeman House Archive, University of Southern California School of Architecture.

4. These drawings, reproduced here, are the architect's set kept in the files at Taliesin. Another copy of the February working drawings used by Lloyd Wright during construction remained in his personal Freeman House job file and was generously shared by Eric Lloyd Wright.

5. Both Wrights had a fine hand, so it is tempting to ask whether someone else in the office was responsible for the south elevation. It would be most ironic if Schindler, who was still somewhat involved with Wright in late 1923, was the author of it and the detail of the roof to the side. In any case, the plans seem to be drawn in the same hand; only the north elevation is anomalous.

6. Awnings designed by Lloyd Wright were installed at the Storer House in 1925. However, they were not the original Frank Lloyd Wright designs, which were more elaborate. During the restoration of the Storer House by Eric Lloyd Wright for Joel Silver, the original designs were

re-created and installed to shelter the small balconies at each side of the house. The art-glass windows perform a similar role at the Ennis House, along with the brightly tiled bathrooms and the glass tile overmantel for the fireplace, although the Wrights designed none of these elements.

7. Robert Sweeney, *Wright in Hollywood* (Cambridge, Mass.: MIT Press, 1994), p. 65.

8. Brendan Gill, *Many Masks: A Life of Frank Lloyd Wright* (New York: G. P. Putnam's Sons, 1987), p. 268.

9. 1935 Sanborn Insurance map, Los Angeles County, vol. 10, p. 109, Hollywood District.

10. As it turns out, the survey was off at the Ennis House as well; the impact of that on the design is not known.

11. Gill, *Many Masks*, p. 254.

12. Kathryn Smith, *Frank Lloyd Wright: Hollyhock House and Olive Hill* (New York: Rizzoli, 1992), chapters 12 and 13.

13. The owner's copies of these documents are in the Freeman House Archive, University of Southern California School of Architecture.

14. The famous HOLLYWOOD sign was built in 1923 to advertise a new subdivision called Hollywoodland. The last four letters came down some years later.

15. See Chapter 3 for a further discussion of the geometrical relationship between squares and octagons.

16. The Frank Lloyd Wright Foundation lists the version with the vertical strips of wood and glass as part of the January 1924 set. However, both show the planter and lower kitchen roof found only in the February set, and appear to have been drawn by the same hand at the same time.

17. This claim of the Freemans first shows up in articles written about the house in the 1940s. There is no other evidence, except that which the observer might find for him or her self.

18. Henry-Russell Hitchcock, *In the Nature of Materials: The Buildings of Frank Lloyd Wright, 1887–1941* (1942; repr. Cambridge, Mass.: Da Capo Press, 1975), fig. 260.

19. Sam Freeman's comments are taken from an interview program on Pacifica Radio, "The Architect and His Clients," produced by Bruce Rodde and first broadcast on June 5, 1969, on KPFA.

20. Kanner, "Freeman House Deeded to USC."

21. In an undated letter to Lloyd, probably written in early 1925, Frank Lloyd Wright claimed that he had defended him to Dr. Storer, "who broke out bitterly against you." Gill, *Many Masks*, p. 283.

3. INTERPRETING THE DESIGN

1. This phrase was introduced by anthropologist Clifford Geertz in 1973.

2. Kathryn Smith, *Frank Lloyd Wright: Hollyhock House and Olive Hill* (New York: Rizzoli, 1992), pp. 166, 221n.

3. Baker Brownell and Frank Lloyd Wright, *Architecture and Modern Life* (New York: Harper and Brothers, 1937), p. 1.

4. Frank Lloyd Wright, "In the Cause of Architecture, VII. The Meaning of Materials—Concrete," *Architectural Record*, August 1928, pp. 98–104.

5. Ibid.

6. Thomas Hines, *Irving Gill and the Architecture of Reform: A Study in Modernist Architectural Culture* (New York: Monacelli Press, 2000) p, 36,

7. Robert C. Twombly, *Frank Lloyd Wright: His Life and His Architecture* (New York: John Wiley & Sons, 1979), p. 337, citing an essay by Wright in *Architectural Forum*, January 1938, using a slightly simplified version of the quote as it is frequently reproduced.

8. In *An Autobiography* (New York: Horizon Press, 1977), p. 515, Wright quotes his January 1938 *Architectural Forum* essay, since reprinted in Bruce Pfeiffer, ed., *Frank Lloyd Wright Collected Writings, Vol. 3, 1931–1939* (New York: Rizzoli 1993), pp. 284–285. The same language can also be found in, Frank Lloyd Wright, *The Natural House* (New York: Horizon Press 1954), p. 79.

9. Also known as the Ready-Cut or Standardized System-Built Homes, Wright's work on this idea led to at least thirty-six separate designs, from small single-family homes to duplex apartments, of which nine were built. Although the system was licensed to several builders, production was halted by America's entry into World War I. William Allin Storrer, *The Frank Lloyd Wright Companion* (Chicago: University of Chicago Press, 1993), pp. 202–7; Shirley du Fresne McArthur, *Frank Lloyd Wright: American System-Built Homes in Milwaukee* (Milwaukee, Northpoint Historical Society, 1985), p. 87.

10. Wright himself discusses this phenomenon in various essays over the span of his career. Also see Theodore Prudon, *Preservation of Modern Architecture* (New York: John Wiley & Sons, 2008), p. 76.

11. Frank Lloyd Wright, *The Natural House*, pp. 174-175.

12. See especially the Richards Bungalow, Lake Bluff, and the Hunt Residence II, Oshkosh, Wisconsin, with their windows between the kitchen and dining areas. Storrer, *The Frank Lloyd Wright Companion*, pp. 204–5.

13. Frank Lloyd Wright, *An Autobiography*, p. 373.
14. Ibid, p. 262.
15. Frank Lloyd Wright, *The Living City* (New York: Horizon Press, 1958), p. 21.
16. Kenneth Frampton, "Frank Lloyd Wright and the Text-Tile Tectonic," in *Studies in Tectonic Culture: The Poetics of Construction in Nineteenth and Twentieth Century Architecture* (Cambridge, Mass.: MIT Press, 2001), pp. 93–120.

4. CONSTRUCTION

1. Hackenschmidt is on the payroll as foreman, according to the Lloyd Wright job records.
2. Charles Lockwood, "LA Homes Mark Architect's Most Turbulent Period," *Los Angeles Times*, January 30, 1983, Section VII: pp. 1, 6–10.
3. Descriptions of specific materials, tools, and other supplies purchased or used in the construction of the Freeman House, along with their costs and sources, are taken from the receipts in Lloyd Wright's job files that were made available to the author by Eric Lloyd Wright.
4. Crew on the Freeman House included Allen Bannister, Pedro Payan, Cornelius Payan, E. P. Hard, Jose Suares, Ignacio Unsoy, Byron Vandegrift, Jim Putnam, Jerome Henry, E. M. Fitzgerald, Paul Gale, J. E. Willis, Ed Dias, J. A. McCann, Fred Miller, G. Hamilton (laborers, some of whom would later advance to other positions); Carl Steensen, A. H. Cassavoy, Fred C. Matthias, H. B. Judkins (carpenters); and L. G. Stevens, H. H. Stevenson, Thornhill, Tre Decker, Joe Cortinas, M. C. McFall, V. E. Hill, Jones, W. Lobe, E. Doser, N. S. Bryan, Frank Brophy, C. Ringhauser, Converse, Herr (various positions, often more than one); E. Loomis (filling gaps in the floor, cleaning lumber, helping stone setters); W. A. Dixon (roof framing); Emil Hackenschmidt, Arthur Judevine (foremen); Carl Beck (pointing); T. Waldro, T. Revener, K. Guerski (glaziers).
5. Charles Lockwood, "Searching Out Wright's Imprint in Los Angeles," *New York Times*, December 2, 1984. Available online at: http://www.nytimes.com/1984/12/02/travel/searching-out-wright-s-imprint-in-los-angeles.html
6. Comment by Hazel Roy to the author, at the Freeman House, 1992.
7. The mortgage documents are from the Freeman House Archive, University of Southern California School of Architecture.
8. Byron Vandegrift, interviewed by the author at the Freeman House, 1988. He was also interviewed by Robert Sweeney for *Wright in Hollywood* (Cambridge, Mass.: MIT Press, 1994).
9. Dry-tamp concrete was considered inherently vulnerable to failure because of its porosity, and it was thought that increasing pressure would not overcome this problem (see Chapter 5 for a more in-depth discussion). In fact, pressure can help to a point, as can steam-curing and other techniques that introduce sufficient moisture for hydration but not so much that the mix no longer holds its shape.
10. This list, the result of several years of study, makes some assumptions. Possible additional variations may have been overlooked, some variants may have been created informally in the field by cutting or knocking off parts of the block so as to achieve a fit, and more blocks may be in use in the foundations than was estimated here.
11. The telegrams quoted in this chapter are part of Lloyd Wright's Freeman Job File, courtesy of Eric Lloyd Wright.
12. Telegram from Lloyd Wright to Frank Lloyd Wright, August 1924.
13. From two undated worksheets prepared by Frank Gately, Auditor, for the Aetna Life Insurance Company, to be used in calculating workman's compensation payments. Lloyd Wright job files for the Freeman House, courtesy of Eric Lloyd Wright.
14. Letter from A. W. Zindel, of Union Hardware and Metal Company, dated September 30, 1924, to Lloyd Wright.
15. Distribution Sheet, Lloyd Wright, approx. October 1, 1924, from the Freeman job files, courtesy of Eric Lloyd Wright.
16. Block Cost Data 9-30-24, handwritten notes by Lloyd Wright, from the Freeman job files, courtesy of Eric Lloyd Wright.
17. Statement, Samuel Freeman Residence, handwritten list of items and costs, approx. October 1, 1924, from the Freeman job file, courtesy of Eric Lloyd Wright.
18. In the job file, there are a number of pages of notes and numbers that do not have a project name on them; because they could be connected with the Ennis or Storer Houses, they are not referenced here.
19. Letter from Wright to Lloyd, September 15, 1924, copy viewed at the Getty Research Institute Research Library. Call number 870496.
20. For more discussion of Wright's involvement with A. M. Johnson, see David DeLong, *Frank Lloyd Wright: Designs for an American Landscape, 1922–1932* (Harry N. Abrams, 1996), and Sweeney, *Wright in Hollywood*.
21. Sam Freeman, in an interview program on Pacifica Radio, "The Architect and His Clients," produced by Bruce Rodde and first broadcast on June 5, 1969, on KPFA.

22. Letter from Wright to Lloyd, June 2, 1925, courtesy of Eric Lloyd Wright.
23. Freeman job file, Lloyd Wright Archives, courtesy of Eric Lloyd Wright.
24. Diane Kanner, "Freeman House Deeded to USC: Hollywood House Designed by Frank Lloyd Wright," *Los Angeles Times*, March 25, 1984, section VIII, pp. 25, 34.
25. This information was provided to the author by Robert Sweeney.
26. Letter from Lloyd Wright to the Ennises, February 25, 1925, "List of the Serious Errors and Changes Made in the Construction of the Ennis Residence from December to Date . . ."
27. From a document in the Freeman House Archive, University of Southern California School of Architecture.
28. Kanner, "Freeman House Deeded to USC."
29. Ibid.
30. "The California House: 1924," *Los Angeles Times*, July 19, 1953, p. H16.
31. Wyn Evans, Hazel Roy, et al., in interviews with the author.
32. Rodde, "The Architect and His Clients."
33. "The California House: 1924."
34. Art Seidenbaum, "The Southland Houses that Frank Lloyd Wright Built," *Los Angeles Times*, October 17, 1965, p. Q2.

ed. Christian Schittich (Oxford: Architectural Press-Elsevier, 2004), pp. 12–15.
8. Freeman House Specification. See Appendix 1.
9. Interview with Norman Weiss, June 17, 2010.
10. Maurice M. Sloan, *The Concrete House and Its Construction* (Philadelphia: Association of American Portland Cement Manufacturers, 1912), p. 206.
11. Robert Sweeney, *Wright in Hollywood* (Cambridge, Mass.: MIT Press, 1994), p. 209.
12. These numbers were arrived at by totaling the amounts found on the job site invoices, minus what was returned. Because of the possibility of missing invoices, errors in notation at the time, or in the math today, the totals should be viewed as rough approximations only.
13. Martin Weil, with Linda Lefever, "Investigation and Analysis of Original Finishes for the Freeman Residence," report prepared for the University of California School of Architecture. May 23, 1989.
14. Denise Hamilton, "Floor Show", *Los Angeles Times*, July 11, 1999, p. K1.
15. Frank Lloyd Wright, *An Autobiography* (New York: Horizon Press, 1977), pp. 280–81.
16. Frederick Gutheim, ed., *In the Cause of Architecture: Frank Lloyd Wright* (New York: Architectural Record Books, 1975), p. 199.

5. MATERIAL REALITIES

1. Andrew N. Rebori, "Frank Lloyd Wright's Textile-Block Slab Construction," *The Architectural Record*, vol. 62, no. 6, December 1927, pp. 453–455.
2. See note 4, Chapter Four.
3. From the "Specification" included in the contract documents signed by Wright, Lloyd Wright, and the Freemans. Freeman House Archive, University of Southern California School of Architecture. See Contract Documents.
4. Michael Hoffman, "Fog, Cloud and Dew Chemistry," California Air Resources Board, February 28, 1989. http://www.arb.ca.gov/research/abstracts/a4-075-32.htm, accessed July 1, 2010.
5. Richard Coffman and William S. Ginell, "Consolidation Tests on Samuel and Harriet Freeman House Textile Blocks," Scientific Program, The Getty Conservation Institute, Final Report, August 20, 1992.
6. See Sweeney, *Frank Lloyd Wright in Hollywood*, chapter eight; Miles Lewis, "Knitlock," *Australian Building: A Cultural Investigation*, Section 7.07, http://mileslewis.net/australian-building/, accessed June 16, 2010.
7. Edward R. Ford, "The Pioneering Age of Concrete Blocks—Frank Lloyd Wright's Textile Block Houses," in *Architectural Details 2003*,

6. INHABITATION AND CHANGE

1. Gary and Hap Lovell, interviewed by the author at the Lovell Beach House, Newport, CA, 1988.
2. Brendan Gill, *Many Masks: A Life of Frank Lloyd Wright* (New York: G. P. Putnam's Sons, 1987), p. 282.
3. Though there is documentation for the initial painting of the exterior woodwork in records at the Schindler Archive, most of the sequence and timing of subsequent painting campaigns is based on the paint analysis undertaken by Martin Weil.
4. According to a recollection of Murray Niedich, who grew up near the Freeman House and became a lifelong friend of Sam Freeman, interviewed by the author in 1989.
5. There is also a project at the Schindler Archive naming "A. Friedman" as the client, which raises the possibility that the Romaine Street project was actually for Sam, looking for a new home in 1926. However, it seems most likely that the project for Friedman was a rental property, while the one for Sam Freeman was the house intended for his parents.
6. Schindler often did not date his drawings, so the chronology is based on receipts at the Schindler Archive, photographs, and interviews, but it is a bit imprecise.

7. Wyn Evans, interviewed by the author in 1987.
8. Gjura Stojano was a French-born artist of Serbo-Croatian heritage who was best known for painting one of the dramatic murals in the new Bullocks Wilshire store near MacArthur Park, "The Spirit of Sport." At the Lovell Beach House, there is a small wooden relief carving also by Stojano.
9. Bennie (Benvenuto) Bufano was a well-known sculptor, and political progressive, from the San Francisco Bay area.
10. The scenario described here is based on drawings, interviews, and paint analysis. However, it is possible that the work happened in stages over the course of a decade.
11. Gary and Hap Lovell suggested that the two projects were linked in a chat with the author at the Freeman House in 1989.
12. Henry-Russell Hitchcock, *In the Nature of Materials: The Buildings of Frank Lloyd Wright, 1887–1941* (1942; repr. Cambridge, Mass.: Da Capo Press, 1975), fig. 262.
13. Estimate based on an analysis of the professions listed by Hollywood Heights' residents in the 1930 US Census.
14. Bella Lewitzky; although an oft-repeated sentiment in many interviews of the Freemans' friends and neighbors.
15. Rosalind Schaeffer DeMille, in an interview with the author in 1990. DeMille grew up in the home at 1958 Glencoe Way, immediately to the west of the Freeman House.
16. In the 1940s, Lester Horton, then in New York, wrote a long (undated) letter to Katherine Stubergh, a former member of his dance troupe and long-time supporter, that included a description of an evening out in the city, a weekend at Claude Rains's home in New Jersey, and a trip to Bennington. Among those accompanying Horton were Harriet, Hazel Roy, Esther and Albert van Dekker, and Bella Lewitzky. The letter is in the Horton collection at the Library of Congress.
17. Sam Freeman, in an interview program on Pacifica Radio, "The Architect and His Clients," produced by Bruce Rodde and first broadcast on June 5, 1969, on KPFA
18. For more information on the John DeKeyser house, including its connection to the Freeman House, see Sheine, *R. M. Schindler*, pp. 178–81.
19. Gary and Hap Lovell interview, 1988.
20. Ibid.
21. Wright was a noted collector of Japanese prints, and often gave them as gifts.
22. The actor Albert van Dekker was sometimes referred to only as Albert Dekker. This has led to some confusion, regarding attributions of Schindler's projects, as his work for the Dekkers is listed under both names.
23. Letter from Esther van Dekker to the author, February 1987.
24. DeMille interview, 1990.
25. Information on Chace's life comes from Robert Sweeney's essay: "Life on Kings Road: As It Was, 1920–1940," in *The Architecture of R. M. Schindler*, ed. Michael Darling and Elizabeth A. T. Smith (New York: Harry N. Abrams, 2001).
26. Al Keiser and Murray Niedich, interviewed by the author at the Freeman House, March 1988.
27. Gary and Hap Lovell interview, 1988.
28. Keiser and Niedich interview, 1988.
29. Charles Lockwood, "Searching Out Wright's Imprint in Los Angeles," *New York Times*, December 2, 1984. Available online at: http://www.nytimes.com/1984/12/02/travel/searching-out-wright-s-imprint-in-los-angeles.html.
30. Hitchcock, *In the Nature of Materials*, caption for figs. 259–60.
31. Wyn Evans, interviewed by the author, 1986.
32. Robert Clark, interviewed by the author, June 1988.
33. Ibid.
34. Ibid.
35. Keiser and Niedich interview, 1988.
36. This directionality was the first clue we had that 1) the flooring under the carpet was not the original flooring, and 2) that the original flooring was probably still in place. Because the newer wood floor ran east to west, we knew that it couldn't have been original. Early photographs showed how Wright had the flooring run in the same direction as everything else in the room, north to south. And the original must have still been there, or else the new floor would have run north–south because the underlying framing ran east–west. A small bit of destructive investigation soon proved us correct.
37. This number comes from a reading of her extant passports, now part of the Freeman House Archive, USC.38. Gary and Hap Lovell interview, 1988.
39. His houses are well known from films. The Elrod House in Palm Springs was used in the movie *Diamonds Are Forever*, the Sheats-Goldstein House in *Charlie's Angeles II*, *The Big Lebowski*, and *Bandits*, the Chemosphere House in *Body Double*, Silvertop in *Less Than Zero*, the Rainbow House in *Lethal Weapon II*, etc.
40. The information on Lautner and Newiadamsky's involvement comes from interviews with Lautner and Newiadamsky by the author at the Freeman House, 1988, and from the Gary and Hap Lovell interview, 1988.
41. Ibid.
42. From a telephone interview with James Reneau by the author, 2003.

43. This anecdote comes from an interview with Eric Lloyd Wright by the author in March 2004, at the architect's home in Malibu.

7. STEWARDSHIP

1. Editorial, *Los Angeles Times*, March 27, 1984.
2. Undated note from Harriet Freeman to Robert Harris, Freeman House Archive, University of Southern California School of Architecture.
3. We know that Clark Gable's agent lived in the laundry apartment because of the story told by the Freemans in later years that when he visited her at the house, he helped push the ivy back out her bathroom window.
4. F. Harold Weber Jr., Geologist, California Department of Conservation, Division of Mines and Geology, "Whittier Narrows Earthquakes—Los Angeles County. October 1 and 4, 1987," *California Geology*, vol. 40, no. 12, December 1987,
5. http://www.cr.nps.gov/hps/tps/standguide/
6. Bruce Brooks Pfeiffer, *Frank Lloyd Wright Monograph 1914–1923* (Tokyo: A.D.A. EDITA, 1985), p. 243.
7. Barlith is identified in an article on page 39 of *The Building Review*, vol. 22, no. 3, September 1922 (published by the San Francisco Chapter of the American Institute of Architects), as a "white, milky liquid which does not alter the appearance of even the most delicately tinted building stones," and which consists of "an insoluble, elastic water repellant material resembling synthetic rubber, into a permanent solution and that when the water carrying this composition evaporates the compound is deposited in infinitesimally thin layers on the inside surfaces of the pores so that materials are waterproofed and yet free circulation of air is not restricted."
8. All quotes in this section are from the unpublished "Program for Future Use and Restoration Philosophy, Samuel and Harriet Freeman House, University of Southern California School of Architecture" (October 1989, revised in 1992), written by Jeffrey Chusid.
9. http://www.nps.gov/nr/

8. IMPLEMENTATION

1. http://www.nps.gov/history/hps/tps/standguide/
2. Timme was a native of Texas, co-founder of Taft Architects in Houston, and dean of the College of Architecture at the University of Houston before coming to USC in 1996.
3. The apposite phrase used by Robert Harris to describe many of the details at the Freeman House, which were often optimistic in terms of what they sought to accomplish. The first example that occasioned the phrase was the roof drain that emptied just above the footing for a major column supporting the living room.
4. Jeff Guh, interviewed by the author at USC, March 2004.
5. Ibid.
6. Stan Westfall, interviewed by the author at USC, March 2004.
7. Arne Mikkelson, interviewed by the author at Mikkelson's home, March 2004.
8. Theodore Prudon, *Preservation of Modern Architecture* (New York: John Wiley & Sons, 2008), pp. 45–46, has an interesting discussion of the process of deconstruction (or controlled demolition) and reconstruction as a reflection on the nature of modern architecture versus more traditional buildings.
9. Robert Timme, interviewed by the author at the Freeman House, November 2001.

9. WRIGHT AND HISTORIC PRESERVATION

1. "Simulacra and Simulations," in *Jean Baudrillard; Selected Writings*, ed. Mark Poster (Stanford: Stanford University Press, 1988), pp.166–84.
2. Stan Westfall, interviewed by the author at USC, March 2004.
3. See, for example, Kent Kleinman, "Archiving/Architecture," *Archival Science*, vol. 1, 2001, pp. 321–32.
4. For a heuristic discussion of authenticity and preservation in Modernist architecture, especially as concerns Wright, see Neil Levine, "Building the Unbuilt: Authenticity and the Archive," *Journal of the Society of Architectural Historians*, vol. 67, no. 1 (March, 2008), pp. 14–17.
5. Jim Erickson, Taliesin Estate Manager, in a telephone interview with the author, December 2010.
6. E-mail from Keiran Murphy, Historic Researcher for Taliesin Preservation, Inc., to the author, September 2010.

REFERENCES

Alofsin, Anthony. *Europe and Beyond*. Berkeley: University of California Press, 1999.

——. *Frank Lloyd Wright—The Lost Years, 1910–1922: A Study of Influence*. Chicago: University of Chicago Press, 1994.

Banham, Reyner. *A Concrete Atlantis*. Cambridge, Mass.: The MIT Press, 1986.

Baudrillard, Jean. "Simulacra and Simulations." In *Jean Baudrillard; Selected Writings*, edited by Mark Poster. Stanford: Stanford University Press, 1988, 166–84.

Bolon, Carol R., Robert S. Nelson, and Linda Seidel. *The Nature of Frank Lloyd Wright*. Chicago: University of Chicago Press, 1988.

Brilliant III, Ashleigh. *The Great Car Craze: How Southern California Collided with the Automobile in the 1920s*. Santa Barbara, Calif.: Woodbridge Press, 1989.

Brownell, Baker, and Frank Lloyd Wright, *Architecture and Modern Life*. New York: Harper and Brothers, 1937.

Berns, Marla C., ed., *The Furniture of R. M. Schindler*. Santa Barbara, Calif.: University Art Museum, 1996.

Bock, Richard. *Memoirs of an American Artist*. Los Angeles: C. C. Publishing Co., 1989.

Buckland, Michael and John Henken, editors. *The Hollywood Bowl: Tales of Summer Nights*. Los Angeles: Balcony Press, 1996.

Buhle, Paul, and Patrick McGilligan. *Tender Comrades*. New York: St. Martins, 1999.

——, and David Wagner. *Hide in Plain Site*. New York: Palgrave Macmillan, 2003.

Chappell, Sally Kitt, and Ann Van Zanten. *Barry Byrne and John Lloyd Wright: Architecture and Design*. Chicago: University of Chicago Press, 1982.

Dailey, Victor, Natalie Shivers, and Michael Dawson. *LA's Early Moderns: Art/Architecture/Photography*. Glendale, Calif.: Balcony Press, 2003.

Coffman, Richard and William S. Ginell. "Consolidation Tests on Samuel and Harriet Freeman House Textile Blocks," Scientific Program, The Getty Conservation Institute, Final Report, August 20, 1992.

Davis, Mike. *City of Quartz*. London, New York: Verso Press, 1990.

DeLong, David. *Frank Lloyd Wright: Designs for an American Landscape, 1922–1932*. New York: Harry N. Abrams, 1996. Accessible on line at http://www.loc.gov/exhibits/flw/

Farr, Finis. *Frank Lloyd Wright: A Biography*. London: Jonathan Cape, 1962.

Federal Bureau of Investigation, *Communist Infiltration-Motion Picture Industry (COMPIC)*. Excerpts. File Number: 100-138754, Serial: 251x1, Part 7 of 15: 125, 126. http://aboutfacts.net/DocsHollywoodFBI/compic7b.pdf. Accessed July 20, 2011.

Ford, Edward R. "The Pioneering Age of Concrete Blocks—Frank Lloyd Wright's Textile Block Houses." In *Architectural Details 2003*, edited by Christian Schittich. Oxford: Architectural Press/Elsevier, 2004, 12–15.

Frampton, Kenneth. "Frank Lloyd Wright and the Text-Tile Tectonic." In *Studies in Tectonic Culture: The Poetics of Construction in Nineteenth and Twentieth Century Architecture*. Cambridge, Mass.: MIT Press, 2001, 93–120.

Friedrich, Otto. *City of Nets: A Portrait of Hollywood in the 1940s*. London: Headline Book Publishing, 1987.

Gebhard, David and Harriet Von Breton. *Lloyd Wright, Architect*. Santa Monica, Calif.: Hennessey + Ingalls, 1998.

Gill, Brendan. *Many Masks: A Life of Frank Lloyd Wright*. New York: G. P. Putnam's Sons, 1987.

Goodwin, George. "Frank Lloyd Wright's Usonian Houses for Jewish Clients," *American Jewish Archives Journal*, 51, 1 and 2 (1999): 67–92.

Graff, Ellen. *Stepping Left: Dance and Politics in New York City, 1928-1942*. Durham, N.C.: Duke University Press, 1997.

Gutheim, Frederick, editor. *In the Cause of Architecture: Frank Lloyd Wright*. New York: Architectural Record Books, 1975.

Hamilton, Denise. "Floor Show," *Los Angeles Times*, July 11, 1999, K1.

Hanks, David A. *The Decorative Designs of Frank Lloyd Wright*. New York: E. P. Dutton, 1979.

Hasbrouck Hunderman Architects. *Historic Structure Report for the Dana-Thomas House, Springfield, Illinois*. Professional report submitted to the Capital Development Board and the Department of Conservation of the State of Illinois, 1984.

Hines, Thomas. *Irving Gill and the Architecture of Reform: A Study in Modernist Architectural Culture*. New York: Monacelli Press, 2000.

Hitchcock, Henry-Russell. *In the Nature of Materials: The Buildings of Frank Lloyd Wright, 1887–1941*. 1942. Reprint. Cambridge, Mass.: Da Capo Press, 1975.

Hoffman, Michael. "Fog, Cloud and Dew Chemistry," California Air Resources Board, February 28, 1989. http://www.arb.ca.gov/research/abstracts/a4-075-32.htm. Accessed July 1, 2010.

Hoppen, Donald W. *The Seven Ages of Frank Lloyd Wright*. Santa Barbara, Calif.: Capra Press, 1993.

Jackson, John Brinkerhoff. "Truck City." In *A Sense of Place, A Sense of Time*. New Haven: Yale University Press, 1994, 171–85.

Jandl, H. Ward. *Yesterday's Houses of Tomorrow: Innovative American Homes 1850 to 1950*. Washington, D.C.: Preservation Press, 1991.

Kamerling, Bruce. *Irving J. Gill Architect*. San Diego: San Diego Historical Society, 1993.

Kane, Paula. "Wright in Los Angeles," Research paper, July 1974.

Kanner, Diane. "Freeman House Deeded to USC: Hollywood House Designed by Frank Lloyd Wright," *Los Angeles Times*, March 25, 1984, VIII, 25, 34.

Kaufmann jr., Edgar. *9 Commentaries on Frank Lloyd Wright*. New York: Architectural History Foundation and Cambridge, Mass.: The MIT Press, 1989.

Kleinman, Kent. "Archiving/Architecture," *Archival Science* 1 (2001): 321–32.

Laseau, Paul, and James Tice, *Frank Lloyd Wright: Between Principle and Form*. New York: Van Nostrand Reinhold, 1992.

Levine, Neil. "Building the Unbuilt: Authenticity and the Archive," *Journal of the Society of Architectural Historians*, 67.1 (2008): 14–17.

———. *The Architecture of Frank Lloyd Wright*. Princeton: Princeton University Press, 1996.

———. *Modern Architecture: Representation and Reality*. New Haven: Yale University Press, 2010.

Lewis, Miles. "Knitlock," *Australian Building: A Cultural Investigation*, Section 7.07. http://mileslewis.net/australian-building/, Accessed June 16, 2010.

Lipman, Jonathan. *Frank Lloyd Wright and the Johnson Wax Buildings*. New York: Rizzoli, 1986.

Lloyd, Margaret. *The Borzoi Book of Modern Dance*. New York: Alfred A. Knopf, 1949.

Lubell, Sam, and Douglas Woods, *Julius Shulman Los Angeles: The Birth of a Modern Metropolis*, New York: Rizzoli, 2011.

MacCormac, Richard C. "The Anatomy of Wright's Aesthetic." In *Writings on Wright: Selected Comment on Frank Lloyd Wright,* edited by H. Allen Brooks. Cambridge, Mass.: MIT Press, 1981, 163–74.

MacDowell, Syl. "The Magic Story of Hollywood," *Los Angeles Times Sunday Illustrated*, September 28, 1924.

Maldre, Mati, and Paul Kruty. *Walter Burley Griffin in America*. Champaign, Ill.: University of Illinois Press, 2000.

Marmorstein, Gary. "Steel and Slurry: Dr. Philip M. Lovell, Architectural Patron," *Southern California Quarterly* 84, nos. 3/4 (Fall/Winter 2002): 241–70.

McArthur, Shirley du Fresne. *Frank Lloyd Wright: American System-Built Homes in Milwaukee*. Milwaukee: Northpoint Historical Society, 1985.

McCoy, Esther. *Five California Architects*. 1960. Reprint, New York: Praeger Publishers, 1975.

———. *The Second Generation*. Salt Lake City: Peregrine Smith Books, 1984.

———. *Vienna to Los Angeles: Two Journeys*. Santa Monica. Calif.: Arts + Architecture Press, 1979.

McWilliams, Carey. *Southern California: An Island on the Land*. Santa Barbara, Calif.: Peregrine Smith, 1973,

Moore, Abby. *Californian Textile Block*. London: PRC Publishing, 2002.

Morton, Terry B., ed. *The Pope-Leighey House*. Washington, D.C.: Preservation Press,1983.

National Park Service, Standards and Guidelines for the Treatment of Historic Properties. http://www.nps. gov/history/hps/tps/standguide/.

Navasky, Victor S. *Naming Names*. New York: Hill and Wang, 2003.

" A New Waterproofing." *The Building Review* 22, no. 3 (1922), 39.

Onderdonk, F. S. *The Ferro-Concrete Style*. 1928. Reprint. Santa Monica: Hennessey + Ingalls, 1998.

Pappas, Bette K. *Frank Lloyd Wright: No Passing Fancy: A Pictorial History*. St. Louis: Bette K. Pappas, 1985.

Pfeiffer, Bruce Brooks editor, *Frank Lloyd Wright Collected Writings*, Vol, 3, *1931–1939*. New York: Rizzoli, 1993.

———. *Frank Lloyd Wright Monograph 1914–1923*. Tokyo: A.D.A. EDITA, 1985.

Plastering and Fireproofing, International Library of Technology 498. Scranton, Penn.: International Textbook Company, 1919.

Prudon, Theodore. *Preservation of Modern Architecture*. New York: John Wiley & Sons, 2008.

Rebori, Andrew N. "Frank Lloyd Wright's Textile-Block Slab Construction," *Architectural Record*, 62.6 (1927).

Rodde, Bruce. "The Architect and His Clients," Produced for Pacifica Radio and first broadcast on June 5, 1969, on KPFA.

Sergeant, John. *Frank Lloyd Wright's Usonian Houses: The Case for Organic Architecture*. New York: Whitney Library of Design, 1984.

Scott, Margaret. *Frank Lloyd Wright's Warehouse in Richland Center*. Richland Center Wis.: Richland County Publishers, 1984.

Scott, Randy Chris. *The Concrete House in America*. MSAS thesis, The University of Texas at Austin, 1992.

Sheine, Judith. *R. M. Schindler*. London: Phaidon, 2001.

Slaton, Amy E. *Reinforced Concrete and the Modernization of American Building, 1900–1930*. Baltimore: Johns Hopkins University Press, 2001.

Sloan, Maurice M. *The Concrete House and Its Construction*. Philadelphia: Association of American Portland Cement Manufacturers, 1912.

Smith, Kathryn. *Frank Lloyd Wright: Hollyhock House and Olive Hill*. New York: Rizzoli, 1992.

Starr, Kevin. *Material Dreams: Southern California Through the 1920s*. New York: Oxford University Press, 1990.

Storrer, William Allin. *The Frank Lloyd Wright Companion*. Chicago: University of Chicago Press, 1993.

Sweeney, Robert. *Wright in Hollywood*. New York: The Architectural History Foundation, 1994.

———. "Life at Kings Road: As It Was, 1920–1940." In *The Architecture of R. M. Schindler*, Elizabeth Smith et al. Los Angeles: The Museum of Contemporary Art in association with Harry N. Abrams, 2001.

Tilton + Lewis Associates. *Historic Structure Report for the Isadore J. and Lucille Zimmerman House*. Manchester, N.H.: Currier Gallery of Art, 1989.

Twombly, Robert C. *Frank Lloyd Wright: His Life and His Architecture*. New York: John Wiley & Sons, 1979.

Warren, Larry. *Lester Horton: Modern Dance Pioneer*. New York: Marcel Dekker Inc., 1977.

Weber Jr., F. Harold. "Whittier Narrows Earthquakes—Los Angeles County. October 1 and 4, 1987," *California Geology* 40.12 (1987).

Wagener, Wolfgang. *Raphael Soriano*. New York: Phaidon Press, 2002.

Weil, Martin, with Linda Lefever, "Investigation and Analysis of Original Finishes for the Freeman Residence." Report prepared for the University of California School of Architecture, May 23, 1989.

Weil, Zarine, ed. *Building A Legacy: The Restoration of Frank Lloyd Wright's Oak Park Home and Studio*. San Francisco: Pomegranate, 2001.

Weintraub, Alan, Thomas Hines, and Eric Lloyd Wright, *Lloyd Wright: The Architecture of Frank Lloyd Wright Jr.* New York: Harry N. Abrams, 1998.

Wright, Frank Lloyd. "In the Cause of Architecture, VII. The Meaning of Materials—Concrete," *Architectural Record*, August 1928: 98–104.

———. *An Autobiography*. New York: Horizon Press, 1977.

———. *The Living City*, New York: Horizon Press, 1958.

———. *The Natural House*, New York: Horizon Press 1954.

Zygas, Paul, and Linda Nelson Johnson, *Frank Lloyd Wright: The Phoenix Papers*. Tempe: Arizona State University Herzberger Center for Design Excellence, 1995.

PHOTO CREDITS

INDEX

[Buildings cited are by F. L. Wright unless otherwise indicated.]